Lawyers and Mediation

Bryan Clark

Lawyers and Mediation

Springer

Bryan Clark
University of Strathclyde
Law School
Glasgow
United Kingdom

ISBN 978-3-642-23473-6 ISBN 978-3-642-23474-3 (eBook)
DOI 10.1007/978-3-642-23474-3
Springer Heidelberg New York Dordrecht London

Library of Congress Control Number: 2012935225

Printed on acid-free paper

Springer is part of Springer Science+Business Media (www.springer.com)

Preface

It is perhaps best at the outset to remark that I write this book with no axe to grind. I am neither a practicing mediator nor practicing lawyer (although as a university educator of would-be lawyers as well as current and potential mediators I have a vested interest in both). This book is no practice guide or 'how to' manual for lawyers interested in mediation (of which there are many excellent examples). Nor, it should be said, is the book a mediation purist's diatribe warning against the perils of lawyer entanglement with the process. Rather, I hope through this work to tread a cautious and balanced path through the thorny terrain of the lawyer's relationship with, and role within and on the fringes of mediation.

This project was inspired by my own research begun some 16 years or so ago into mediation in Scotland, my field work and observations since and discussions with lawyers, mediators, mediation users and academics on the complex and controversial nature of the lawyer's interaction with the process. This book owes a heavy debt to the wealth of empirical studies and theoretical analyses into mediation and lawyers undertaken by scholars internationally. The breadth of scholarship is breathtaking. Mirroring this international academic interest, the modern mediation movement is itself a global one, albeit that progress across different jurisdictions and in relation to distinct dispute areas within and across countries has occurred at widely diverging paces. As I shall illustrate in the chapters to come, to some extent at least, it may be said that the pace has been set by lawyers. They can be considered both accelerator and brake.

I cannot claim a fully comprehensive geographical coverage in this work but the book's reach at times spans an examination of salient developments, experience and debates regarding lawyers and mediation in Scotland, England and Wales, the USA, Australia, New Zealand, Canada, South East Asia and across continental Europe. I hope I shall be forgiven for devoting perhaps a disproportionate time to matters in Scotland. Most of my own empirical work has been carried out in my native shores. Moreover, research in civil justice issues in Scotland—a small 'mixed' jurisdiction—does not travel particularly well and tends to be shunned in favour of studies from its larger, English and Welsh neighbouring jurisdiction, which are all too often depicted as "UK" research.[1]

[1]Excellent though much of the scholarship in England and Wales is.

It should be noted, however, that the bulk of the key literature in the field has emerged in the USA—arguably the birthplace of modern mediation and also one of the most developed nations (at least in some US States) in terms of recognition, promotion and use of the process. Comparable development in mediation elsewhere lies at different developmental stages. So for example, Australia and Canada mirror the USA in being relatively advanced; England and Wales can be considered not too far off the pace; Scotland lies probably somewhere further back on the evolutionary road and across much of continental Europe (although there are notable exceptions), at least in its modern form, mediation still lies at a somewhat embryonic stage. No doubt though (the problems of cultural and legal transplants aside for the moment) evidence gleaned from experience in one jurisdiction may signal future prospects in others. Given the disparity in developments and available literature evident across jurisdictions, the book's treatment by no means achieves equality of coverage across different geographical areas (and I must concede that my own linguistic limitations have curtailed examination of many no doubt pertinent developments and material in non-English speaking jurisdictions).

As one would expect the interaction of lawyers within mediation, like growth in the process itself, similarly varies considerably across different nation states. Lawyers in their droves have rushed to take up their place in the brave new world of mediation. Nonetheless, many more remain on the fringes unconvinced by the promise of mediation. In short, it can be said that the more 'mainstream' mediation has become in a jurisdiction, the more it tends to be populated by lawyers, at least in certain dispute areas. This is no coincidence. As we shall discuss later in this book, lawyers have often been the authors of mainstream developments.

It should also be stressed here that the term 'mediation' is not an easy one to pin down in a definitional sense. Process pluralism abounds. Distinct mediation approaches have developed across a range of different contexts. *In extremis*, one 'mediation' process may be barely recognisable to another. While in some settings, mediation is no more than negotiation-with-bells-on; a quick way perhaps to bang heads together aided by the promptings of a third party, in the words of Carrie Menkel-Meadow, "[i]n its most grandiose forms, mediation theorists and proponents expect mediation... to achieve the transformation of warring nation states, differing ethnic groups, diverse communities, and disputatious workplaces, families and individuals, and to develop new and creative human solutions to otherwise difficult and intractable problems...it is a process for achieving interpersonal, intrapersonal and intrapsychic knowledge and understanding."[2] The effect that lawyers have had on creating particular normative mediation forms in different contexts and how easily they 'fit' into distinct manifestations of the process are key facets of this book.

In keeping with the heterogeneous nature of mediation, equally I would not pretend that lawyers represent a homogenous grouping across borders. The notion that the legal profession, even in the context of one jurisdiction, is a unified body

[2]Menkel-Meadow (2001), pp xiii–xiv.

singing from the same specialised and esoteric hymnbook is no more than a folk concept. For the purpose of this book, this term at times encompasses autonomous legal practitioners, employed 'in-house' lawyers and judges. Given the disparity in make up and composition of legal professionals in different jurisdictions, it is notoriously difficult to undertake comparative study into lawyers—especially spanning the civil law and common law divide.[3] My task here is easier in that this work is not a comprehensive comparative study of lawyers but rather a mere snapshot of lawyers' involvement with mediation in different jurisdictions coupled with a search for overarching trends, commonalities and divergences.

As this book shall illustrate, the interaction between lawyers and mediation is a complex, controversial and often emotive issue. Rivers of ink have been spilled over the matter. Opinions, when expressed, are often hotly contested. In my work I examine the motives of those lawyers who have become involved in mediation and equally those who have set their face away from the process. In both senses lawyers' motives may be practical or principled; altruistic or selfish; informed or fuelled by bare unfamiliarity or wilful blindness. This work also analyses the appropriateness of lawyer involvement (as well as the law that they carry with them) in mediation and the effect that the addition of lawyers has had upon the practice of mediation. It has been argued cogently, for example, that in certain contexts, lawyers have co-opted mediation and begun to reconstruct the process in their own image with legal bargaining taking the foreground. By contrast, mediation in some contexts has been subject to cogent critiques regarding it as a 'law-less' process, often foisted upon the weak and disempowered. In this context, many would see the inclusion of lawyers, either as mediators or party advocates, as a necessary legal fillip to protect the rights of participants.

On the flip side of the lawyer–mediation relationship, it is undeniable that the elevation of mediation within new settlement-driven cultures of civil litigation has begun to impact upon the practice of law and the work, even the professional identity perhaps, of lawyers. This may in part be due to the lawyer's proclivity for adapting to new circumstances. Whether lawyers are always willing (and able) to adapt to new, cultural imperatives within their professional sphere is questionable, however. The role of judges in promoting mediation, thus affording the process legitimacy (from the lawyers' perspective at least) and shifting mediation from outside of the traditional justice system to within its boundaries, is also of great import. The same importance may be placed upon the role of academic lawyers, both in respect of the 'academic capital' that their writings afford to mediation, and importantly in their role in the education and training of would-be legal practitioners (and judges) and how conducive this may be to expediting legal practice norms commensurate with the development of mediation.

The debate about the place of lawyers in and around mediation runs to the very heart of mediation itself. Jostling between lawyers and others in the mediation arena represents a battle for the ground upon which the mediation process is built.

[3] Abel (1989), p 81.

In particular, disputes over the role of the lawyer in mediation cut across the facilitative/evaluative divide in mediation discourse.[4] This is no coincidence, in the sense that as we shall note in Chap. 1, mediation's modern development as part of the 1970s Alternative Dispute Resolution (ADR) movement in the USA was characterised by the unexpected meeting of diffuse groups promoting two disparate policy aims: one the one hand, the 'quality' proponents seeking empowerment for communities and a transference of 'ownership' of disputes away from lawyers and legal processes into the hands of parties themselves; and on the other, court administrators, governments and certain influential lawyers, motivated by a desire to streamline, unburden and thus preserve traditional civil justice systems by diverting cases towards extra-judicial settlement. While the early community pioneers might have dreamt of a utopian world of dispute resolution clothed in community empowerment and transformation, far removed from the trappings of lawyers and the legal process, under the 'efficiency proponents'"[5] view, mediation became a by-product of litigation and a repository for cases deemed suitable for diversion by the courts. Generally, lawyers became to be recognised as natural inhabitants of this environment in which mediation was seen as an adjunct, rather than alternative to, litigation.

The structure of this book is set out as follows: Chap. 1, a snapshot of the historical development of mediation in the modern context, across the common law and civil law world and a similar tracing of lawyers' involvement in the process; Chap. 2, an analysis of the evidence surrounding the extent and nature of global lawyer resistance towards mediation; Chap. 3, an examination of lawyers' motives for involvement in mediation and some of the tactics they have deployed in gaining a foothold in the field; and an analysis of evidence supporting the notion that lawyers have sought to co-opt mediation at the expense of other would-be mediators; Chap. 4, an analysis of whether the 'cap-fits'—i.e. reviewing the evidence as to the benefits and drawbacks of lawyer involvement in mediation both acting as lawyer-mediators and party advocates within the process, with a further discussion of the merits of judicial mediation; Chap. 5, an examination of the impact and consequences that the increasing institutionalisation of mediation and its linking with and embedding within formal civil litigation systems holds both for the mediation process and civil justice itself as well as a discussion of the role of lawyers in court-connected mediation; and Chap. 6, a short concluding chapter setting out a prognosis for the future regarding lawyers' interaction with mediation including such matters as determining appropriate ethical codes for mediation practice, training and educational needs, and the impact that the continued exposure to mediation may herald for legal professions generally.

---

[4]In short, whether the mediator will simply facilitative the participants' discussion to assist them to reach a settlement or in addition, evaluate for example, their legal claims, commercial or personal interests and potential settlement options.

[5]The terms 'quality proponents' and 'efficiency proponents' have been borrowed from Sibley and Sarat (1989).

I hope the book will be of interest to students of law, dispute resolution, regulation and the social sciences; mediation professionals; policy makers; judges and court officials; legal practitioners and academics. I have endeavoured to state the applicable law and mediation developments as at 1 November 2011.

References

Abel R (1989) Comparative sociology of the legal professions. In: Abel R, Lewis P (eds) Lawyers in society, comparative theories. University of California, Berkley

Menkel-Meadow C (2001) Introduction. In: Menkel-Meadow C (ed.) Mediation: theory, policy and practice. Ashgate/Dartmouth, Aldershot

Sibley S, Sarat A (1989) Dispute processing in law and legal scholarship: from institutional critique to the reconstruction of the juridical subject. Denver Univ Law Rev 66(3):437–498

Acknowledgment

Writing a book such as this is an arduous task, particularly when juggling a busy working life and two small children! The somewhat rocky path was smoothed, however, in many different ways by the contributions of a number of people that I must thank here. First, I owe a debt of gratitude to those with whom I have discussed many of the issues raised in this book. Those whose insights I have profited from over the years include Charlie Irvine, David Semple, John Sturrock, Ewan Malcolm, Sheriff Marcus Stone, Richard Mays, Sue Prince, Jeremy Scuse, Loukas Mistellis, Penny Brooker, Ian McDonough, Simon Roberts, John Lande, Archie Zariski, Don Peters, Andrew Agapiou, Datuk William Lau, Debbie De-Girolamo, Margorie Mantle, Margaret Ross, Hazel Baxter, Esther Gathier, anonymous journal referees, countless conference participants, my PhD students as well as those in my mediation classes, and the research subjects who gave up their valuable time to talk to me and fill out my questionnaires. Thanks are also due to Danielle McLaughlin, Charles Dawson, Madeline Stachura, Angela Taylor and Gerry Keegan for the research assistance which over the past few years has supported completion of this work. I am very grateful to Donald Nicholson and Roy Poyntz for providing insightful comments on draft content of this work. Karen Howatson stepped in at a late stage to compile the index for which I am very grateful. The doses of good humour, solace and empathy provided by Nicole Busby, Calum McLeod and my pals and colleagues at Strathclyde University Law School also helped chivvy me along as the book neared completion. Parts of the book were written while on sabbatical generously granted by the Law School at the University of Strathclyde. Library, research facilities and decent coffee were provided by the University of Stirling. I should also record that without the unfailing encouragement, patience and much-needed prodding by my commissioning editor Anke Seyfried at Springer, this book would never have been written. My mum and the Clark and Fairgrieve clans were a great support network throughout. Finally, my heartfelt appreciation goes out to Kathleen, Dylan and Maisie for the patience, laughs and love that helped sustain me throughout this project.

Bryan Clark

Contents

Chapter 1
The History of Lawyers and Mediation

1.1 Historical Development

A detailed examination of the history of mediation is beyond the scope of this book but as Nadia Alexander has recently noted, "[m]ediation is a process which is both new in terms of its emergence in the legal arena and old in terms of its timeless universality."[1] Despite the generally espoused view of mediation as a modern, alternative to longstanding, traditional dispute resolution mechanisms, it should not be forgotten that across myriad cultures, forms of mediation have been present historically for centuries.[2] Indeed, "mediation is a folk concept which existed prior to the evolution of state law, legal system and lawyer-litigators."[3] So, for instance, mediatory forms of dispute resolution were practised in pre-capitalist, tribal societies, in ancient Greek cultures as well as in mediaeval England.[4] Since its earliest stages of establishment, the USA has experienced a gradual development of the use of extra-judicial forms of dispute resolution such as mediation.[5] The post-industrial era in the developed world also saw mediation flourish in particular contexts; witness the twentieth century growth of labour mediation, for example, in the USA and other parts of the western world.[6] Equally it should be noted that mediatory processes have historically been embedded within the legal systems of many civil law countries including much of continental Europe primarily through the role of the 'settlement judge' (including the *Juge de Paix* in France and *Vrederechters* in the Netherlands) as part of an 'inquisitorial' system of civil

---

[1] Alexander (2006), p. 1.

[2] See generally Roebuck (2007).

[3] Mulcahy (2002), p. 205.

[4] Abel (1983) cited in Roebuck (2007), p. 105; Levinson (1994).

[5] An excellent review can be found in Auerbach (1983), Chap. 1.

[6] See Murray et al. (1996), p. 75.

B. Clark, *Lawyers and Mediation*, DOI 10.1007/978-3-642-23474-3_1,

justice. Equally some judges have traditionally sought to actively settle disputes brought before their courts in the common law world.[7]

More modern times, however, have been characterised by what can be termed a 're-institutionalisation' of mediation as part of a wider "Alternative Dispute Resolution" ('ADR') movement. The modern ADR movement can be largely traced back to its emergence in the 1970s, USA deriving primarily from the National Conference on the Causes of Popular Dissatisfaction with Administration of Justice (the 'Pound Conference') in Minnesota in 1976 in which Professor Frank Sander is credited with first coining the phrase, "Alternative Dispute Resolution".[8] Although modern mediation is thus often viewed as a characteristically Anglo-American development, in the Pound Conference era parallel debates regarding the establishment of alternative forms of dispute resolution were concurrently taking place in Europe, such as those promoted by the Florence Access to Justice Project.[9] Unlike its European equivalents, however, the Pound conference had a major and almost immediate impact on expediting the process of mediation in its native land.

1.1.1 The Lawyer Pioneers of ADR

In some senses, it can be said that despite its 'alternative' billing, the modern ADR movement was something that lawyers, peddlers of traditional dispute resolution, largely constructed themselves.[10] While the father of the term 'ADR', Professor Frank Sander, is an academic lawyer, more importantly perhaps, the pioneering ADR movement was propelled by the significant support lent to it by a spate of leading figures prominent in the US legal profession of the time, including most prominently Chief Justice Warren Burger. The pro-ADR rhetoric of these lawyers was often fierce and somewhat paradoxically directed against themselves and the very legal system in which they inhabited. Burger was blunt in his assessment of a society dominated by the law and lawyers: "we may well be on our way to a society overrun by hordes of lawyers, hungry as locusts, and brigades of judges in numbers never before contemplated".[11]

All is not what it appears, however. Although the Chief Justice cautioned against the ills of hordes of hungry lawyers, locusts even, his arrows were not targeted

---

[7] See, for example, the discussion of American judges in Hensler (2003), p. 175. This practice has expanded in more recent times, see the discussion in Chap. 4.

[8] Sander (1979). The theoretical origins of modern mediation can be charted back to the works of Lon Fuller and other eminent legal jurists. For a stimulating summary of mediation's theoretical nascence, see Menkel-Meadow (2000).

[9] Cappelletti (1978).

[10] Roberts and Palmer (2005), p. 66.

[11] Sibley and Sarat (1989), fn 19.

against the lawyer and the law *per se*. For 'efficiency'[12] proponents like Burger, ADR was seen primarily as a remedy for the ills of an increasingly litigious society straining the seams of the formal justice system. It should then be understood that such legal proponents' aims for the ADR movement were somewhat modest and unsophisticated: the basic rationale was to dampen down a perceived American litigation explosion,[13] provide a more efficient means for handling disputes, help alleviate the perceived crippling court case loads of the day, and in particular, siphon off what can rather unfairly be termed 'garbage' cases[14] from the system. In this sense, the agenda espoused by Burger and his ilk were both anti-law and pro-law simultaneously: anti-law in that ADR was perceived principally as a way of shifting certain litigants out of the formal legal system, underplaying the legal dimensions of such disputes and removing them from the jurisdiction of lawyers, but also pro-law in that such diversion would help preserve the formal legal system for its use in more important cases. As Sibley and Sarat have suggested: "[for] the establishment bar and legal elites who... promoted ADR as a way of dealing with the contemporary crisis of the courts...[t]heirs is not a critique of the essence or ideals of adjudication; instead they seek to save adjudication by limiting it, to preserve the space of law by not overtaxing its institutional capacity".[15] So a prominent factor in developing ADR was to answer the courts' *crie de coeur*. Hence, far from decrying the inherent value of traditional adjudication, ADR in this sense, reaffirmed the importance of litigation's (and hence the lawyer's) role in society.[16]

1.1.2 ADR In and Out of the Traditional

A consequence of linking ADR's role with the fate of litigation allied to the involvement of lawyers and judges in the movement was an intertwining of the alternative with the traditional. ADR thus became to be generally promoted not on its own footing but rather as an appropriate diversion from the court generally for cases of perceived lesser import. Thus in practice ADR programmes became yoked to the traditional system by the means of court-sponsored programmes in low value

[12] This terminology is borrowed from Sibley and Sarat (1989).

[13] Whether or not there was in fact a litigation explosion taking place at this time has been hotly contested—see, for example, Galanter (1985).

[14] Of no significant value in either monetary or legal terms.

[15] Sibley and Sarat (1989), p. 446.

[16] It would be misleading to suggest, however, that all those involved in the Pound Conference could be described as efficiency proponents. Analysis of the Pound Conference proceedings reveal that many of the participants were primarily interested in expanding access to justice rather than simply being concerned with ADR's capacity for institutional efficiency—see Welsh and McAdoo (2005), pp. 401–405.

matters with appropriate cases channelled to ADR from the judiciary. While the rhetoric of the efficiency proponents was thus often cloaked in arguments promoting an eschewing of lawyers and adversarialism (for the 'garbage' cases at least) the reality was that ADR programmes began to mirror, in at least some aspects, the very courts and attendant processes from which their referrals emanated. This 'contamination' can be seen as an inevitable repercussion of ADR's institutionalisation.[17]

Nonetheless, some mediation programmes began life far removed from the dusty confines of the courtroom. While court-based ADR programmes were gathering pace in the USA, grassroots founders of community mediation were concurrently establishing programmes with scant concern for the preservation of litigation systems but rather placing an emphasis on increasing the *quality* of process and settlement outcomes for disputants, above and beyond those offered by traditional legal paradigms.[18] Putting clear blue water between mediation and formal dispute resolution, these 'quality proponents'[19] viewed mediation as a true alternative to litigation, characterised by a paradigm shift in dispute handling: from the pursuit of individual legal rights to maximisation of mutual interests; from the imposition of decisions to party empowerment and self-determination; from adversarialism and conflict to harmony, compromise and community. Inherent in such mediation pioneers' vision of dispute resolution was a marked condemnation of the traditional legal system in general (and hence the role of lawyers therein). While such a jaundiced view of formal dispute resolution was mirrored by the efficiency proponents, it was heavily diluted and stopped short of the often unbridled nature of the assault of 'legal justice' launched by grassroots, quality proponents of mediation.

Many early community programmes were thus designed to sit outside rather than within the confines of litigation systems. Such programmes often resisted any link whatsoever with traditional litigation processes and, for example, would not accept referrals from courts at all. Lawyers - seen at best as an irrelevance and at worst, a menace - were generally absent from participation in such programmes and in many cases proscribed. Viewed through the quality proponent's lens, mediation was thus fundamentally concerned with wresting control back from lawyers and legal processes into the hands of disputants (and communities) themselves. The preservation of litigation through purifying its case-load was not a consideration. Unlike the efficiency proponents' implicit view that legal justice ought to be rationed and sacrificed in cases of lesser import, quality proponents thus challenged the general notion that legal precepts were the only legitimate norms against which disputes should be settled and within which true 'justice' could be found. Theirs was a pluralistic notion of justice in which other identifiable social norms based, for

---

[17] This tainting of the mediation process may not necessarily be seen in a negative light. These matters are discussed in detail in later chapters of this book.

[18] Welsh (2001), pp. 15–16.

[19] Sibley and Sarat (1989).

example, on shared community values and mutual party interests, might act as a barometer of justice.[20]

Despite the enthusiasm of these grassroots pioneers, many of their programmes quickly fell into abeyance and those that survived were often subsumed into traditional justice systems. While some community programmes appeared to enjoy a measure of 'success'[21] willing participants were generally a scant commodity. As Nancy Welsh has noted "[u]nfortunately, a relatively small number of disputants actually chose to take advantage of the new process. Most disputants continued to turn to the courts for resolution of their disputes. By the mid-1980's, despite [community] mediation's genesis out of a marked dissatisfaction with the judicial process, many grass roots mediation activists were advocating for the institutionalization of mediation *within* the courts because that is where parties and their disputes could be found."[22] It is of course true that many such early initiatives were poorly resourced and lacked the oxygen of publicity to attract disputants. Equally, there is some evidence to suggest that would-be participants in general simply placed more value in the potential for rights vindication through the courts rather than seeking harmonious, community-based resolution.[23] In any case, the demarcation between efficiency proponent's schemes and those of quality proponents began to fall away as binds began to form between the courts and mediation programmes.[24]

Thus, the modern development of mediation is characterised by the meeting of two disparate groups, with two largely separate agendas. Evidence suggests that across the globe in the modern context, mediation tends not to develop well without some form of institutionalisation or embedding within traditional legal processes. Such relocating within traditional dispute resolution sites has led to the development of models of mediation which may implicate rather than eschew the role of the lawyer. While such practice norms may commonly be far removed from the original vision of grassroots mediation aficionados, keen to see their efforts to promote the process bear fruit, pioneers often accepted the fertilizer that the courts could apply to their programmes.[25]

---

[20] These are issues that we shall return to in Chap. 5.

[21] In terms of settlements produced and user satisfaction -see Welsh 2001, p. 20.

[22] Welsh (2001), p. 20 (internal citations omitted).

[23] See generally Engle Merry (1990). I discuss this issue further in Chap. 2 at Sect. 2.3.1.

[24] In terms of why many early schemes failed, in their review of the early 'Community Boards' experiment in San Francisco, Merry and Milner (1995) found that the reality of a 'community' upon which shared values could provide a basis for settlements, did not in fact exist in modern life and was no more than a romantic reflection of an indigenous community that no longer existed. The case-load was low and had little effect on community empowerment and settlements reached tended to reflect individual interests of disputants rather than any shared community norms.

[25] Welsh (2001), p. 2-.

On the one hand then mediation holds out the possibility of empowerment, disputant control (over process and outcome) and even the 'transformation'[26] of disputants and the communities in which they inhabit. Likewise, mediation also represents an efficient means to garner settlement, diversion from court adjudication, and the promise of savings of time and money for both disputants and the state. The extent to which these disparate aims are incompatible is an issue which has dogged mediation's development over the years. These are key matters discussed in this book.

One's vision of mediation is thus important in terms of the legitimacy of lawyers in the process. Where mediation is promoted as some form of 'litigation-lite', emerging in the legal arena through pre-trial litigation proceedings or court-initiated schemes then a natural place for lawyers may be found.[27] Where mediation lies outside of the legal sphere and its ethos is seen as antithetical to the law, lawyers may in a like fashion be perceived as anathema to the process. This presentation is of course overly simplistic. Modern mediation practice is nuanced and pluralistic. The process of mediation arises in many different contexts and takes many forms. Schisms between official discourse in how the mediation process is painted and its actual practice abound. As I shall proceed to discuss in this book, the place of law and lawyers within the process diverges significantly both in terms of naturally occurring phenomena and also in a normative sense.

1.2 Mediation and Lawyers in the Post-Pound Era

In many jurisdictions, mediation has developed quite separately across different dispute fields, generally without any significant partnering or alliances between mediation proponents in each discreet area, at least until the process has reached a more mature stage. The involvement of lawyers in each dispute area can be seen to have also varied significantly within and across different jurisdictions. Across the globe lawyers now populate the mediation field as mediators, client representatives, academic commentators, trainers and educators, and judicial gatekeepers. While I do not claim to offer universal coverage, to establish a baseline for the analysis in this book, here I offer a snapshot of global developments in mediation[28] over the past two or three decades with a particular focus on the involvement of lawyers.

It is worth making a few general points to begin with. The dalliance with mediation in different jurisdictions, although respectively often widely divergent

[26] For a discussion of transformative mediation see Baruch- Bush and Folger (2005).

[27] Although conversely part of this 'lightness' may in fact entail the absence of lawyer representatives.

[28] I have focused on some principal jurisdictions representative of mediation developments across the common law and civil law tradition. Absence from discussion in this chapter will not preclude examination of any particular jurisdiction's experiences in later chapters.

in terms of pace of development and time of origin, has tended to follow a similar pattern: first, there is 'discovery' of the process by interested professionals; second, there is 'experimentation' by these professionals who may organise themselves into groupings to promote the practice of the process; and third, there is some form of underpinning, promotion or legitimisation by government or the formal legal system and an attendant institutionalisation of the process occurs. Experience suggests that this latter element may be most instrumental in expediting the process and can, for example, take the form of state funding of mediation programmes and financial imperatives for parties to mediate; explicit recognition of the process, and enacting of governing provisions in law in areas such as confidentiality, enforcement of settlements and mediator redress; court promotion, judicial referral and compulsory rules to mediate; and some form of legal regulation and mandated training for those who purport to offer mediation services.

1.2.1 USA

The legacy of the Pound Conference was profound in the USA. Recent decades have seen a rapid expansion of mediation across the USA in different dispute contexts. The public arena was quick to respond to the wave of enthusiasm for ADR which crashed into the firmament in the aftermath of Pound. Arguably the most striking feature of recent US experience in mediation has been its enmeshment with court processes. In 1998, after significant *ad hoc* court-based experimentation,[29] Congress enacted the Alternative Dispute Resolution Act requiring all federal courts to establish ADR programmes, many of which included mediation as the 'flagship' ADR process.[30] Such programmes have since been rolled out across civil courts the length and breadth of the country across a wide spectrum of disputes.

Aside from court promotion, the state has over time been a key supporter of mediation in the USA in other ways. In the 1990s consecutive US Presidents weighed in to the mediation debate. In 1992 an executive order on mediation was issued by George Bush espousing the value of mediation and in 1998, Bill Clinton issued a memorandum pledging that federal agencies would make greater use of mediation and other ADR process. Public agencies and federal government thus began to embrace mediation in a significant fashion. In one significant move, in 1994 the US Postal Service established Resolve Employment Disputes, Reach Equitable Solutions Swiftly ('REDRESS'), a pioneering, 'transformative' model of mediation for the handling of disputes arising within its workplace.[31]

[29] Hensler (2003), pp. 185–186.

[30] U.S.C 28 §651(a) & (b) (1998).

[31] See generally Blomgren Bingham (2002).

Private sector developments in mediation soon also occurred in the aftermath of the Pound Conference. In particular, lawyers were quick to establish or take up a significant presence in numerous professional mediation associations. In 1979, the Center for Public Resources (now the CPR Institute for Dispute Resolution) was established by a group of general counsel drawn from Fortune 500 companies. Concurrently the longstanding American Arbitration Association, expanded the services it provided to encompass mediation. Other important commercial ADR organisational developments included the inception of the National Institute of Dispute Resolution (NIDR) and the Society of Professionals in Dispute Resolution (SPIDR) (now the Association of Conflict Resolution). Family mediation services also began to emerge in which both lawyers and psychologists sought to embrace 'better ways' of resolving matrimonial disputes, through organisations such as the Academy of Family Mediators. Many family mediation programmes became subsequently linked to the public realm by way of court referral, leading to further expansion.[32]

Mediation is thus incredibly well established in many parts of the USA. The process has moved from the fringes of disputing culture squarely into the mainstream. Writing in 2000 John Lande asserted that "the current wave of adr developments seem much broader than prior waves... the current wave is intended to change what some might call the 'heartland' of disputing, touching virtually all types of disputes and disputants...closely linked to the diffusion of an ideology supporting this expansion"[33]

Unarguably, American lawyers have become key players in mediation's renaissance. Many legal practices have developed mediation departments as part of their core activities. Lawyers have increasingly mined the rich vein of professional opportunity that mediation has afforded them and moved into mediation practice in a number of fields. While such issues are explored in depth in chapters three and four of this book, it can be noted here that lawyers are most prominent in 'institutionalised' mediation, for example, court-annexed schemes and court-initiated practice. Typically selected in such contexts either by judges or their fellow attorneys, mediation practice in the shadow of the court is often dominated by lawyers. Writing in 2003, Deborah Hensler noted that "most court mediators are lawyers or retired judges, many of whom hope that mediation programmes will provide sufficient numbers of cases to generate significant income".[34] Often mediation in this context reflects the norms of the court, and thus provides a natural environment for lawyer involvement as party representatives or mediators.[35] In fact in some programmes only lawyers may mediate and non-lawyer mediators are

[32] Stipanovich (2004), fns 132 and 133.

[33] Lande (2000), p. 147.

[34] Hensler (2003), p. 187.

[35] See the discussion in Chap. 4.

proscribed.[36] Mediation is now taught in all law schools[37] and can increasingly be seen as part of mainstream legal education and legal practice.[38]

1.2.2 The Common Law World

Other nations have embraced mediation with various degrees of enthusiasm. Generally, although there are notable exceptions, common law countries were quicker to dip their toes into the hitherto unchartered waters of mediation than their civil law counterparts. In the main, it can be said that the key themes of Pound—a desire to unearth solutions to alleviate crippling delays and costs in the civil justice system—particularly resonated in many common law jurisdictions, which to various degrees shared such problems.

1.2.2.1 United Kingdom: England and Wales

In the UK, mediation developments across different dispute areas such as family, general civil and commercial fields have occurred both outside and within the civil court process. From a jurisdictional perspective, the legal systems of England and Wales on the one hand, and Scotland on the other,[39] are substantially distinct and hence I will deal with mediation developments in each separately.

As ADR flourished in the USA in the 1980s the winds of change blew over the Atlantic and began to impact upon the civil justice scene in England and Wales.[40] Lawyers were quick to show their hand in the emerging ADR field with the inception of 'Solicitors in Mediation', a group of solicitors offering family mediation services. This in turn led to the development of the 'Family Mediation Service', set up under the auspices of the Law Society in 1988. Perhaps not to be outdone, barristers set up a 'Conciliation Board' again offering a family mediation service in 1985. A further commercial grouping of lawyers involved in commercial mediation, IDR (Europe), was established in 1989 (later transformed into the ADR Group). Probably the flagship ADR organisation in the UK, 'CEDR', was

---

[36] Nolan-Handley (2002). Debates over whether mediation amounts to the practice of law are longstanding—see the discussion in Chap. 3 at Sect. 3.3.4.

[37] Although the extent of its embedding across core teaching in law schools has been questioned—see the discussion in Chap. 2 at Sect. 2.5.1.3.

[38] See generally Macfarlane (2008).

[39] Scotland has a 'mixed' legal system, being influenced by both common law and civil law traditions, although the incumbent formal court system is principally in the common law, adversarial mode.

[40] Including through developments under the auspices of CEDR (The Centre for Effective Dispute Resolution).

established in 1990 and mainly driven by commercial law firms. While the bulk of English lawyers may have shown scant regard for mediation in its early days of development, institutional legal interests viewed mediation as no passing, fringe side-show. Important reports by both the Law Society[41] and the Bar[42] in the early 1990s, showed a keen proprietary interest in ADR by the profession.[43]

Indeed by the mid 1990s ADR had begun to develop rapidly and lawyers were at the forefront. In the words of Loukas Mistelis: "[i]t is intriguing that in England the driving force for all [ADR] reforms came from lawyers involved in commercial litigation, a few academics and the courts."[44] A culmination of this interest and boasting significant lawyer involvement, 'The Civil Mediation Council' was created in 2003 as an independent body charged with promoting the development of mediation as an alternative form of dispute resolution.

Aside from the foregoing developments, reforms to the English civil court system have had a profound impact on the fate mediation. The Civil Procedure Rules implemented in 1999 led to a 'court as last resort' ethos in civil disputing which propelled mediation forward.[45] Taking up this mantel with gusto, civil courts began to cajole and twist the arms of litigants into attempting mediation prior to taking a case to trial.[46] Concurrently a number of court pilot mediation services were established, often, but not limited to, small claims disputes.[47] While mandatory mediation was generally eschewed by the English courts,[48] the practice has recently become a reality in the family dispute context: under Ministry of Justice Protocols,[49] divorcing couples require to attend mediation information sessions prior to taking a case to court. At the time of writing it is known that it is planned to extend this practice to all civil cases of a low monetary value.

In more recent years, lawyers have continued to plough a furrow in the mediation market primarily in commercial and family fields through organisations such as ADR Chambers, a mediation panel comprising former judges and retired and practising barristers and solicitors, and the solicitor-populated Association of Northern Mediators. Empirical research has illustrated an upsurge in interest in lawyers to mediation in a number of fields including in general commercial and

---

[41] Representing solicitors.

[42] Representing barristers.

[43] Bedlam (2001); Brown (2001). For a fuller discussion of this issue see Chap. 3 at Sect. 3.4.

[44] Mistelis (2006), p. 145.

[45] For a discussion see generally Shipman (2006).

[46] Primarily through the medium of costs sanctions for unreasonable refusals to mediate—see *Halsey v. Milton Keynes General NHS Trust, Steel v. Joy* [2004] EWCA Civ 1651.

[47] Cases under £5000 in value. See for example the evaluations by Doyle (2006); Prince (2007); Genn et al. (2007).

[48] See the discussion in Chap. 5 at Sect. 5.2.3.

[49] Practice Direction 3A—Pre-Application Protocol for Mediation Information and Assessment.

construction spheres.[50] Lawyers do not dominate across all civil mediation dispute areas. Areas such as family and employment/workplace matters find the mediator population more diverse in terms of professional background. In the commercial field, however, particularly at the top end of the market, lawyers have a tight stranglehold on practice. In 2005, for example, it was reported by CEDR that 80% of their mediators were lawyers.[51] Research by Nick Gould et al. conducted in 2010 in the context of English construction mediation found that, in respect of successful mediations charted in the study, some 84% of mediators were lawyers.[52] Recent research of mediators and repeat mediation users in London, found that 68% of commercial mediators were lawyers.[53] Additionally, in pilot, court-annexed mediation schemes in England and Wales, such as those in Exeter and Guilford county courts, it also appears that lawyers have been heavily involved in the design and delivery of such programmes.[54] Educational provision at university level for lawyers at undergraduate and post-graduate levels, has increased steadily in recent years reflecting the growth of interest and practice in the area, although in terms of embedding within the core legal curriculum, mediation's growth remains modest.[55]

1.2.2.2 United Kingdom: Scotland

The development of mediation, far less lawyers' involvement therein, is still at a relatively early stage in Scotland.[56] Early English developments trickled over the border as mediation began to make an, albeit modest, mark upon Scotland.[57] A smattering of Scottish lawyers was quick to respond to mediation's promise. One of the first such developments, 'CALM', an association of family lawyer-mediators, was established in 1990. The Faculty of Advocates first established a commercial mediation service in 1996. The Law Society of Scotland[58] followed suit with the inception of ACCORD—a grouping of commercial solicitor-mediators trained in mediation techniques.[59] Some Scottish lawyers also became members of

[50] Bourne out in particular by the work of Penny Brooker—see Brooker (2001); Brooker (2005).

[51] South (2005).

[52] Some 41% were solicitors, 35% barristers and 7% judges - Gould et al. (2010), pp. 10–11.

[53] Bucklow (2007), p. 44.

[54] Prince and Belcher (2006), pp. 30–34.

[55] A joint CMC/Civil Justice Council project seeking to ascertain levels of mediation coverage in legal education is at the time of writing currently on-going.

[56] See generally Mays and Clark (1996); McDonald (2004); Ross (2006).

[57] For a review of early developments see generally Mays and Clark (1996), Chap. 1.

[58] Representing solicitors.

[59] Mays and Clark (1996). A Law Society of Scotland committee on ADR was set up at this time, although later disbanded.

the now defunct 'Mediators' Association'.[60] Outside of family and community mediation, these early initiatives, however, fell into abeyance largely due to a lack of client demand for their services. Nonetheless, rising from the ashes of these early endeavours, new developments have since taken root: lawyers have become involved in providing *pro bono* mediation for the Edinburgh sheriff court pilot mediation service and similar later pilots in Glasgow and Aberdeen sheriff courts[61]; recent times has seen the development of commercial mediation providers in Scotland such as 'Core Mediation' and 'Catalyst Mediation', both of whom boast significant lawyer representation on their mediation panels[62] and a new Faculty of Advocates Mediation Service was set up in 2007. The Scottish Legal Complaints Commission established a mediation scheme as part of their consumer complaints handling processes.[63] A Law Society of Scotland Steering Group has also recently been launched seeking to devise an action plan to expand the use of mediation throughout the legal profession in Scotland. Such initiatives reflect perhaps a new, reinvigorated interest in mediation in, at least, certain sectors of the Scottish legal profession. Indeed recent field work suggests that a growing cadre of lawyers in Scotland are keen to embrace mediation in a wide range of civil disputes.[64]

Steps in setting consistent standards for practice have tentatively begun. The Scottish Mediation Network, an interdisciplinary linking body for mediation activity across the spectrum of civil dispute spheres, was established in 2005 with a view to introducing and developing common standards in training and regulation in mediation practice. University level education in mediation remains sparse in law schools although in recent years, instruction has increased.[65] While mediation has not yet benefited from significant linking with the civil court process in Scotland,[66] a recent Scottish civil justice review may lead to reforms providing for the increased enmeshment of the process in the formal justice system.[67] Mediation

[60] Formed in (1995). The author was a member of the original steering committee—there was much talk but sadly little action!.

[61] Evaluated in Samuel (2002); Ross and Bain (2010).

[62] The panels boast mediators drawn from many other professions, however.

[63] By virtue of the Legal Profession and Legal Complaints Act (2007), s. 8.

[64] My empirical work in the field confirms this, see Clark and Dawson (2007); Agapiou and Clark (2011).

[65] An 'ADR' elective exists at undergraduate level at the University of Aberdeen and a Post Graduate Qualification is available at the University of Strathclyde.

[66] Beyond pilot mediation schemes in "small claims" civil cases (see Ross and Bain (2010); Samuel (2002) and specific (and little used) court rules in certain circumstances - in consistorial matters, courts are empowered to refer certain matters to mediation -Rules of the Court of Session, 49.23; Sheriff Court Rules, 33.22 & 33A.22) and in respect of the commercial procedure in the sheriff court, matters may also be referred to mediation (Sheriff Court Rules, 40.12).

[67] Gill (2009), pp. 165–187 and Annex D. It has been argued that it does not go far enough, however—see Irvine (2010). The Scottish Government has since made positive noises as to mediation's future potential and signalled an intention to better embed the process within the civil justice system—Scottish (2010).

has been bolstered by legislative underpinning in certain dispute contexts however. For example, the process is recognised as part of the statutory process for the resolution of Scottish planning disputes[68] and is a key aspect of statutory dispute resolution processes in the field of Additional Support Needs in education.[69]

1.2.2.3 Australia

The developmental pattern of mediation in Australia has followed similar evolutionary lines to other parts of the common law world. In terms of modern development, the first mediation initiatives in Australia began to take root in the 1980s arising at least in part as an antidote to a perceived upsurge in litigious behaviour and attendant civil court malaise. While initially it seemed that lawyers were lukewarm in their response to mediation, by the late 1980s some lawyers were beginning to embrace its practice and philosophy as initial developments began to take a hold across the spectrum of civil disputes. Mediation and other ADR processes began to be taught in law schools and an increasing number of legal professionals took training in mediation.[70] Court-connected mediation projects began in 1980 in New South Wales in the context of small civil disputes (and minor criminal actions).[71] Provision soon expanded to other States and also took root at Federal level. Australia quickly became known as a trailblazer in terms of mediation development. As early as 2001, it was said that "[c]ourt-related ADR exists in every court and tribunal in Australia; community mediation and private mediation exist in all Australian jurisdictions".[72] In the present time, Federal and State courts in Australia now routinely refer parties to mediation, in some cases without the consent of parties.[73] Compulsory steps to settle family cases prior to litigation have been in place since 2006.[74] The recent Civil Dispute Resolution Act 2011[75] is likely to promote mediation further. The Act mandates that any parties seeking recourse to the civil courts must prove to the court that they have first taken "genuine steps" to resolve the dispute. Such steps may include recourse to mediation.

Government has also lent its weight behind the process, principally through the National Alternative Dispute Resolution Advisory Council (NADRAC) established in October 1995 by the Commonwealth Attorney-General. This lawyer-dominated, independent body is charged with, *inter alia*, providing policy advice to the

---

[68] Under the Planning etc (Scotland) Act (2006).

[69] Under the Education (Additional Support for Learning) (Scotland) Act 2004.

[70] Tidwell (1999).

[71] Under the Community Justice Centres (Pilot Projects Act) 1980.

[72] Alexander (2001), p. 2.

[73] In, for example, Queensland and Victoria.

[74] Family Law (Shared Parental Responsibility Act) 2006.

[75] Act nº 17 of 2011.

Attorney General on the appropriate use of ADR, promoting increased publicity and knowledge of ADR processes, commissioning research into ADR and developing appropriate training and educational provision in ADR. A National Mediator Accreditation System (NMAS) was also established in 2008, designed to establish recognised, national standards in requisite training and regulation for mediators.

According to Tidwell, "[t]here has been an evolutionary process in which the legal profession has moved from questioning the usefulness of mediation to a position where mediation is largely dominated by the law".[76] Lawyers have become key players in the mediation field and have either established or are instrumental in a number of professional bodies including LEADR (Lawyers Engaged in Alternative Dispute Resolution), the Institute of Arbitrators and Mediators Australia (IAMA) and Australian Commercial Disputes Centre.

1.2.2.4 New Zealand

New Zealand also stands as a well developed country in mediation terms. Court-annexed mediation has become especially well established. In the Family Court, provisions have been in place to allow referral to mediation since 1980.[77] While initially mediation may have been slow to be embraced by lawyers, in the past decade or so the interest and activity of lawyers in the process has increased.[78] Lawyers now play a significant role in the mediation process, in no small part aided by the institutionalised nature of its practice. The two main professional bodies in the mediation field are LEADR and the Arbitrators' and Mediators' Institute of New Zealand (AMINZ), both of whom are heavily populated by lawyers.

Under Family Court rules, disputants may be referred on a voluntary basis to either 'counsel-led' mediation, in which parties are referred to an external lawyer mediator, and 'judge-led' mediation, undertaken in-court by a sitting Family Judge.[79] Future fundamental changes to the civil justice system in New Zealand are likely to lead to a significant upsurge in use of mediation generally. In the District Court in particular, recent reforms implemented in November 2009 placing the pursuit of settlement at the centre of the court process, are likely to propel mediation's use further in this context. A mediation pilot project has also been recently launched in the High Court[80] and a court-annexed mediation scheme also exists in the Environment Court.[81] Furthermore, mediation enjoys a long history in

[76] Tidwell (1999), para 11.

[77] Family Proceedings Act 1980, ss.8–19.

[78] See Freeman-Greene (2001).

[79] For a further discussion see http://www.courts.govt.nz/courts/family-court/what-family-court-does/mediation Accessed on 1 November 2011.

[80] See http://www.lawfuel.co.nz/releases/release.asp?NewsID=1406. Accessed on 1 November 2011.

[81] Under the Resource Management Act s.268. See also Oliver (2007).

the employment field.[82] The government seems committed to embedding it further in this field. On 18 July 2010 Minister of Labour Kate Wilkinson announced changes to the Employment Relations Act to further promote the use of labour mediation.[83]

1.2.2.5 Canada

While Canada has a history in labour mediation stemming back to the early twentieth century, it is only over the last two decades or so that mediation has steadily taken a hold. Some of the earliest initiatives occurred in the family field mainly through private, out of court developments in common law provinces and court-annexed mediation in the civil law province of Quebec.[84] Compulsory mediation information sessions on a *gratis* basis for disputing couples seeking access to formal adjudication were subsequently instituted in 1997 to help expedite the process in the family setting.[85] Mediation in other civil matters also began to develop, first through pilot programmes in the Superior Court of Montreal, which were later rolled out to the entire Quebec province.[86] Practice models have since developed across Canada involving both judicial mediation and also court-annexed mediation by external mediators. While mediation in Quebec remains a voluntary process, mandatory mediation in non-family matters has been established in Ontario in the districts of Ottawa, Toronto and Windsor and can be seen to now form part of the mainstream legal culture.[87] Unsurprisingly, lawyers have become prominent in the mediation field. Redolent of the settlement-judge role prevalent in civil law systems, sitting judges in Quebec also often mediate cases. Suitably trained lawyers, amongst other professionals, serve as mediators in family matters and other civil dispute areas. As Prujiner notes, in the report, *Comite du suivi* of 1999, the majority of mediators (some 65%) were lawyers[88] and "[a]t the turn of the twenty-first century offers of private commercial mediation were virtually non-existent; now they are expanding rapidly into an increasingly active professional market dominated by jurists".[89] Many law schools are now offering educational provision in mediation as part of their standard legal education.

---

[82] See, for example, Corby (1999).

[83] See the report at http://www.aminz.org.nz/Section?Action=View&Section_id=20&Story_id=1371 Accessed 1 November 2011.

[84] Through the Rules of Practice of the Superior Court Of Quebec in Civil Matters.

[85] Through the Act to Institute, under the Code of Civil Procedure, Pre-hearing Mediation in Family Law Cases and to Amend other Provisions of the Code (1997) c.42.

[86] See Prujiner (2006), p. 89.

[87] For a review see Macfarlane (2002).

[88] Prujiner (2006), p. 100.

[89] Prujiner (2006), p. 101.

1.2.2.6 Hong Kong

Significant Hong Kong governmental effort has been expended in attempting to promote the use of mediation in civil disputing. Mediation in Hong Kong first emerged in the construction sector when in 1984, the government introduced a mediation scheme into certain construction contracts.[90] Although of limited success, this initial programme led to a subsequent embedding of mediation in government construction contracts in 1990. Standard mediation rules were subsequently introduced by the Hong Kong International Arbitration Centre (HKIAC) in 1991. Outside of the construction arena, developments in family and commercial mediation also began to occur in the early 1990s. Family mediation in particular was bolstered by a 3 year pilot court-annexed scheme introduced in 2000.[91]

In the present day context, fundamental recent reforms to the civil justice system in Hong Kong have the potential to lead to the rapid development of mediation across the spectrum of civil disputing. An interim report produced by a working party established by the Hong Kong Chief Justice to review civil procedure in the High Court published in November 2001 proposed a number of radical reforms to the incumbent system and afforded star billing to mediation. Important proposals included: the introduction of mandatory mediation in certain cases; measures to stay proceedings while mediation is attempted; costs sanctions for parties who unreasonably refuse to attempt mediation (where it remains voluntary); and mediation becoming a pre-requisite for legal aid. The final report published in 2004 diluted some of the more radical aspects of the interim proposals but nonetheless efforts to expedite mediation remained clear.[92] While plans to introduce mandatory mediation were shelved, financial imperatives to attempt mediation through costs sanctions for unreasonable refusals to attempt mediation and by way of legal aid rules remained. The provisions of the Final Report came into force on April 2 2009.

Although much of the current crop in mediators in Hong Kong is comprised of lawyers,[93] it has been reported that lawyers, especially the Bar, have been particularly resistant to mediation developments, witnessed particularly in their opposition to the recent reforms to the High Court civil procedural rules.[94] Furthermore in his 2007–2008 policy address, the Chief Executive of the Hong Kong Special Administrative Region ('HKSAR') lamented the lack in voluntary uptake of mediation and partially laid the blame for this state of affairs at the feet of lawyers.[95] Other

[90] See Wall (2009), pp. 78–79.

[91] The scheme received a largely positive evaluation—see generally Hong Kong Polytechnic (2004).

[92] Chief Justice's Working Party on Civil Justice Reform (2004).

[93] In 2010, for example, 100 out of 251 Hong Kong International Arbitration Centre general panel mediators were lawyers.

[94] Wall (2009), pp. 82–83.

[95] Cheung (2010), pp. 67–68.

efforts to promote the process abound, however, and it may be that lawyers will have little choice but to be swept along on the wave of current mediation developments. A spate of new pilot mediation schemes, for example, in the area of construction disputes, has been developed to promote mediation use.[96] In addition, a recent Practice Direction commencing in 2010 introduced an 'ADR certificate' under which lawyers are bound to discuss the merits of mediation with their clients and present cost-comparisons with other forms of dispute resolution.[97]

1.2.3 Continental Europe

As noted above, despite the embedded early prevalence of mediatory forms of settlement in civil law systems, such as the role of the settlement judge, in the main, continental European countries were relatively slow to react to mediation's modern promise. In terms of why this was so, at least some European civil law countries did not feel the same efficiency driven impetus for mediation stemming from an overburdened legal system and burgeoning culture of litigiousness that helped propel the progress of modern mediation in common law countries. Across continental Europe there may have also existed a suspicion that mediation was some kind of new fangled American import that had no place in the civil law tradition.[98] Additionally, unlike the courts in common law countries that tend to be vested with rights to alter their own procedural rules, in most civil law countries the ability to achieve this has remained the preserve of the legislature, which may have served to stifle innovation in court-based mediation initiatives.[99] Nonetheless it can be seen that in many civil law jurisdictions, mediation has moved swiftly from inception to a heavily regulated phase (often bypassing the 'experimental phases' which have characterised early development in most common law countries) although not always accompanied by success in terms of growth of the process.[100]

---

[96] See Cheung (2010).

[97] Wall (2009), p. 84. At the time of writing a Mediation Bill seeking to further underpin the process on a statutory footing is set to be tabled at the Hong Kong Legislative Council—see http://www.news.gov.hk/en/categories/law_order/html/2011/11/20111116_161052.shtml Accessed 18 November 2011.

[98] Although see Macfarlane (2004), suggesting that acceptance of mediation, at least in the family context, may have been quicker in civil law countries than Anglo-Saxon nations in part because of the adversarial systems prevalent in the common law world.

[99] Alexander (2006), p. 20.

[100] See generally Alexander (2001).

1.2.3.1 The Netherlands

In European terms, the Netherlands can be seen as a somewhat developed nation with well established practises in such areas as family, commercial and employment disputes.[101] Although forms of settlement practices akin to mediation have been practised for many years in the Netherlands stemming back to the sixteenth century, primarily through judicial settlement activities, modern mediation was first imported into the country in the late 1980s.[102] In family matters, an association of lawyer mediators was launched as early as 1989.[103] Initial private sector initiatives developed in 1992 with a heavy lawyer presence, led the way in seeking to expedite the future development of mediation. Hard on the heels of these endeavours, after engagement with government, the *Nederlands Mediation Instituut* (Netherlands Mediation Institute) NMI was established in 1993 by practising and academic lawyers with a view to promoting mediation, educating the public about its merits and establishing appropriate standards in training and regulation.[104] Significant governmental support has since been lent to mediation, primarily through Ministry of Justice initiatives.[105] In particular, a number of court-annexed mediation programmes have been established in the Netherlands, beginning with the introduction of mediation pilot projects in 2000[106] with subsequent expansion occurring on the back of a pro-mediation policy statement by the Minister of Justice in 2004.[107]

In terms of mediator composition, lawyers currently share the mediation market with other professionals. While competition between different professionals is the norm, in family mediation practice it is not uncommon for lawyers to co-mediate with psychology professionals in serious cases.[108] In the non-family court-connected context, lawyer mediators are likely to outnumber those drawn from other professional backgrounds.[109]

---

[101] See De Roo and Jagtenberg (2002).

[102] De Roo and Jagtenberg (2002).

[103] The *Vereniging van Familierecht Advocaten-Scheidingsbemiddelaars* (Association of Family Law Lawyers-Divorce Mediators).

[104] NMI regulatory rules were published in 1995 and amended in 2000 governing such issues as confidentiality in the process, the voluntary nature of the process and independence of the mediator.

[105] Platform ADR (1998); Ministry of Justice *Meer wegen naar het recht Beleidsbrief ADR 2002*.

[106] *Mediation naast rechtspraak* (Court Encouraged Mediation) and *Mediation Gefinancierde Rechtsbijstand* (Mediation and Legal Aid). De Roo and Jagtenberg (2006).

[107] Macfarlane (2006), p. 182.

[108] De Roo and Jagtenberg (2006).

[109] See, for example, Neimeijer and Pel (2005), p. 359. The research revealed that 75% of the mediators in the five participating districts covered by the research were lawyers and they handled 81% of overall cases.

1.2.3.2 France

One of the earliest of the civil law European countries to dabble with mediation was France.[110] The first French developments occurred in the mid 1980s and mediation is now deployed across a wide range of dispute areas including the commercial, community, family and employment spheres.[111] Early experimentation in France[112] arose primarily from mediation developments in French-speaking Quebec in Canada and in particular the exposure of influential professionals to mediation practice there.[113] In the realm of civil disputes, family mediation is the most well developed practice area in France and the emphasis placed in French society on the importance of maintaining family ties in the rearing of children post-divorce, may render mediation especially suitable in this area.[114] The practice of family mediation has received institutional underpinning from the law: Article 21 of Law No. 95-125, for example, provides that judges may refer civil cases to mediation with the parties' consent.[115] The more recent legislation of 4 March 2002 affords judges the right to direct parties to an introductory information session on mediation in custody disputes over children. An influential report to the National Assembly by Monique Sassier in 2001 resulted in the inception of a State Diploma of Family Mediation, a mandatory educational provision for all those seeking to practice as family mediators.[116] Mediation in other contexts is not so well grounded but steady progress has been made in the field generally over recent years. Judicial involvement in other strands of mediation can be detected even if court-sponsored mediation in non-family areas remains patchy.[117]

While the initial interest in mediation arose from professionals in the social work and psychology fields, lawyers have increasingly shown an interest in the process. One important pan-European initiative which was born in France is the "European Group of Magistrates for Mediation" ("GEMME"), seeking to promote the use of mediation by magistrates and sound the horn for mediation to litigants and their lawyers. In the commercial mediation arena, lawyers have also established partnerships with the business community in developing mediation

---

[110] This can be seen as fitting given its status as the "mother system" of the European civil law family—see De Roo and Jagtenberg 2004, Chap. 2.2.1.

[111] Macfarlane (2004).

[112] As distinct from well established, judicially sponsored conciliation procedures.

[113] Macfarlane (2006), p. 181.

[114] This is a feature shared across many European countries. For a discussion see Macfarlane (2004).

[115] February 8th 1995. While the provision was aimed principally at family mediation it is applicable across the civil dispute spectrum.

[116] Sassier (2001).

[117] See, for example, the experience of the Grenoble Court of Appeal in labour disputes.

organisations.[118] Many lawyers, amongst other professionals have trained as mediators in general civil matters, on programmes accredited by bodies such as the Paris Mediation and Arbitration Centre ('CMAP'), a branch of the Paris Chamber of Commerce. Most recently legislation was passed to comply with the terms of the recent European Mediation Directive.[119]

1.2.3.3 Germany

Germany has been slow to react to mediation's promise. Despite earlier academic interest in the subject by law, criminology and sociology scholars,[120] initial developments occurring in the context of family mediation did not surface until 1989 through *ad hoc* regional practice.[121] These developments became formalised through a new collaborative body, the Federal Working Group for Family Mediation, established in 1992 and a pilot, court-annexed mediation pilot scheme quickly followed in the state of Lower-Saxonia.[122]

General civil and commercial mediation developments did not occur until the late 1990s and although practice levels continue to be modest rather than spectacular, the process has risen in popularity of late through promotional bodies such as the National Association for Mediation in Business and the Workplace.[123] Mediation has also been increasingly bolstered by support provided by the courts.[124] The most important provision in this sense is section 15a of the Introductory Law of the Code of Civil Procedure enacted in 2000, which facilitates, but does not require, the inception of mandatory mediation schemes in certain civil disputes in German courts.

Much early regulatory provisions as to mediation in Germany prescribed that only lawyers could mediate.[125] Lawyers are prominent in mediation developments and have aggressively asserted their right to inherit the mediator's crown, particularly through attempts to render mediation 'the practice of law' and hence the sole preserve of legal practitioners.[126] The Federal government has recently entered the fray by way of the Legal Services Act 2008. While this provision stipulates that

[118] See, for example, the CMAP (*Le Centre de Mediation et d'Arbitrage de Paris*) established in 1995.

[119] Available at http://www.legifrance.gouv.fr/affichTexte.do?cidTexte=JORFTEXT000024804821&dateTexte=&categorieLien=id. Accessed 1 November 2011.

[120] See Hoffman (2007), pp. 518–519.

[121] See, Alexander et al. (2006), p. 224.

[122] Hoffman (2007), p. 520.

[123] Hillig and Huhn (2010), p. 47.

[124] See Osten (2011).

[125] See the discussion in Alexander (2000).

[126] See discussion in Hoffman (2007), pp. 533–534.

generally mediation is not to be deemed a legal service,[127] it prohibits the giving of legal advice by non-lawyer mediators and therefore fundamentally limits the ability of non-lawyer mediators to engage in evaluative techniques.[128] While traditionally mediation has featured little in German legal education, the 2003 Law on the Reform of Legal Education, led to the introduction of mediation into the standard law curriculum.[129]

1.2.3.4 Italy

Italy has again been characterised by a steady growth in mediation over the past two decades or so. The practice of mediation in Italy can now be found across a wide spectrum of civil disputes including consumer, commercial, matrimonial and public law issue areas. Initial interest stemmed primarily from growing disquiet concerning the Italian civil justice system which had become increasingly blighted by crippling delays.[130] At an early stage of its development, Italy moved to implant mediation within the court system. Initial such endeavours included a 1991 law empowering "Judges of the Peace" to mediate small claims disputes coming before their courts[131] and laws empowering Chambers of Commerce to mediate disputes involving pre-contracting issues prior to cases proceeding to trials.[132]

In common with many civil law European nations, Italy moved quickly to regulate mediation activities through law. In 2003 legislation was passed seeking to regulate many key facets of mediation in business disputes and expedite further development of the process.[133] Regulations were propounded, *inter alia*, to define the process, underpin confidentiality within mediation and enforceability of mediation agreements, provide for private and public sector mediation bodies, prescribe minimum training requirements for mediators and allow judges to propose mediation to litigants.

In terms of most recent legislative inroads, in March 2010 legislative decree n. 28/2010[134] was passed to enact the EU directive on Mediation.[135] In addition to

---

[127] § 2 Abs, 3 Nr 4.

[128] The measure does allow, however, for the provision of legal information. This distinction is discussed further in Chap. 3 at Sect. 3.4.3.3.

[129] Article 1(2c).

[130] Writing in 2003 Giuseppe De Palo, Paola Bernadini and Luigi Cominelli reported that the average duration of a civil trial amounted to some three and a half years - see De Palo et al. (2003), p. 51.

[131] Law No 374 (1991).

[132] Law No 580 (1993) and Law No 192 (1998).

[133] Law No 5 (2003).

[134] D.Lgs. 4-3-2010 n. 28, "Attuazione dell'articolo 60 della legge 18 giugno 2009, n. 69, in materia di mediazione finalizzata alla conciliazione delle controversie civili e commerciali", Italian Official Journal, March 5, 2010, n. 53.

[135] See Sect. 1.2.4.

placing obligations upon lawyers to inform their clients about mediation, in a wide range of commercial and civil disputes mediation has become a mandatory first step which must be taken by disputing parties prior to litigating their case. A particular controversial characteristic of court-referred mediation in this context is that where the case looks set to fail the mediator is empowered to issue a settlement offer which the parties may either decline or accept. Failing to accept such an offer, however, may deprive a winning party of their court expenses consequently.

Despite early[136] and continued[137] evidence of opposition to mediation developments, Italian lawyers have become instrumental in offering mediation services particularly in the commercial dispute resolution sphere[138] and in some contexts law is seen as a 'preferred' professional background for mediators.[139]

1.2.4 Supra National, European Developments

It is also prudent to reflect on supra-national initiatives on mediation pursued by the European Union (EU) which provide an abiding subtext to the individual efforts of the EU countries. Over recent decades, the EU has become a keen a supporter of mediation. In the family mediation context, a Recommendation of the European Council was made in 1998 which sought to promote mediation, by furnishing a homogeneous framework of reference for European countries and making recommendations about training, regulation and improving the accessibility of the process to disputing couples.[140]

More recently, the EU has shown its support for mediation through the development of the European Code of Conduct for Mediators in 2004 which sought to develop non-binding guidelines for such issues as training and regulation of mediators,[141] and most importantly by way of the European Directive on Mediation, adopted on 21 May 2008.[142] The Directive was some 8 years in gestation and

[136] De Palo and Hartley (2005), p. 475.

[137] At the time of writing a recent strike had been called by Italian lawyers in protest at recent legislation mandating mediation in civil litigation.

[138] For example, in respect of the 1996 Rome Bar Association conciliation service.

[139] See, for example, the requirements for inclusion on approved rosters under Article 4.4 of the decree no 222 of 2004.

[140] Recommendation 98/257/EC. A European Mediation Network was established in 2007 with a view to sharing best practice and consistent policies across Europe as well as promoting research—see http://www.mediationeurope.net/ Accessed 1 November 2011.

[141] Available at http://ec.europa.eu/civiljustice/adr/adr_ec_code_conduct_en.pdf Accessed 1 November 2011.

This has been adopted as a model by some regulatory bodies across Europe, e.g. the Civil Mediation Council in England and Wales.

[142] Directive 2008/52/EC of the European Parliament and of the Council of 21 May 2008 on certain aspects of mediation in civil and commercial matters.

makes arrangements for the promotion and use of mediation across the broad spectrum of civil and commercial disputes. The original premise of the directive, that is should apply to all member states' domestic mediation activities was watered down, and the provision now only applies directly to cross border disputes.[143] Nonetheless, the directive makes it clear that nothing within its terms precludes states from applying its provisions to domestic disputes. The Directive does not seek to alter individual state laws on mediation to any real degree but it does seek to provide institutional support for the development of mediation by, for example, ensuring the enforceability of mediation agreements and the confidentiality of the mediation process. It also seeks to encourage the increased use of mediation and in particular to ensure a sound relationship between mediation and judicial proceedings by, for example, encouraging courts to refer disputing parties to mediation. The provisions do not prescribe compulsory referral by courts to mediation, but it expressly states that there is nothing in the Directive to prohibit states from doing so if they so wish. The terms of the Directive required its implementation in all Member States[144] by 21 May 2011. Its impact is due to be reviewed in 2016.

At the time of writing, many Member States have implemented the terms of the Directive through domestic legislation. The respective approaches to implementation are interesting not least because of the marked divergence in approach than can be seen. Some Member States have taken the opportunity to legislate significantly across the mediation field in general, while others, such as Scotland and England and Wales have been more cautious in their legislative interpretation, limiting the focus squarely on cross-border disputes. At the time of writing, some Member States have failed, however, to cement the terms of the Directive within their domestic legal system. In response to this recalcitrance, the European Commission has recently sent letters of formal notice of impending legal action to the Czech Republic, Spain, France, Cyprus, Luxembourg, the Netherlands, Finland, Slovakia and the UK[145] for their non-compliance.[146] The European Parliament has also stepped into the pro-mediation fray by recently passing a resolution on the implementation of mediation in Member States. This resolution seeks further action on issues such as confidentiality in, and enforceability of mediation, the expanding of mediation take-up amongst lawyers, other professions and society in general and the development of common standards in training and regulation.[147]

---

[143] Where one party is domiciled on one country and the other in another EU state.

[144] Except Denmark.

[145] In respect of Gibraltar.

[146] See the report at http://europa.eu/rapid/pressReleasesAction.do?reference=IP/11/919&format=HTML&aged=0&language=EN&guiLanguage=en Accessed 1 November 2011.

[147] European Parliament resolution of 13 September on the implementation of the directive on mediation in Member States, its impact on mediation and its take-up by the courts (2011/2026 (INI)).

In terms of lawyer engagement specifically, concurrently the European Commission has established a spate of research projects under the auspices of "Lawyers in ADR", an initiative designed to promote knowledge and use of mediation in the context of the new Directive amongst legal professionals. Ongoing work includes research into the costs of cross border disputing, studies into the current state of mediation activity across Europe and a book on mediation advocacy.[148] Similar studies have been conducted in the consumer redress field, with recent attempts made to chart all current ADR schemes (including mediation) in this dispute sphere as well as gaps in coverage across all EU member states.[149] Some 750 ADR schemes dealing with consumer disputes across EU nations were identified in the research.[150]

1.3 Conclusion

Globally, the modern mediation movement has at least in part been instigated and propelled by lawyers. Progress has clearly been uneven both within and across different jurisdictions. In the historical development of mediation, however, the pursuit of efficiencies and diversion from traditional courts were clearly significant drivers for reform from, amongst others, the legal profession. As this book shall discuss in the foregoing chapters, while pro-mediation policy makers and members of the judiciary in particular may stand accused of seeking to further the interests of efficiency and expediency in civil justice matters to the detriment of litigants in society, lawyers involved in mediation may be charged with seeking to advance their own professional interests at the expense of other potential service providers, through lawyer-to lawyer-mediator referrals, practice models that suit lawyer-mediators and party representatives, and tactical manoeuvres designed to exclude lay-persons from mediation practice. As noted in the review presented in this chapter, while mediation developments that sit outside of the formal legal disputing practices have generally fared moderately at best, many countries have actively forged strong bonds between formal adjudicative forms of civil justice and mediation which thus may herald a lawyer-dominated future for mediation. Whether lawyers, products of their own traditional legal training and practice norms, are even suited for mediation practice is by itself a controversial issue. Such matters shall be discussed in later chapters of this book.

Nonetheless, while some lawyers and judges are champions (whatever their motives might be), many remain on the fringes apathetic, others are openly

---

[148] See http://www.adrcenter.com/international/cms/?page_id=259 Accessed 1 November 2011.

[149] Alleweldt et al. (2009).

[150] Alleweldt et al. (2009).

sceptical or even anti-mediation in their posturing, and a smattering can be described as doomsayers, predicting an untrammelled glut of mediation riding roughshod over the purity of the application of law and legitimacy of formal justice systems. Against this backdrop, the next chapter analyses the notion of lawyer resistance to mediation and investigates the motives of those lawyers who may be seen as a roadblock to mediation's progress.

References

Abel RL (1983) Mediation in pre-capitalist societies. Windsor Yearbook of Access to Justice 3:175–185

Agapiou A, Clark B (2011) Scottish construction lawyers and mediation: an investigation into attitudes and experience. Int J Law Built Environ 3(2):159–181

Alexander N (2000) German law paves the way for mandatory mediation. ADR Bull 2(9):87–88

Alexander N (2001) What's law got to do with it? mapping modern mediation movements in civil and common law jurisdictions. Bond Law Rev 15(2):1–29

Alexander N (2006) Introduction. In: Alexander N (ed) Global trends in mediation, 2nd edn. Kluwer International, Alphen aan den Rijn

Alexander N et al (2006) Mediation in Germany: the long and winding road. In: Alexander N (ed) Global trends in mediation, 2nd edn. Kluwer International, Alphen aan den Rijn

Alleweldt F et al (2009) Study on the use of alternative dispute resolution in the European Union. Final Report. Civic Consulting of the Consumer Policy Evaluation Consortium (CPEC), Berlin 16 October 2009. http://ec.europa.eu/consumers/redress_cons/adr_study.pdf. Accessed 1 Nov 2011

Auerbach J (1983) Justice without law, resolving disputes without lawyers. OUP, New York

Bedlam LJ (2001) Committee on ADR. General Counsel of the Bar, London

Blomgren Bingham L (2002) Why suppose? let's find out: a public policy research program on dispute resolution. J Dispute Resolut 1:101–126

Brooker P (2001) Commercial and construction ADR: lawyers' attitudes and experience. Civ Justice Q 20:327–347

Brooker P (2005) Construction lawyers' experience with mediation post-CPR. Const L J 21(1):19–46

Brown H (2001) ADR Report. The Law Society, Courts and Legal Services Committee, London

Bucklow A (2007) The "everywhen" mediator: the virtues of inconsistency and paradox: the strengths, skills, attributes and behaviours of excellent and effective mediators. Arbitration 73 (1):40–48

Bush RAB, Folger JP (2005) The promise of mediation: responding to conflict through empowerment and recognition, 2nd edn. Jossey-Bass, San Francisco

Cappelletti M (ed) (1978) The florence access to justice project, vol 1–IV. Sijthoff and Noordhoff Int, Alphen aan den Rijn

Cheung SO (2010) Construction mediation in Hong Kong. In: Brooker P, Wilkinson S (eds) Mediation in the construction industry: an international review. Spon Press, London

Chief Justice's Working Party on Civil Justice Reform (2004) Final report. http://www.civiljustice.gov.hk/fr/paperhtml/toc_fr.html. Accessed I Nov 2011

Clark B, Dawson C (2007) Scottish commercial litigators and ADR: a study of attitudes and experience. Civ Justice Q 26:228–249

Corby S (1999) Resolving employment rights through mediation: the new zealand experience. Institute of Employment Rights, London

De Palo G, Hartley P (2005) Mediation in Italy: exploring the contradictions. ABL/INFORM Global 21(4):469–479

De Palo G et al (2003) Mediation in Italy: the legislative debate and the future. ADR Bulletin 6(3):51–53

De Roo A, Jagtenberg R (2002) Mediation in the Netherlands, past, present and future. Electron J Comp Law 6.4

De Roo A, Jagtenberg R (2006) The Dutch landscape of court-encouraged mediaiton. In: Alexander N (ed) Global trends in mediation, 2nd edn. Kluwer International, Alphen aan den Rijn

Doyle M (2006) Evaluation of the small claims mediation service at Manchester county court. Dept of Constitutional Affairs, London

Engle Merry S (1990) Getting justice and getting even: legal consciousness among working-class Americans. University of Chicago Press, Chicago

Freeman-Greene S (2001) Mediation: can we ignore it? http://www.leadr.co.nz/db/index.php/articles-mainmenu-162/78-mediation-can-we-ignore-it. Accessed 1 Nov 2011

Galanter M (1985) The Legal malaise; or, justice observed. Law Soc Rev 19(4):537–556

Genn H et al (2007) Twisting arms: court referred and court linked mediation under judicial pressure. Ministry of Justice, London

Gill, Lord (2009) Report of the Scottish civil courts review. Scottish Civil Courts Review. Edinburgh

Gould N et al (2010) Mediating construction disputes: an evaluation of existing practice. Centre for Construction Law, Kings College, London

Hensler DR (2003) Our courts, ourselves: how the alternative dispute resolution movement is reshaping our legal system. Penn St L Rev 108:165–197

Hillig J, Huhn M (2010) Construction mediation in Germany. In: Brooker P, Wilkinson S (eds) Mediation in the construction industry: an international review. Spon Press, London

Hoffman A (2007) Mediation in Germany and the United States. Eur J Law Reform 9:505–551

Hong Kong Polytechnic (2004) Evaluation study on the pilot scheme on family mediation. http://www.judiciary.gov.hk/en/publications/hkpu_finalreport.pdf. Accessed 1 Nov 2011

Irvine C (2010) The sound of one-hand clapping: Gill's faint praise for mediation. Edinb Law Rev 14(1):85–92

Lande J (2000) Getting the faith: why business lawyers and executives believe in mediation. Harv Negot Law Rev 5:137–227

Levinson D (1994) Aggression and conflict: a cross-cultural encyclopaedia. ABC-Clio Inc, Santa Barbara

Macfarlane J (2002) Culture change? a tale of two cities and mandatory court-connected mediation. Journal Dispute Resolut 2:241–366

Macfarlane D (2004) Family mediation in France. Journal Fam Stud 10(1):97–113

Macfarlane D (2006) Mediation in France. In: Alexander N (ed) Global trends in mediation, 2nd edn. Kluwer International, Alphen aan den Rijn

Macfarlane J (2008) The new lawyer: how settlement is transforming the practice of law. UBS Press, Toronto

Mays R, Clark B (1996) Alternative dispute resolution in scotland. Scottish Office Central Research Unit, Edinburgh

McAdoo B (1997) Does ADR really have a place on the lawyer's philosophical map?". Hamline J Pub L Pol Y 18:376–393

McDonald F (2004) The use of mediation to settle civil justice disputes: a review of evidence. Scottish Executive Legal Research Studies Programme, Edinburgh

Menkel-Meadow C (2000) Mothers and fathers of invention: the intellectual founders of ADR. Ohio State J Dispute Resolut 16:1–37

Merry S, Milner N (1995) The possibility of popular justice: a case study of community mediation in the United States (law, meaning, and violence). University of Michigan Press, Michigan

Mistelis L (2006) ADR in England and wales: a successful case of public private partnership. In: Alexander N (ed) Global trends in mediation, 2nd edn. Kluwer International, Alphen aan den Rijn

Mulcahy L (2002) Can leopards change their spots: the role of lawyers in mediation. Int J Legal Profession 8(3):203–224

Murray JL, Rau AS, Sherman EF (1996) Mediation and other non-binding ADR processes. Foundation Press, New York

Neimeijer B, Pel M (2005) Court-based mediation in the Netherlands: research, evaluation and future expectations. Penn State Law Rev 110:345–379

Nolan-Handley J (2002) Lawyers, non-lawyers and mediation: rethinking the professional monopoly from a problem-solving perspective. Harv Negot Law Rev 7:235–286

NPWC/NBCC (1990) No dispute – strategies for improvement in the Australian building and construction industry. Report for the National Public Works Council and National Building Council joint working party Dickson, A.C.T. : National Public Works Conference. Melbourne

Oliver M (2007) Implementing Sustainability – New Zealand's environment court-annexed mediation. Indian Society of International Law (ISIL) Fifth International Conference on International Environmental Law, New Delhi, India. http://www.leadr.co.nz/db/images/M_PDFs/marlene%20oliver%20paper.pdf. Accessed 1 Nov 2011

Osten P (2011) Court based Mediation in Germany and transposition of the mediation directive 2008/52 EC. Contribution to the training seminar at the Hungarian Judicial Academy, Budapest, May 12th, 201. http://www.gemme.eu/en/news/download/352. Accessed 1 Nov 2011

Platform ADR (1998) Conflictbemiddeling; eindrapport platform ADR. Ministerie van Justitie, Den Haag

Prince S (2007) Institutionalising mediation? An evaluation of the Exeter small claims mediation pilot 5 *Web JCLI*

Prince S, Belcher S (2006) An evaluation of the effectiveness of court-based mediation processes in non-family civil proceedings at exeter and guilford county courts. Department of Constitutional Affairs, London

Prujiner A (2006) Recent developments in mediation in Canada. In: Alexander N (ed) Global trends in mediation, 2nd edn. Kluwer International, Alphen aan den Rijn

Roberts S, Palmer M (2005) Dispute processes: ADR and the primary forms of decision-making, 2nd edn. Cambridge University Press, Cambridge

Roebuck D (2007) The myth of modern mediation. Arbitration 73:105–116

Ross M (2006) Mediation in Scotland: an elusive opportunity? In: Alexander N (ed) Global trends in mediation, 2nd edn. Kluwer International, Alphen aan den Rijn

Ross M, Bain D (2010) In court mediation pilots: report on evaluation of in court mediation schemes in Glasgow and Aberdeen Sheriff courts. Scottish government, courts and constitution analytical team. http://www.scotland.gov.uk/Resource/Doc/310104/0097858.pdf

Samuel E (2002) Supporting court users: the in-court advice and mediation projects at Edinburgh Sheriff court phase 2. Scottish Executive Central Research Unit, Edinburgh

Sander FEA (1979) Varieties of dispute processing. In: Levin AL, Wheeler RR (eds) The pound conference: perspectives on justice in the future. West, Massachusetts

Sassier M (2001) Arguments and proposals for a statute of family mediation in France. Ministry of Family, Childhood and Handicapped Persons, Paris

Scottish Government (2010) Scottish government response to the report and recommendations of the Scottish civil courts review. http://www.scotland.gov.uk/Resource/Doc/330272/0107186.pdf. Accessed 1 Nov 2011

Shipman S (2006) Court approaches to ADR in the civil justice system. Civ Justice Q 25:181–218

Sibley S, Sarat A (1989) Dispute processing in law and legal scholarship: from institutional critique to the reconstruction of the juridical subject. Denver Univ Law Rev 66(3):437–498

South J (2005) Expanding your portfolio: training as a mediator. New Law J 155(7167):366

Stipanovich T (2004) ADR and the 'Vanishing Trial': the growth and impact of 'alternative dispute resolution'. J Empir Leg Stud 1(3):843–912

Tidwell A (1999) It's the process that counts: professionalising mediation in new south wales. Murdoch Univ Electron Law 6(2)

Wall C (2009) The framework for mediation in Hong Kong. Arbitration 75(1):78–85

Welsh N (2001) The thinning vision of self-determination: the inevitable price of institutionalization? Harv Negot Law Rev 6:1–96

Welsh N, McAdoo B (2005) Look before you leap and keep on looking: lessons from the institutionalization of court-connected mediation. Nevada Law Rev 5:347–432

Chapter 2
Lawyer Resistance to Mediation

2.1 Introduction

It was seen in Chap. 1 that lawyers have often been instrumental in propelling mediation onwards in a number of jurisdictions globally. Surveys of lawyers' attitudes to mediation often paint a picture of a generally appreciative legal community positive in its outlook on mediation, at least in the abstract,[1] although that does not seem to have necessarily translated into an upsurge in voluntary engagement with the process. Indeed, the pace of development of the process has varied significantly across different countries and in respect of distinct dispute areas within each jurisdiction. Despite decades of promotion and publicity, in many nations the practice of mediation remains on the fringes of mainstream disputing. In the main, significant progress has been made only in the aftermath of some legislative underpinning or form of linking with traditional justice systems.

Notwithstanding their key role in the modern re-emergence of the process and their oft self-espoused positivity, lawyers, as 'gatekeepers' to mediation,[2] have long been suspected of acting as a roadblock to mediation's advancement. Global speculation as to lawyer recalcitrance to mediation is rife. The issue is one that has consistently reared its head in my own discussions with mediation enthusiasts—non-lawyers and lawyers alike—over the last 16 years or so at home and abroad. More important of course than the anecdotal musings regaled in these conversations, significant empirical evidence suggestive of lawyer intransigence towards mediation does exist. Research into court-annexed mediation schemes in Scotland[3] and

[1] See for example the following studies: Brooker (2001) (England and Wales); Clark and Dawson (2007), Agapiou and Clark (2011) (Scotland); Zariski (1997) (Australia); Lande (2000), Kakalik et al. (1996) (USA); ADR Center (2010) (European Union); Sela (2009) (Israel); Saville-Smith and Fraser (2004) (New Zealand).

[2] The extent to which lawyers are in fact gatekeepers is discussed below at Sect. 2.3.

[3] Samuel (2002), para 4.2.50. See also Ross and Bain (2010), Chap. 7 where lawyer resistance to the introduction of the sheriff court mediation pilots was reported.

B. Clark, *Lawyers and Mediation*, DOI 10.1007/978-3-642-23474-3_2,

England,[4] for example, where some parties may be represented by lawyers and others not, reveals that the presence of lawyer party representatives leads to lower uptake of mediation by litigants. In the family context in England and Wales it has recently been reported that lawyers remain reluctant to refer parties to mediation.[5] Research in the court-connected context in Netherlands similarly suggests that lawyers may have a negative influence on mediation referrals rates.[6] Similar findings were elicited in a study of mediation schemes in a number of European countries.[7] These findings tie in with a wealth of international evidence pointing to the indisputable finding that lawyers *sometimes* appear in practice reluctant to embrace mediation. Writing recently, Don Peters, citing research from the USA, Italy, Poland, Germany, France and the UK goes so far to suggest that "the majority of the globe's attorneys resist mediating".[8] While the empirical basis for that proposition is perhaps questionable, lawyers are certainly often open in their hostility to mediation, or at least the imposition of mediation within particular dispute resolution settings. Witness, for example, the active resistance of lawyers to civil justice reforms which sought, *inter alia*, to promote mediation in Hong Kong[9]; and more dramatically, the recent strike called by Italian lawyers in response to their government's initiative to instigate compulsory mediation in the civil courts.[10]

If it is accepted that there is substantial evidence that lawyer resistance to mediation does exist, it is a pertinent question to ask why this is the case. A whole raft of different factors may be relevant to lawyers' resistance to mediation. Some reasons may appear legitimate or altruistic in their nature, while others seem less acceptable and perhaps, it may be suspected, even emanate from somewhat dishonourable motives on the part of lawyers. Although clearly the categories overlap, I broadly group those that might be perceived as illegitimate reasons for resisting mediation as: selfish financial imperatives; ignorance of the process and its potential utility; and linked to the second, cultural biases in traditional legal practice militating against mediation use. Reasons for objections to mediation, which may, *prima facie* at least, appear more legitimate, include: concerns about the lack of quality assurance in mediation services and unregulated practice; simple lack of client demand[11]; fears over disingenuous use of the process by opponents and arguments based around the efficiency of mediation (e.g. how quick or cheap it

---

[4] Genn (1998); Prince (2004); Doyle (2006); Genn et al. (2007).

[5] Melville and Laing (2010).

[6] Niemeijer and Pel (2005–2006), particularly the studies cited at fn 5.

[7] de Roo and Jagtenberg (2003).

[8] Peters (2011a).

[9] Wall (2009).

[10] Guardian Newspaper (2011). At the time of writing it has been reported that a second strike is planned.

[11] To what extent this is a chimera in that client demand for mediation may be created or suppressed by lawyers themselves is discussed below at Sect. 2.3.3.

actually is) relative to other forms of dispute resolution. Additionally, certain principled objections may be held, including: 'justice-based' assertions focusing on the notion that channelling disputants towards mediation and away from formal adjudicative processes is anathema to their rights to pursue justice; and worries over the suppression of public norms occurring under the weight of increased private settlement.

The latter two principled concerns set out above, which may tend to emanate more from academics and judges[12] rather than practising lawyers,[13] are dealt with in Chap. 5 (on the consequences of institutionalisation of mediation) rather than the present one. With that caveat in mind, this chapter seeks to review the evidence regarding to what extent lawyer resistance has stifled mediation's promise and probes the rationale for the lawyer disinterest and hostility that does exist. Two issues which provide an abiding subtext to the analysis are dealt with first, namely: a brief foray into the public perception of lawyers; and an examination of the notion of lawyer as 'gatekeeper' to dispute resolution methods and how this impacts upon client demand for mediation.

2.2 The Public Perception of Lawyers

Before examining on what basis 'bad' lawyers might be stifling 'good' mediation, it is worth reflecting on the fact that the wealth of speculation that lawyers' resistance may emanate from less than altruistic reasons may to some extent at least merely reflect an historical antipathy towards the profession as a whole. A proclivity for caricature does not make for compelling discourse and a brief foray into the poor reputation that lawyers suffer in the public eye suggests that this reputation alone may go some way at least towards casting them as the villains of the piece - a haughty, narrow-minded, penny-pinching, anti-mediation brigade.

Although surveys often indicate that clients are generally satisfied with their own lawyers and the service they receive,[14] such upbeat individual appraisals do not translate into a favourable general public perception of legal professionals as a whole. Research over the years across different jurisdictions has consistently indicated that the general population view lawyers in a somewhat negative light. Indeed, lawyers suffer an unfavourable perception in the public arena

---

[12] Although by contrast in many countries judges have been targeted by academics for their seemingly unbridled support of mediation.

[13] Who one may suspect may have scant concern for such lofty matters when compared to the micro issues affecting their cases.

[14] For example, for Scotland, Campbell (1976); for the USA, Post (1987), p. 380, Galanter (1994), p. 663; for Canada, Lafontaine (1985), p. 177.

when compared with most other professions.[15] Disparaging jokes about lawyers are rife.[16] The internet is awash with blogs and notice boards lambasting the legal profession. While recent times have seen the expression of heightened fears of a decline in legal professionalism, which at least in part may have increasingly driven a backlash against lawyers,[17] the public antipathy towards lawyers is not a modern phenomenon; it can be traced back for centuries.[18]

Research reveals a number of widely held negative perceptions of lawyers' traits which may fan the flames of public antipathy towards them. Perhaps the main strand of attack is that the lawyer is a cynical professional motivated by money to the expense of all else—one who bathes in paupers' tears and caviar. Allied to this critique is the notion that lawyers service the rich while disregarding the needs of the poor. The argument follows that lawyers habitually put up barriers for the disenfranchised to gain access to justice whilst happily bending legal rules for the powerful in society.[19] In terms of the adversarial perception of lawyers, although we typically value the worth of our own lawyers, thrusting forward rapier-like, as 'champions' to further our cause, by contrast we take a dim of view of those lawyers that act in such a fashion for others.[20]

The poor image that lawyers suffer in public life may also, of course, be linked to the fact that consumers of legal services often turn to lawyers at emotionally distressing and financially detrimental times in their lives, e.g. when buying a house, contesting a civil action, facing criminal charges, buying a business or winding up the estate of a deceased loved one. There is something inherently distasteful in the notion that money can be made from the misery of others. It is then a natural consequence of the social space in which lawyers inhabit—one often filled with their clients' discomfort, angst and conflict—that negative views of such professionals may be held.

The images of lawyers portrayed in the popular media arguably both reflect and also shape and reinforce negative public attitudes towards lawyers.[21] Although throughout history a number of prevalent lawyer-stereotypes have been manifest, both on screen and within literature the dominant image portrayed is that of the

---

[15] For example, for the USA, Daicoff (1997), p. 1344; Galanter (1994), p. 663; Gross 1999; for Germany, Bohlander (1998), p. 128; for Italy, Cappelletti et al. (1967) p. 97.

[16] See generally Galanter (2005).

[17] Kronman (1993).

[18] In December 1891, for example it was reported in *Vanity Fair* that "[lawyers] are specimens...who fatten while their clients are ruined. They work well, and no fair as better specimens, nor more knowing in the law, which they make more complicated as they go: in recompense for which they have promoted a very beautiful system by which their clients are allowed no more access to them than is needed for the payment of their high fees", cited in McIlwaine (2004), p. 243.

[19] Parker (1999), p. 1.

[20] Parker (1999), pp. 10–11.

[21] Macfarlane (2008) at fns 5 and 6.

lawyer as a sharp, devious, cunning, unscrupulous sort, often motivated principally by money and power.[22] In many cases, the depiction of the lawyer as charlatan is also compounded by an attack on his or her emotional state and social characteristics, thus the lawyer may be portrayed, for example, as a loner, unable to hold down relationships, and/or dependent on drugs or alcohol. The issue of actual typical lawyer personality traits and what this might entail for their participation in mediation is an important issue to which I shall return in Chap. 4.

2.3 The Lawyer as Gatekeeper

It is often remarked without too much accompanying fuss, that lawyers are 'gatekeepers' to mediation's development. Given this oft-stated truism, the argument follows that it is crucial that if mediation is to flourish then lawyers must be brought on-side with the process. While lawyers are doubtless often instrumental in legitimising mediation in the eyes of their clients, and empirical studies seem to bear out this assertion in many contexts,[23] the influence of lawyers over their clients in the course of a dispute clearly varies considerably. In fact glib assertions that lawyers act as gatekeepers placing insurmountable barriers to the prospective joys of mediation in the way of their hapless clients have perhaps clouded attempts to ascertain how clients across different dispute areas actually respond to the promise of mediation and what might be done to better sell the process to them. Indeed, as noted above,[24] numerous studies have suggested that lawyers have become increasingly receptive to mediation as a form of dispute resolution, at least in the abstract. Nonetheless, this apparent surge in general enthusiasm does not, it seems, always transfer into the reality of increasing case referrals, save where court or state funding rules propel disputants (and their lawyers) into mediation through various degrees of arm twisting.[25]

2.3.1 Clients and Mediation

In responding to questions as to why mediation has not been taken up, lawyers sometimes blame their clients[26]; the premise here being that lawyers are powerless

[22] See for example, Walter Matthau's portrayal of William Gingrich in Billy Wilder's *The Fortune Cookie* (1966) and Al Palcino in The Devil's Advocate (1997) (where the devil is embodied within a New York lawyer); albeit that there are notable exceptions, such as Atticus Finch in *To Kill a Mockingbird* (1962). See generally, Chase (1986).

[23] These are discussed below at Sect. 2.3.3.

[24] At footnote one.

[25] Discussed further in Chap. 5.

[26] Found in my own research—Clark and Dawson (2007), p.235; Agapiou and Clark (2011a), p.169. See also Sidoli del Ceno (2011), p.188 (English property lawyers).

to convince their clients to see the benefits that they themselves see that mediation might hold. While I discuss this issue below,[27] it is first worth noting that while it might be speculated that such explanations represent no more than a socially desired response, masking lawyer intransigence towards the process, a recent EU funded survey of EU lawyers and business corporations conducted by a consortium led by the ADR Center, revealed that generally speaking lawyers held more positive perceptions of mediation than business clients in issues such as potential success rates and time taken to reach settlement in mediation. Moreover, lawyers were reported to be more likely to have established a presumptive policy on the use of ADR than corporations and were more likely to favour the instigation of court rules to facilitate mediation.[28] Similarly, research in the US context conducted by John Lande suggested that lawyers were more appreciative of mediation than business executives.[29]

Despite the research findings described above, there is significant international evidence in some fields of client goodwill towards mediation[30] and many businesses and public sector bodies, for example, have adopted mediation pledges. It is worth noting though that while studies often tell us that clients are appreciative of mediation in the abstract (or satisfied with the process post-mediation) less is known about what the promise of mediation holds for parties actually in a dispute. There is some evidence from studies of individual disputants that mediation is not always seen as a particularly attractive proposition. This may arise simply because of lack of knowledge of the process. For example, a 2007 survey of German lawyers and mediators found that 85% of mediators and 67% of lawyers viewed that lack of knowledge of mediation in the client base was stifling mediation's development.[31] Like findings have been unearthed in research in other jurisdictions.[32] European Union ADR schemes in the consumer field often also appear to struggle to gain recognition in part because of client ignorance.[33] More importantly, client reluctance may arise because parties are seeking to be 'saved' by champions to fight their corner,[34] or because they might prefer an authoritative decision to be rendered on their behalf.[35] In a 2005 study of German commercial enterprises in which only 28% of all firms surveyed had mediated, the authors noted a striking disparity

---

[27] In Sects. 2.3.2–2.3.4.

[28] ADR Center et al. 2010, Chaps. 3–6.

[29] Lande 2000, pp. 172–173.

[30] A number of studies in the US and Latin American contexts are summarised in Peters (2010), pp. 387–392.

[31] Hoffman (2007), p. 538.

[32] My own research into Scottish construction contractors and subcontractors found more than 20% of clients were unaware of the process of mediation—Agapiou and Clark (2011b).

[33] Alleweldt et al. (2009), p. 9.

[34] Genn 1999, p. 100; Genn and Paterson (2001), p. 117.

[35] See, for example, Merry (1990); Merry and Sibley (1984).

between respondents' views on mediation in the abstract and attitudes held towards the process amidst an actual dispute, which were far less in favour of mediating.[36]

Furthermore, many parties in dispute may simply see little worth in mediating given their own strategic goals in the litigation process. This may be so particularly for defendants who are happy to draw out the process either because they want to delay payment or in the hope that their opponent will simply become disheartened and give up or run out of resources to pursue the action.[37] Empirical evidence suggests that defendant insurers, in particular, may often see fit to sit tight with no compunction to settle in cases in which individual plaintiffs face liability for their (the insurers') costs in the event of an unsuccessful claim.[38] Against this backdrop then of potential client ambivalence towards mediation, it is worth exploring the lawyer-client relationship, in particular, seeking to ascertain, "who is in charge"[39] and how that might impact upon the way that a dispute is handled and ultimately disposed of.[40]

2.3.2 *General Ideas*

Traditionally it can be said that the legal profession has shown a desire to exert dominance in the lawyer-client relationship and exercise their status as experts with the clients mere naïfs. In part at least, this has been achieved through history by clothing the law in mystique and shrouding legal practice in arcane language and practices. This kind of activity—creating a chasm between the professional's art and the layman - is of course common to all professions in their quest for control and status.[41] Furthermore, traditional legal education and training peddles, and hence anticipates in practice, a model of resolution of disputes based primarily on legal norms but absent the client and her extra-legal needs and interests.[42] The traditional model of legal practice in which lay clients' dispute 'stories' are

---

[36] Cited in Peters (2010), p. 392.

[37] Genn (2009), pp. 109–110.

[38] See the studies cited in Kritzer 2001/2002, p. 1955. 'Fee-shifting', or the 'English rule', in which an unsuccessful party will pay all or some of the costs of their opponent, is common in many jurisdictions across the common law and civil law world.

[39] The phrase coined by Douglas Rosenthal in his influential book, *Lawyer and client: who's in charge* (Rosenthal 1974).

[40] A separate but linked issue is the way that the power relationship between lawyers and clients impacts upon the acceptability of a dispute resolution process—mediation- that specifically entails client participation and the possible sidelining of lawyers.

[41] Johnson 1972.

[42] Legal Education is discussed further in the context of cultural barriers to mediation at Sect. 2.5.1.3.

reframed by an expert lawyer into a legal narrative[43] thus encourages lawyer-client interactions in which the lawyer calls the shots. Lawyers, in common with other professional agents, holding an informational advantage over their clients in the subject matter of their expertise, are able to exploit this knowledge gap to deliver the upper hand in the relationship with their clients.[44]

2.3.3 Lawyer-Client Relationship in the Dispute Resolution Context

In the realm of dispute resolution processes, recognising the traditional, subservient nature of the client, it has been noted generally that lawyers play a critical role in communicating ideas as to the legitimacy of different dispute resolution methods to their clients through "law talk". Thus, according to the classic study by Austin Sarat and William Felstiner, "lawyers' assimilation, acceptance, rejection, integration, or other response to alternatives to established norms of litigation practice [including mediation] is critical to both the practical consequences and the impact of civil justice reform and innovation."[45] International experience bears out the truth of this notion in respect of mediation, at least in certain contexts. In her review of the development of court annexed mediation programmes in the USA, Roselle Wissler, for example, points to the prominent role of lawyers in directing their clients towards mediation in the court-referred context. She attributes this, *inter alia*, to the limited role that clients play in negotiations outside mediation, the general unfamiliarity of clients towards ADR in general and the significant influence that lawyers hold over their clients generally.[46] Further US studies suggest that particularly in the court-annexed context, decisions relative to mediation use are normally taken by lawyers.[47] In a similar fashion, John Lande found that business executives generally received the bulk of their information about ADR from their attorneys. He further noted that as those attorneys became more experienced in ADR they would be more likely to present themselves as experts in the field with a view to guiding their clients in this respect.[48] Recent research in the Israeli context also supports the notion that lawyers typically remain in control of the decision to mediate or not, with many lawyer respondents signifying that they would rarely raise mediation

[43] Felstiner and Sarat (1980–1981).

[44] Sharma (1997).

[45] Sarat and Felstiner (1989), p. 1664.

[46] Wissler (2004a).

[47] Welsh (2004).

[48] Lande (2000), p. 169. Although he did also note that business executives' "belief" in mediation was related to the amount of information they received about the process from their colleagues (other than lawyers)—p. 200.

with clients without prompting by the court.[49] The study also revealed that suggestions to mediate disputes were very rarely made by clients, with most such suggestions emanating most commonly from the pre-trial judge and secondly, from attorneys.[50] Adrian Borbély's recent work in relation to mediation in France also suggests that lawyers' dominant position as professional agents vis-a-vis their clients in terms of dispute resolution determinations places them firmly in the driving seat when it comes to determinations regarding recourse to mediation.[51]

2.3.4 *Lawyer Control and Client Type*

Against a backdrop of limited take-up of mediation in various contexts and an assumption (and some evidence) that lawyers control their relationship with clients and decisions pertaining to dispute handling, it is easy to leap to the conclusion that lawyers represent a roadblock to mediation development. Nonetheless, it needs to be appreciated that lawyers are not always in the ascendancy relative to their clients. Although the reality of the situation is doubtless more complex and variations on the broad themes espoused here will be found, research has shown that in general, the more sophisticated and powerful the client is, the less the lawyer is able to exert control over that client in their interactions in the classic garb of 'patronage' professions, including how disputes ought to be resolved. In accordance with the traditional stereotype, it is true that lawyers representing disempowered, 'one-shotter' clients in such disputes as personal injury,[52] divorce, consumer and poverty cases may typically view themselves as 'taxi drivers'—in which the client decides on the destination but the route (and thus how the dispute is handled) is determined by the lawyer.[53] This may be unsurprising given the gulf in power that may subsist between lawyers and individual clients in such matters alluded to above.

More powerful clients may present an altogether different proposition for their lawyers, however. In this sense, there may be an inverse relationship, between the client's status and the control the lawyer exerts over that client.[54] In his seminal 1970's work, Joseph Handler noted that although "lawyers dominate the relationship when clients are poor, deviant, or unsophisticated... [s]trong, rich and

[49] Sela (2009), p. 51.

[50] Sela (2009).

[51] Borbély (2011).

[52] Recent research into personal injury actions in Scotland has suggested that lawyers typically remain in control of decisions as to how such disputes are handled: Coope and Morris (2002).

[53] Mather (2003), p. 1075. Albeit that in their classic study of the way that lawyers and clients interacted in divorce cases, Felstiner and Sarat found that typically neither lawyers nor clients dominated their relationship but rather that the power dynamic drifted between them over time, Felstiner and Sarat (1992).

[54] Heinz et al. (1976).

confident clients direct their lawyers. . . ."[55] Commercial clients, in particular, may typically fall into Handler's latter category. First, in general it can be said that as quintessential repeat players in civil disputes, commercial clients will be able to learn more about dispute resolution processes (and lawyers' agendas within the same) than 'one-shotters'. Secondly, empirical research in the USA, for example, has indicated that external corporate lawyers in fact rarely drive their clients' goals and rather are commonly seen as mere 'tools' or 'conduits' of their clients.[56] Accordingly, such lawyers may principally act as 'hired guns' concerned with doing the bidding of their clients rather than exhibiting any real measure of independence and authority within the lawyer/client relationship.

Research in the USA even goes so far as to suggest that increased competition for corporate business discourages client-influencing practices on the part of external lawyers, who fear that if they lean too heavily on clients to follow their lead they may swiftly find themselves replaced by more compliant attorneys.[57] The same phenomenon has been reported in other jurisdictions.[58] Writing in the aftermath of a global economic crisis and time of recession, it can be said that in inclement financial conditions, lawyers may become even more prone to kow-tow to their commercial clients, for which they are increasingly becoming reliant on for their continued financial viability. Evidence across Europe suggests, for example, that lawyers are increasingly amending their practices, reducing costs by varying their standard hourly billing rates, and increasingly seeking to appease their clients in an ever more competitive environment.[59] Such practices may not always be sufficient, however, in the sense that commercial organisations have begun to outsource routine parts of their legal activities to offshore agencies in an effort to reduce their legal outlays.[60]

Such 'bending' to clients may be compounded by the fact that the past two decades or so has also seen a distinct growth in in-house legal counsel.[61] Thus commercial clients have become more informed legally and less reliant on external lawyers. In-house counsel, who may carry none of the suspected incentives of external lawyers to render dispute resolution a drawn out, expensive affair, do not merely carry out prophylactic activities, but may also guide and influence the direction of general legal policy within their corporations. Recent UK research by Herbert Smith has gone so far as to suggest that *the* major factor dictating the attitudes and behaviour of UK blue-chip companies towards ADR is the attitude

[55] Handler (1978), p. 25.

[56] Kagan and Rosen (1985); Spangler (1986), p. 64.

[57] Kelly (1994), p. 212. See also Subrin (2002)/3, p. 213.

[58] including, New Zealand see Freeman-Greene (2001).

[59] See, for example, the series of recent articles by Jonathan Armes (Armes 2010a, 2010b, 2010c).

[60] See the example of Rio Tinto discussed in Susskind (2010), p. xxxii.

[61] See the studies cited in Macfarlane (2008), pp. 5–6.

thereto of their in-house counsel.[62] Nonetheless, it has been argued that in-house counsel may retain a cultural opposition to mediation given the educational background and professional norms and ideology they share with external attorney colleagues[63] as well as the somewhat isolated position they often occupy within their employing organisation.[64]

Even in respect of individual clients, greater access to on-line, generic legal advice and information may be shifting the power dynamic between lawyers and clients, with the latter perhaps now more forthcoming with their own views as to how disputes might be handled.[65] The continued growth of consumerism movements manifest in different jurisdictions[66] and relative decline in the professional status of lawyers[67] may also be tilting the power scales in the clients' direction.

In sum, in those dispute contexts then in which clients are typically dominated by their advisors,[68] and have little choice than to place their trust in the guidance offered as to how those disputes should be handled, then (save rules of court or financial imperatives compelling or encouraging use) lawyers may truly hold the key that may unlock the door to increased mediation activity.[69] In other cases, however, where clients exert more power relative to their external lawyers in their agent-client relationship, expediting the practice of mediation may require a better direct 'sell' to clients themselves.[70] This is especially true because even when clients dominate the decision making process regarding dispute handling, if they lack knowledge of mediation or harbour a negative predisposition towards it, they are likely to baulk at the process.

With the above discussion firmly in mind, I now proceed to analyse some of the reasons why lawyers may seek to resist mediation, beginning with the issue of the lawyer's economic disincentives to mediate.

---

[62] Smith (2007). The methodology deployed in this study can be considered somewhat flawed, however, in the sense that only in-house lawyers were asked this question. See also Macfarlane (2003), pp. 7–8.

[63] The issue of the education of lawyers and how it impacts upon acceptance of mediation is discussed below at Sect. 2.5.1.3.

[64] Borbély (2011), pp. 136–137.

[65] Macfarlane (2008), p. 63.

[66] The leading international consumer organisation is Consumers International—see http://www.consumersinternational.org/.

[67] See the discussion in Chap. 3 at Sect. 3.2.3.

[68] A number of other advisors beyond lawyers may be relevant here including housing associations, law clinics, citizens advice bureaux and their equivalents.

[69] Of course some disputants will have no form of representation at all.

[70] Including, arguably a more 'selfish' sell of mediation to clients—see Ross (2004).

2.4 Money, Money, Money

At the root of the notion that lawyers have blocked mediation's path by dint of their own economic imperatives lies the argument that mediation is more cost-effective for participants[71] than traditional means of resolving disputes. A significant portion of such party cost savings may be found in legal outlays, which otherwise might be expected to line the pockets of lawyers. Indeed, it has been noted, in somewhat pained terms, that for lawyers, 'ADR' does not signal Alternative Dispute Resolution, but rather "Appalling Decline in Revenue". In his seminal article on mediation and lawyers, Len Riskin put it simply: "[m]any lawyers, if they thought about it, would see mediation as an economic threat".[72] Despite bold claims that mediation will save clients money, proving this has not always been easy to establish in an empirical sense. While the matter of the cost-effectiveness of mediation is discussed under Sect. 2.6 below, it is sufficient to point out here that evidence on the issue is mixed. In any case, it may be speculated that some lawyers, open-mouthed, swallowed the hyperbole over the cheapness of mediation and their limited financial prospects within it, thus adding fuel to counter strategies aimed at self-preservation.

2.4.1 *The Case Against Lawyers*

Rivers of ink have been spilled by mediation enthusiasts and other commentators globally speculating on less than honourable, financial motives on the part of lawyers for their failure to embrace mediation. My own early Scottish research conducted in 1996 revealed a frustrated fledgling mediation community laying the blame for the stagnant state of affairs of the time predominantly at the feet of money-grabbing lawyers, with little hard evidence to back up such claims.[73] Similar accusations have since been repeated in Scotland: in 2001, the Scottish Consumer Council, in the context of discussing barriers to mediation, noted that while general ignorance and cultural barriers may have in part caused legal antipathy towards mediation, "it may... be that some solicitors fear that suggesting mediation to their clients will cause them to lose out financially".[74] In England and Wales similar concerns have been voiced.[75] Across Europe such assertions

---

[71] The fact that mediation may entail savings in terms of public costs is, I presume, of less interest to individual lawyers.

[72] Riskin (1982), p. 48.

[73] Mays and Clark 1996.

[74] Scottish Consumer Council (2001), para 5.3.

[75] Russell (2007).

have often been mirrored. According to one leading French arbitrator, for example, "[t]here is a reluctance to use mediation in [Europe]. The reason being loss of potential income. After all, mediation is over in a few days even for massive cases; there are vested interests involved and mediation is simply not as lucrative for legal advisors".[76] While reported initial reluctance to embrace mediation amongst Danish lawyers was defended by those lawyers on the basis of limited appropriate training and regulation for mediators, it has been argued that "it is equally apparent that the possible loss of income resulting from more mediation and less litigation rapidly became an issue for Danish attorneys".[77] Miryana Nedic recounts similar suspicions in Serbia[78] and Adrian Borbély has theorised that the economic incentives of lawyers, has at least in part, been responsible for the limited uptake of mediation in France.[79] Similarly, in Italy, it has been speculated that resistance to a more comprehensive approach to mediation from lawyers has emanated from an "instinct for self-preservation as lawyers face prospects of competition in the business of resolving disputes".[80] In jurisdictions in which mediation is now well grounded, similar views have surfaced, particularly when developments were at an early stage. At the outset of mediation's introduction in Australia, for example, it was argued that while many eminent lawyers had become aware of mediation they represented a small minority and that "[o]thers pay lip service to ADR with little intention of allowing it to disturb what is for many a very comfortable and profitable status quo."[81] In a like manner, in the early days of mediation's re-birth in the USA, prior to the expansion of court-connected mediation,[82] lawyers were believed to be inhibiting use at least in part because of concerns about loss of earnings.[83]

2.4.2 Evidence of Financially Motivated Behaviour

Clearly then there is significant speculation in many countries that lawyers have resisted mediation because of concerns over the detrimental impact on their fee income. Often the rhetoric is sharp. Does the available evidence then tally with such suspicions? I will begin by laying out some general matters concerning financially induced behaviour by legal professionals before narrowing the analysis to the context of mediation.

---

[76] Tromans (2007), p. 20.

[77] Vindelov (2006), p. 131.

[78] Nedic (2008).

[79] Borbély (2011).

[80] De Palo and Harley (2005), p. 470.

[81] Pears 1983, p. 163 cited in Tidwell (1999).

[82] Which has arguably led to legal 'capture' of the process—see Chap. 3.

[83] See for example, Wissler (2004b); Sander (2000), p. 6.

Christine Parker noted that "the profession as a whole seems engaged in a cynical attempt to manipulate the exclusionary capacities of lawyers' justice in the attempt to further their own market advantage and social status".[84] Leaving aside the issue of whether their conduct can be described as 'cynical', lawyers, in a like fashion with other professional groupings, are of course concerned with advancing certain fundamental aims in accordance with what can be termed, the "professional project".[85] Not all such aims are concerned with the generation of income, however. In fact, in contrast to attempts to advance economic interests, it is worth remembering that in many jurisdictions lawyers can historically be seen to have been more concerned with enhancing their social status.[86] Traditionally the law was a gentleman's profession; a noble calling rather than a money-making endeavour *per se*. This can be seen, for example, in the way that the Scottish, English and French professions over time devised status-enhancing practices such as limiting the supply of producers, ceding work to subordinates and competing professionals which was not seen as sufficiently prestigious and fitting for lawyers, and in the process thus limiting the pursuance of economic aims.[87] In a similar vein, it has been argued that generally speaking European lawyers were historically too hidebound by their aristocratic origins to be concerned with the 'vulgar' activities of business or finance.[88]

Nonetheless in more recent years, legal professionals across the globe have become much more business-focused in their outlook, tearing up the roots of their gentlemanly origins and becoming bed-fellows with commerce to such an extent to arguably precipitate a crisis in professionalism.[89] This phenomenon can be detected in such developments as the growth of large firms, directly employed lawyers, the introduction of the billable hour and the establishment of Multi-Disciplinary Practices. Aggression and competition have gained ascendancy. According to Yves Dezalay, "[t]o stay competitive… firms have had to break with the dilettantism cultivated in the epoch of 'gentlemen lawyers'. [Law firms have engaged in] [t]he race for massive expansion, commercial aggressiveness, the cultivation of technique rather than good manners, staff poaching from competitors, and the exploitation of new generations".[90]

---

[84] Parker (1999), p. 1.

[85] Larson (1977).

[86] See for example, Burrage (1988), pp. 226–229.

[87] See for example. Burrage (1988), p. 237; Sugarman (1995), p. 223; Paterson (1988); Abbott (1988), pp. 275–276.

[88] See generally, Osiel (1989).

[89] See for example, Daicoff (1997); Abel (1988a, 1988b); but compare with Paterson (1988), p. 76.

[90] Dezalay (1991), p. 800 (internal citations omitted).

2.4.3 Lawyers' Economic Interests and Disputing Practices

The general argument that lawyers' behaviour in the dispute resolution context may be shaped, amongst other things, by economic considerations has some empirical basis.[91] Research in the USA, for example, has revealed a link between the way that lawyers are remunerated and their approach to disputing. Hence, it has been argued that contingency fee arrangements[92] dictate an approach by lawyers conducive to a quick turnaround of cases to maximise income. This may be unlikely to lead to an increase in uptake in mediation if it is seen as an additional and potentially time consuming process step in a process in which swift resolution is sought. Similarly, lawyers paid on an hourly basis may favour recourse to full discovery and delayed settlement not merely to give their clients extra leverage in negotiations but also to improve their own levels of compensation.[93] The billable hour is a particular contentious way of charging for services that has lent succour to the argument that lawyers are slaves to mammon first and devotees of their clients second. As Christopher Mayson has noted, "[w]hen performance and fees are assessed on [an hourly] basis, it is inevitable that lawyers will try to create as many chargeable hours as possible. Here is a system that rewards the inefficient, the ignorant, and probably even the downright incompetent."[94]

The acute sense of adversarialism inherent in legal practice may itself harbour selfish financial practices by lawyers. In their seminal work, Gilson and Mnookin suggested that American litigators "rarely cooperate to resolve disputes efficiently; instead, shielded by a professional ideology that is said to require zealous advocacy, they endlessly and wastefully fight in ways that enrich themselves but rarely advantage the client".[95] In a like fashion, using a framework developed by Sharma[96] to address professional-agent/principal relations, Adrian Borbély, articulates a convincing argument regarding how French lawyers' control of disputing decision making,[97] preference for adversarial norms, and selfish economic aims, allows them to pursue costly, inefficient forms of dispute resolution and limits the scope for use of mediation in French business disputes.[98]

Mediation may be eschewed by lawyers at least in part then because potentially it can skewer some fundamental characteristics of the traditional adversarial mode of dispute resolution that exacerbate inefficiencies arising in a billable-hour

[91] See, for example, Krizter (1998).

[92] Also known as 'conditional fee' in which clients pay their lawyers only in the event of a successful result.

[93] Wissler (2004b), p. 467 and the research cited therein.

[94] Mayson (1992), p. 4.

[95] Gibson and Mnookin (1994), p. 511.

[96] Sharma (1997).

[97] In part caused by business managers' lack of input in such matters.

[98] Borbély (2011).

grounded regime. Contrary to the client-dominated ethos of mediation, adversarial forms of dispute resolution entail involvement of lawyers at every stage of the process and generally keep the disputing parties apart thus maximising lawyers' time and fee potential.[99] Certain financial arrangements for lawyers may directly militate against the use of mediation. For example, the potential for creative settlements within mediation may resonate negatively with lawyers whose normal form of remuneration is by way of 'success fees'—i.e. a percentage of compensation awarded to a plaintiff. Traditional fee structures for lawyers may militate against mediation's use in more extreme ways. For example, it has been suggested that German lawyers were often resistant to mediation because legal aid fee arrangements designed to remunerate lawyers for advice and representation did not allow payments for lawyers within mediation.[100] Clearly if policy makers are keen to promote mediation then structural rules relative to the process cannot completely disregard the remuneration of legal professionals involved.[101]

In respect of empirical work directly addressing lawyer respondents' interaction with mediation, some evidence of economically-induced resistance can be detected. Roselle Wissler's classic study of American lawyers' views on ADR revealed that respondents' views of long term compensation, advancement and prestige that would result from mediation had an effect upon their views of the process.[102] Comparable evidence has been collected in other jurisdictions. While it was accepted that deep seated cultural norms may be partly to blame for Italian lawyers' initial lukewarm response to mediation, empirical evidence suggests that traditional fee structures for litigation lawyers militate against the use of mediation.[103] Similar evidence of lawyer intransigence due to financial pressures has been cited in Turkey.[104] In a recent EU survey of lawyers and corporations in respect of mediation in the EU, although lawyer respondents typically espoused positive views of the process and were generally in favour of an expansion of the recent European Mediation Directive on Mediation as well as further steps to better embed the process,[105] a significant number pointed out that lawyers generally were a threat to mediation because of the negative impact it might hold for their income.[106] Similarly, in an evaluation of a Scottish Small-Claims Court mediation scheme, some evidence of lawyer reluctance to engage with mediation due to financial

[99] Dzienkowski (1996), p. 56.

[100] Hoffman 2007, p. 534. Similar problems have been reported in Switzerland, see Meiser (2006), p. 385.

[101] Except of course if the intention is to preclude lawyers from the process.

[102] Wissler (2004b), p. 467.

[103] De Palo and Cominelli (2006), p. 262.

[104] Ilter and Dikbas (2010), p. 148.

[105] Such as expanding the terms of the directive to domestic disputes and better integration with the civil court process.

[106] ADR Center et al.(2010), para VI.

imperatives was revealed.[107] Such findings have been unearthed in other, similar UK studies.[108] Furthermore, English research into the attitudes of lawyers in commercial property disputes revealed suggestions from more junior lawyers that their senior colleagues did not encourage their use of mediation because it was not seen as sufficiently lucrative.[109]

Despite the wealth of evidence cited above, lawyers are often coy about the potentially deleterious financial implications that mediation might hold for their own practice. Surveys of lawyers often do not support the notion of a profession quaking in their boots at the prospect of mediation skewering their generous income stream from traditional ways of resolving their client's disputes. Writing in 2000, John Lande found that only 25% of external lawyer survey respondents from Massachusetts, Pennsylvania, Tennessee, and Florida believed that developments in ADR led to a reduction in fee income.[110] My own recent Scottish research has suggested that lawyers do not generally view that mediation developments will put a dent in their fee income. In relation to the statement, "lawyers will lose money if ADR becomes popular", a mere 16% of respondents to a 2005 survey of Scottish commercial litigation lawyers agreed with the statement as opposed to some 65% who disagreed.[111] My recent survey of Scottish construction lawyers was even less equivocal about mediation's potential impact upon levels of lawyer income: only 6% of respondents believed that growth in mediation would be detrimental to their financial interests against 78% that disagreed.[112] English research by Penny Brooker conducted in 2001 into the attitudes of commercial lawyers towards mediation found that "in some sectors of commercial practice, the image of lawyers, fearful of a loss of revenue... can no longer be sustained".[113] Hong-Lin Yu's work with regard to the attitudes of Taiwanese lawyers again found a very small number expressing fears about negative financial consequences of their involvement in mediation.[114] A recent study of lawyers' views towards mediation in Israel again found mixed views on whether mediation developments would lead to a drop in lawyers' revenues, with a mere 5% of respondents admitting that possible financial losses through mediation was ever a factor in resisting the process.[115]

---

[107] Ross and Bain (2010), para 3.38.

[108] Genn (1998); Prince (2004); Doyle, (2006); Genn et al. (2007).

[109] Sidoli del Ceno 2011.

[110] Lande (2000), p. 180.

[111] Clark and Dawson (2007), p. 239.

[112] Agapiou and Clark (2011), pp. 170–173.

[113] Brooker and Lavers (2002).

[114] Yu 2009, p. 539. Yu notes, however, that this may to some extent relate to fee structures in Taiwan where lawyers are typically paid in accordance with the complexity of the case they take on, rather than any hourly rate.

[115] Sela (2009), p. 48.

In surveys like these described above, it should be cautioned that those with more positive attitudes towards mediation are more likely to respond than those with more negative outlooks. We must also remain sceptical about the possibility of the prevalence of socially desired responses. Equally, however, assertions by lawyers that mediation will not impact adversely upon their fee levels may sound alarm bells with those keen to see the process expedited in such a way as to cut back on users' costs of disputing. In short, their question might be: why are lawyers not running scared from mediation? We might then suspect then that increasing levels of mediation are not dampening down lawyer remuneration levels in practice. In some contexts perhaps enlightened practitioners may be reaping the benefits of efficient, cost-effective dispute resolution on behalf of their clients in terms of repeat business. Nonetheless, while I return to such matters in Chap. 3, suffice to say here that there is significant global evidence now suggesting that the legal profession may be profiting handsomely from involvement in mediation. This occurrence has fuelled suspicions that lawyers are milking the mediation cash-cow, lending succour to the thesis of lawyer co-option.

2.5 Ignorance and Cultural Barriers

Lawyer ignorance is a commonly cited barrier to mediation developments globally. Although recent empirical work in the field, for example, in Scotland,[116] England,[117] Australia,[118] the USA,[119] Taiwan,[120] and the EU[121] typically finds that lawyers are almost unanimous in espousing their own knowledge of the process, they often hold far less confidence in their colleagues' awareness levels, pointing the finger at (other) lawyer ignorance. It may be stretching credulity somewhat to believe that after decades of publicity and promotion of mediation in most countries that lawyer ignorance truly continues to exist. Three relevant points made be made here. First, it may be suspected that an element of 'wilful blindness' may exist, redolent of a generally negative and hostile lawyer attitude towards the notion of mediation. Secondly, and connected to the first point, it is worth remembering that the issue of a general ignorance of lawyers towards mediation cannot be examined in isolation of the notion that inherent within the legal profession there may exist cultural barriers in the way of mediation's acceptance. In this sense, a cultural climate that does not view mediation as a legitimate

[116] Clark and Dawson (2007); Agapoui and Clark 2011.

[117] Brooker 2001; Sidoli del Ceno (2011).

[118] Zariski (1997).

[119] Lande (2000).

[120] Yu (2009).

[121] ADR Centre et al. (2010).

activity may nurture continued ignorance of the process, at least in the sense of any informed and meaningful appreciation of the process. Finally the 'newness' of mediation may be a source of angst amongst lawyers, baulking at the prospect of involvement in an unfamiliar process.

In respect of the latter issue it can be said that change, whatever the substance of that change, may bring with it an inherent resistance. Lawyers may classically be seen as traditional and conservative in their outlook. The status quo may hence hold an innate attraction for lawyers.[122] Of course it is true that the nature of the changes mediation heralds may also be troubling. Mediation represents a challenge to traditional legal forms of dispute resolution and the core work of lawyers. It suggests that there is something 'broken', in need of a 'fix'. Mediation may posit a shift from winning to collaboration and from legal positions to vested interests. The process may also entail an abdication of an element of lawyer control with a more central role for the client in brokering settlement, and the novel aspect of the interjection of a third party to assist resolution,[123] along with an admission by lawyers that one is required. In the US context, John Dzienkowski has written that "[t]he most fundamental justification for adversarialism involves the psychology of change.... [L]awyers' entire perspective on lawyering comes from this view that the adversarial system is immutable and they feel very comfortable with the basic tenets of adversarialness. Thus, any change from the current system presents the strains and tension that accompany most changes in human experience".[124] In the context of Italian lawyers' resistance to mediation, it has similarly been stated that, "[a]nything that would challenge the sacred and intangible aura that surrounds legal jurisdiction is unconsciously considered [by lawyers as] taboo."[125] The cultural frameworks that lawyers inhabit that may nurture such views are explored below.

2.5.1 Lawyers and Culture

It is beyond the scope of this book to discuss the concept of 'culture' in any significant depth. In short, culture is a contested term. One useful definition sees the term denoting "the arts, beliefs, habits, institutions, and other human endeavours considered together as being characteristic of a particular community, people, or nation."[126] This definition thus confirms that culture does not simply relate to common practice norms and behaviour within a particular community but in addition, a shared ideology and belief about such activity held by community

---

[122] Although lawyers in many contexts have shown an appetite for adaption to meet new social and economic circumstances.

[123] By contrast to third party adjudicators.

[124] Dzienkowski (1996), p. 55.

[125] De Palo and Harley (2005), p. 47.

[126] Gage Canadian Dictionary, (1997), s.v. "culture".

members.[127] This is important in the sense that it entails the notion that to effect cultural change within a group (and acceptance of innovations), alterations to practice alone, which may, for example, be mandated by the instigation of new legal rules, may be insufficient. Alterations to community members' mind-sets regarding such new behaviours are imperative.[128]

While cultures may be examined in multifarious social contexts, the term "legal culture" can be used to denote the cultural parameters of the 'social space' that lawyers operate within. The issue is complex though and legal cultures operate on many different levels. Thus, there may subsist an overarching general legal culture that legal professionals in any one country (or group of countries) belong to as well as more 'local' legal cultures applicable to particular localities of lawyers.

2.5.1.1 Macro Legal Culture

In the macro sense, it can be argued that lawyers operate within an overarching 'adversarial' legal culture. Although the term 'adversarial' can be used in a technical manner to describe the civil justice systems of common law nations as opposed to the inquisitorial approaches manifest across the civil law world, the phrase can also be used in a looser sense to describe partisan, competitive and aggressive behaviours on the part of lawyers that may transcend legal jurisdictions of both schools. The epitome of an adversarial legal culture is that found in the USA - what Robert Kagan described as 'adversarial legalism'.[129] Key traits of adversarial legalism include highly detailed and transparent legal rules and regulatory procedures as well as a broad platform for the assertion of individual legal rights, significant legal enforcement mechanisms, progressive rules regarding the financing of litigation, emphasis placed on oral evidence in legal proceedings, liberal rules of evidential discovery, adversarial combat between lawyers with the judge as referee, a general right to a jury trial, and rules of court in which party control of the litigation is prevalent.[130] It is contended that the impact of such traits is to encourage the assertion of legal rights in a community through the legal resolution of disputes by litigation and positional bargaining in the shadow of on-going litigation rather than more harmonious means of dispute resolution.[131] In turn, this culture fosters the overtly adversarial behaviour of lawyers, and overinvestment in legal resources by litigants caught in a prisoner's dilemma.[132] While traditional American legal culture may represent adversarialism *in extremis* legal cultures in other common law

[127] See generally Geertz (1973).

[128] Zariski (2000), para 23.

[129] Kagan (1991).

[130] Kagan (1991); Cioff (2009), p. 237.

[131] Kelemen and Sibbitt (2004).

[132] Fearing the adversarial conduct of one's opponents, disputants (and their lawyers) may feel they have no choice but to take up legal arms with gusto—see Ashenfelter and Bloom (1993).

countries may be seen as 'watered-down' variants to different degrees. Hence, although other common law nations may exhibit many of the above features of adversarial legalism, they may lack the full gamut of traditional characteristics found in the USA.[133]

In civil law nations with inquisitorial legal systems, institutional structures and court rules traditionally militate against some of the greater incentives to litigate. So, for example, limitations on rules of discovery in civil systems (e.g. Germany) may limit the benefits of litigation for claimants. Similarly, the greater interventionist role of the judge and settlement culture within court systems in civil law countries may render litigation a less attractive proposition for disputants. It is misleading to suggest, however, that clear blue water lies between justice systems in civil law and common law nations. For example, it has been argued recently that adversarial approaches have begun to infuse continental European systems in certain areas.[134] Equally it can be observed that aspects of inquisitorial approaches (particularly a shift to a perception that court-sponsored settlement is a legitimate aim of a civil justice regime, and more interventionist case-management by judges) have begun to pervade common law systems. Nonetheless, certain adversarial traits may imbue the workings of lawyers across a range of jurisdictions of all every ilk - common law, civil law and 'mixed'.[135] For example, Alan Lempereur has eloquently articulated the argument that the cultural norms of the civil law tradition inherent in France may militate against the development of ADR processes.[136] It is argued that this is so, at least in part, because in general the civil law tradition nurtures within lawyers an orientation predisposed to conflict rather than cooperation.[137] Despite their 'inquisitorial' nomenclature, lawyers in civil law systems, while perhaps generally less aggressive and more deferential to the judiciary than their common law counterparts, are just as likely to indulge in uncooperative and competitive behaviours with their opponents.[138]

2.5.1.2 Local Legal Culture

In addition to cultures operating on a national or supra-national level, equally there may operate smaller, more local cultures. Local legal cultures may, for example,

---

[133] So, for example, civil jury trials are typically more rationed in other common law jurisdictions and discovery may be more limited.

[134] Cioff (2009).

[135] 'Mixed' systems, such as Scotland and South Africa, exhibit influences of both the common law and civil law world.

[136] Lempereur (1998), pp. 161–163.

[137] Lasserre (2003).

[138] For a useful comparative discussion of the American and German legal system, see Kotz (2003). For a review of the respective adversarial traits of US and Latin-American lawyers see Peters (2010).

arise by regional, geographical area, distinct professional grouping (e.g. by subject specialism), or within particular firms or organisations. As Lynn Mather has noted, "[a]n emerging literature focusing on lawyers' ideologies and practices suggest that they develop standards of professionalism in concert with one another... lawyers articulate and share particular norms of professional conduct through daily interactions with their peers through 'communities of practice', 'arenas of professionalism', 'local legal cultures' or through the 'culture... of practice organizations'.[139] In this sense, any innovations in the field (such as mediation) must hence be recognised in the pervading local legal culture that lawyers inhabit before they can gain legitimacy. In professional theory terms this is redolent of the notion of institutional theory. According to Lande, "institutional theory contends that professional networks are important media of diffusion and that the extent to which professionals adopt an innovation promoted by their profession is related to their ties to the profession."[140] Lande continues that the "perceived power, success, and professional prestige of those who promote the innovation" is also of significant importance.[141]

In short, lawyers' cultural norms, practices and ideologies can thus be established on both macro and micro levels. Cultural elements may emanate from a range of sources including formal legal and procedural rules, as well as professional codes, practices and customs. So while legal rules mandating and encouraging mediation can clearly have an influence on lawyers' cultural acceptance of mediation,[142] so too may the views thereto of professional bodies, in addition to the posturing of judges and other 'champions' within the profession.[143] The conduct and attitudes of peers at a local level relative to mediation—bread and butter practitioners on the ground - is also of significant importance in creating and retaining cultural norms in Mather's terms, particularly where there are strong bonds between lawyers in the local cultures they inhabit. One other especially formative issue in terms of lawyers' cultural norms is legal education. It is hence worth here briefly sketching out the position of mediation within present paradigms of legal education.

[139] Mather (2003), pp. 1070–1071 (internal citations ommitted). For an interesting disussion of culture and the adoption of mediation by lawyers see A Zariski "Disputing culture: lawyers and ADR" (2000) Vol 7, No 2 Murdoch University Electronic Journal of Law.

[140] Lande (2000), pp. 155.

[141] Lande (2000), pp. 155–156.

[142] Or at the very least that mediation may be accommodated into a preferred form—see the ensuing discussion in Chaps. 3 and 5.

[143] Macfarlane (2008), pp. 19–20.

2.5.1.3 Legal Education

Although evidence suggests that life in legal practice may deviate significantly from what goes on in the class room,[144] legal education is nonetheless incredibly important in crafting the normative shape of a lawyer's practices. Fledgling lawyers often enter the profession with scant awareness of mediation. As noted below, across the globe, mediation does not typically feature significantly in core legal education. Even in the most advanced jurisdictions, such as the USA, mediation may represent no more than a fringe sideshow within mainstream legal education. Don Peters has recently written that 91% of the core law curriculum in the USA amounts to traditional legal content and that the majority of law students (some 73%) get no exposure to non-adversarial, interest-based bargaining processes.[145] If this is the position in the flag-bearer for modern mediation, the prospects for less advanced nations would seem bleak. For example, despite the efforts of a handful of enthusiasts, in Scotland there is currently very little provision made in terms of mediation education for law students.[146] Similarly, despite its relatively mature stage of development, Lord Neuberger has recently decried the lack of mediation coverage in standard legal education in England and Wales.[147] As one would expect, mediation coverage is relatively well established in the university law curriculums of those countries where the process is better established such as Canada and Australia, even if such content is generally non-mainstream.[148] Across Europe, while mediation education within law schools has been progressing slowly over recent years, coverage remains uneven. For example, in Germany, where traditionally speaking law teaching has generally followed traditional, conservative lines,[149] since 2003, greater emphasis has been placed on adoption of skills subjects such as mediation into the standard curriculum. Nevertheless, the numbers exposed to the process remain in the minority.[150] In many other parts of the world, it is suspected that mediation's presence in legal education is minimal.[151]

It is not simply the absence of express mediation coverage in legal education that may be galling for mediation enthusiasts but also the fact that traditional legal education and training is arguably anathema to the whole ethos of non-adversarial forms of dispute resolution. The classic model of law teaching in the common law world is a narrow one. The bulk of law school education is devoted to case analysis, statutory interpretation and the application of the law to narrative facts absent of

---

[144] Abel (1999), p. 117 suggesting that lawyers make 'scanty' use of what is learned in their university studies while in practice.

[145] Peters (2011).

[146] Irvine (2010).

[147] Neuberger (2010).

[148] Prujiner (2006), p. 101.

[149] Hoffman, 2007, p. 544; Alexander et al. (2006), p. 240.

[150] By way of the 2003 Law on the Reform of Legal Education.

[151] See for example. de los Angeles 2011 (Philippines); Ooi (2005) (Malaysia).

any mention of clients and their extra legal interests.[152] Where client facing activities are introduced (typically at post-degree stage), the standard forms of client-lawyer relationship depicted and client counselling activities developed entail the lawyer firmly in control. Substantial coverage of mediation skills and the lawyer-client dynamics that underpin the process are conspicuously absent within this model. While mooting and advocacy are often highly prized within the traditional model, law students are not typically taught how to mediate or trained in the integrative problem-solving techniques central to mediation. The tradition of law teaching in civil law countries across Europe may similarly find little place for mediation and its ilk. Given the traditional emphasis placed upon legislation and codified forms of law as sources of law, precedence is placed on such matters in terms of legal study.[153] Such an approach can be seen as 'scientific or theoretical'.[154] Large classes and traditional lecturing remain the norm, with interactive, facilitative, 'skills-based' classes more exceptional. In the late 1990's, Lempereur, painted a damning picture of the law taught in a rote fashion by French lecturers absent of any mention of the relevance of other disciplines such as business or finance or the interests of the client.[155] It has been argued recently that the position has not shifted much since in France, at least in part stifling mediation's growth.[156]

2.5.2 *Lawyer Cultural Biases and Mediation*

What evidence then exists of ignorance and cultural reasons for lawyer resistance to mediation specifically? This is a difficult question to address. General cultural norms that pervade any particular group may mask significant differences in individual beliefs and behaviours. Establishing cause and effect relative to culture and behaviour may also be no easy task. So in the context of mediation, does a culture of negativity drive behaviour that resists mediation or does such behaviour lead to the formation of cultural norms set against it? With this in mind, nonetheless, some evidence of lawyers' cultural dissonance with mediation can be detected. It should at the outset be noted that greater cultural acceptance of mediation in legal circles in more developed mediation nations may have occurred as a consequence of increased participation by lawyers, the institutionalisation of the process and embedding within formal civil dispute resolution processes.[157] The extent that

[152] For a cogent critique of this model of learning see Macfarlane (2008), pp. 30–34; Bok (1983).

[153] Lempereur (1998), p. 163.

[154] Hoffman (2007), p. 544.

[155] Lempereur (1998).

[156] Borbély (2011), p. 138.

[157] See for example, Macfarlane (2002) charting the experience with Canadian lawyers.

cultural change has actually taken place in such environments, as opposed to grudging acceptance as well as questions as to whether mediation has become moulded into a process more suited to lawyers' traditional disputing cultures, are discussed in later chapters in this book. In any case, while at the very least it may be said that lawyers' cultural resistance towards mediation may have become less pronounced over time in more developed parts of the world, less mature environments may still see mediation struggle in a quagmire of misinformation and cultural jarring.

In its infancy, it is clear that mediation has often struggled to gain a foothold within legal circles. American scholars charted significant evidence in mediation's early journey that resistance by dint of unfamiliarity was blighting developments.[158] Unfamiliarity was only part of the issue, however. Cultural dissonance was just as much of a problem. John Van Winkle, reflecting the anathematic nature of mediation with regard to traditional disputing practices, put it colourfully: "[t]rial lawyers were driving the train, and [mediation] efforts were not only outside their experience, they were counterintuitive and ideologically inconsistent with the rumble of the litigation train".[159] In terms of change and losing control of dispute disposal, one prominent American lawyer (and later convert to the ways of mediation) put it with simplicity: "I thought of mediation as a denigration of my own ability to settle".[160]

Expanding on this theme it will be recalled that in Sect. 2.3 above I examined the traditional notion of lawyer/client relationships with the lawyer firmly in control. While that discussion focused on the issue of controlling the pathway to be taken regarding dispute resolution, equally lawyers traditionally call the shots in crafting agreements with their counterparts in lawyer-led negotiated settlements.[161] Mediation potentially represents a significant challenge in the above regard in that, at least in its classic formulation, party empowerment and self-determination is central to the process.[162] It may thus be unsurprising that lawyers may be uncomfortable with a process that purports to usurp their traditional role in resolving the dispute either in favour of their clients or a neutral third party. Equally, disputes are routinely resolved by lawyers in the shadow of the law and in particular, against a backdrop of negotiating the procedural steps of a litigation process. The well-worn route taken by lawyers in the resolution of disputes by what Marc Galanter famously

[158] Rogers and McEwen (1998); Wissler (2004b).

[159] Van Winkle (2001), p. 18.

[160] Shestack (2001), p. xi.

[161] See the discussion in Macfarlane (2008), pp. 71–75; Evidence of this standard practice can be found in many fields—Voegeli (1992), p. 291 (German family law), Hedeen and Salem (2006) (US law professors, attorneys and law students unlikely to recognise the importance of involving clients in decision making).

[162] In Chap. 4 I will discuss evidence from mediation research suggesting that lawyers often struggle with the ceding of control to clients within mediation. Equally I shall also examine the issue as to whether clients also seek such control.

described as 'litigotiation'[163] has been comprehensively charted. The lawyer's journey to settlement often entails significant time negotiating the procedural hurdles of litigation with little attempt at the outset to engage the merits of the dispute with their opposite number (if at all) with late settlement commonplace.[164] In this latter sense, lawyers may habitually delay negotiation efforts until after evidential discovery has taken place so that settlements agreed can be more informed in a legal sense. At best then, mediation may be seen as a valid option or 'set-piece' for achieving late settlement but lawyers may resist potential utility of the process at an early stage.

There has also been some speculation that lawyers may perceive any participation in mediation as anathema to the 'macho' adversarial climates that they operate within and in particular, that suggesting mediation to an opponent would be seen as a sign of weakness.[165] My own research probing lawyers on this issue has suggested that this is generally not true.[166] I would concede, however, that directly questioning lawyers on such a specific issue may not be overly instructive in providing evidence of lawyers' general cultural responses to mediation.

Archie Zariski's empirical work of Australian lawyers' relationship with mediation conducted in 1999 found that although the process was becoming well known amongst the legal fraternity, cultural barriers to its acceptance remained.[167] In this sense, an Australian Civil Justice Reform Paper in 2005 highlighted the problem of the prevailing legal culture in limiting scope for mediation's growth. The paper also pointed out that procedural reform may be insufficient, *per se*, to perpetuate cultural acceptance of mediation amongst players in the legal scene, which could perhaps only be achieved by shifting lawyers' mindsets rather than by procedural means alone.[168] In the early days of development in Canada it was noted that "[a]lthough [mediation] was legally possible, it did not agree with the dominant judicial and legal culture of using accusatory procedures to obtain a legal solution".[169] Yes, settlements were commonplace, but lawyer-led within the confines of an adjudicative framework. Such an approach is redolent of a "default to rights" paradigm. As noted above, the macro legal cultures of modern legal systems, legal education and professional history and current norms of practice dictate this fundamental construct of a lawyer's professional role. According to Macfarlane, "[t]his commitment to individual rights means that the primary responsibility of the lawyer is the

[163] Galanter (1984).

[164] Macfarlane (2008), pp. 69–71.

[165] Peters and Mastin (2007); (SCC 2001), p. 25.

[166] Clark and Dawson (2007), p. 242; Agapiou and Clark (2011), p. 173. Zariski's work in respect of Australian lawyers similarly found few viewing that recourse to mediation was a sign of weakness. Zariski (1997) Appendix A.

[167] Zariski (2000).

[168] MacDonald (2005), section IV.

[169] Prujiner 2006, p. 85.

furtherance of her clients' goals framed as legal ends."[170] She continues, "she must focus her energies and talents on convincing decision makers—real or imagined—that she has the stronger rights-based argument. There is no need to convince the other side or to propose mutually agreeable solutions".[171] With its focus on disputing parties' interests, including those of the mutual variety and legal parameters merely one of a matrix of relevant issues which may inform dispute settlement, mediation may seem an unnatural proposition for lawyers.

In my own jurisdiction of Scotland, where growth is steady rather than rapid, commentators have long averred that mediation may only begin to flourish with an attendant cultural change in the profession.[172] In a recent Scottish court-annexed pilot study of mediation, cultural barriers to mediation's utility seen in solicitors (and sheriffs[173]) were ascertained.[174] The adversarial training of Scottish lawyers and the traditional working environment they inhabit has been pointed to as an inhibiting factor for mediation's development.[175]

For England and Wales, the recent findings of the evaluation of the mediation projects within the Central London County Court suggested that significant cultural barriers to the development of mediation in the English legal profession remain.[176] In particular, despite the high profile that mediation has enjoyed in England and Wales over recent years and significant support from the government and the judiciary, evidence from that study suggested that many lawyers seemed to habitually dismiss court referral to mediation, often without any discussion with their clients, as something irrelevant and anathema to their general *modus operandi*. Mediation simply did not 'fit' into their general scheme of practice in respect of dispute handling.[177] Across Europe a similar picture can be painted, where progress has often been stilted despite significant government recognition of the process. An empirical study into German lawyers' attitudes to mediation suggested that many German legal professionals were too risk averse to attempt a relatively untried and untested process such as mediation.[178] Such cultural barriers within the ranks of lawyers have been detected across Europe, for example, in Italy,[179] Denmark and France.[180] The same may be true in many other parts of the world. In Turkey it has been reported that despite concerted efforts of late to promote the process, "lawyers

---

[170] Macfarlane (2008), p. 49.

[171] Macfarlane (2008), p. 49.

[172] Mays and Clark (1996); SCC (2001), para 44.

[173] Lower court judges in Scotland.

[174] Ross and Bain (2010).

[175] SCC, para 44.

[176] Genn et al. (2007; Russell (2007).

[177] See also Neuberger (2010); Sidoli del Ceno (2011).

[178] Hoffman (2007), pp. 548–549. To some extent this is considered to emanate from traditional German societal traits of perfectionism and risk averse behaviour.

[179] De Palo and Hartley (2005), p. 475.

[180] Vindelov (2006); Borbély (2011).

often regard mediation with scepticism."[181] It has also been suggested that mediation efforts in Malaysia have stalled in part because "the adversarial approach has long been established within the Malaysian system and is ingrained in lawyers' training and their mindset".[182] Evidence from a recent study in the Philippines has also been found that lawyers are reluctant to refer disputing parties to mediation a least in part because of their adversarial training and lack of awareness of the potential benefits of the process.[183]

2.5.3 *Shifting Trends?*

The self-espoused knowledge and favourable views of many lawyers towards mediation may point to a shifting cultural view of mediation in legal professions in many countries. Add to this the increasing promotion of mediation through court rules, acknowledgement within legal professional bodies, developments in education and increased numbers of lawyers training in mediation in many jurisdictions and it may be thought that the cultural tide as regards mediation is turning. Particularly in jurisdictions in which mediation has started to take root as a legitimate form of civil dispute resolution, the process may be seen to be infiltrating standard legal practice. US scholars have found that lawyer resistance could be surmounted when mediation is experienced. Repeat players are commonplace.[184] Canadian research has also revealed that although lawyers were often resistant to rules mandating or encouraging its use, continued exposure to the process led to increased acceptance and accommodation of the process.[185] While, my own recent empirical work in the Scottish contexts has thus far detected modest levels of engagement with mediation by commercial and construction lawyers, it has nonetheless revealed that those who do engage with the process are very likely to seek out further mediation experiences. Moreover, their satisfaction with mediation tends to increase the greater their involvement.[186] Tamara Relis's research into medical negligence mediation in Canada, found significant evidence "of mediation experiences resulting in many practising lawyers reconceptualizing both their cases and their roles within them, with extralegal considerations becoming inherent within lawyers' thinking".[187]

---

[181] Ilter and Dikbas, p. 148.

[182] Ameer Ali (2010), p. 86. Archie Zariski recently reported that attempts to survey the attitudes of Malaysian lawyers towards mediation elicited a response rate of a mere one percent (Zariski 2011).

[183] de los Angeles (2011), p. 10.

[184] Riskin (1982), p. 42;Wissler (2002); Wissler, (2004b).

[185] Macfarlane (2001, 2002).

[186] Clark and Dawson (2007). p. 236; Agapiou and Clark (2011), pp. 165–166.

[187] Relis (2009), p. 17.

The issue of cultural change is a two way street, however, and equally in some contexts, it may be said that traditional legal culture is beginning to infiltrate and override mediation culture to a greater extent than the reverse. Altered behaviours without shifting belief systems do not, *per se*, evince cultural changes. Many lawyers who have dipped their toes into mediation or been pushed into new waters by compulsory rules may be accommodating mediation rather than embracing it. Thus their beliefs about dispute resolution may largely remain unchanged even if mediation use is on the rise. In this sense, I shall explore this issue and some of reasons why lawyers have embraced mediation in Chap. 3.[188]

2.6 Fears Over the Efficiency of Mediation

Lawyers sometimes appear to reject mediation on the basis that they believe that recourse to the process is not economically efficient. This belief may at times at least be intrinsically linked to client unwillingness to shell out monies on a process that may be perceived as relatively untried, untested and counterintuitive[189] as well as the lawyer's belief that he can negotiate a settlement to a dispute without the need for third party intervention. In respect of the latter issue, empirical research often suggests that lawyers resist mediation because of the potential for negotiated settlement.[190] This may be expected given the fact that in many contexts, lawyer-crafted settled outcomes are the norm. Such views doubting mediation's worth may often be fuelled by a perception that mediation does not offer anything particularly distinct from, or beneficial to negotiation itself. As Dame Hazel Genn explains in the context of the English civil justice system, "[l]awyers... find it difficult to envisage what value mediation might add to normal negotiation in a system that is in any case settlement dominated. Since most lawyers argue that their objective in litigation is to achieve a settlement rather than go to trial, many consider that they are already 'doing mediation' themselves".[191]

It may be difficult of course to determine whether lawyers are conveniently hiding behind such assertions to indulge their cultural prejudices or mask financial imperatives. As I shall discuss below, the evidence regarding mediation's worth in monetary terms is not so clear cut as to suggest that this is always the case. Nonetheless, those who genuinely believe that mediation offers little in terms of economic efficiency may at times be labouring under a misconception. First, it is suggested that mediation may allow for a quicker and superior settlement to

---

[188] The particular issue of mediation's enmeshment with the traditional legal system is examined in Chap. 5.

[189] See the discussion at Sect. 2.3.1 Disputing parties may often be impatient to wait for 'jam tomorrow'—i.e. spend money in the short term to save in the future.

[190] Clark and Dawson (2007), pp. 235–236; Sela (2009), pp. 43–44. See also Shestack (2001), p. xi.

[191] Genn (2009), p. 110.

disputes and deliver better substantive satisfaction and procedural justice for parties involved.[192] Mediation also holds out the prospect of widening the pie of what is on offer to disputing parties in the way of creative settlements beyond the limited menu of remedies offered by the courts and standard lawyer negotiations.[193] Evidence of creativity of settlement, especially in the court-connected context practice is mixed, however, and it seems that in the main, mediated settlements are often mere financial compromises.[194]

Nonetheless, the notion that negotiated settlement potential renders mediation an unnecessary accoutrement may to some extent be linked to lawyers' (and clients'[195]) limited understanding of, and cultural prejudices towards the process. This idea is backed by empirical evidence. A study of Israeli lawyers' interactions with mediation, for example, found that use of mediation may be sufficient to often dispel the belief that the prospect of settlement is a good reason for rejecting mediation.[196] Other research routinely finds recalcitrant lawyers transformed into enthusiastic repeat players in the process.[197] Experience of mediation may often, it seems, lead to a conversion of sorts and an eye-opening as to the merits of the process.[198]

Particular ways in which mediators may help expedite resolution or improve the quality of settlement norms, include the notion that the intervention of a mediator to the dispute resolution process may effectively overcome certain heuristic biases of parties and their lawyers which can scupper bilateral negotiations. In this sense, lawyers involved in direct negotiations may engage in 'reactive devaluation', discounting offers made by their opponents and indulging their 'messianic certainties', taking an overly optimistic view of the merits and risks inherent in their own case.[199] Such unbridled optimism may fuel unrealistic posturing in settlement discussions.[200] As Carrie Menkel Meadow has noted, "[d]istortions in thinking like reactive evaluation, availability, recency, primacy, loss and risk aversion, as well as overconfidence and labelling theory tell us that adversarial processes (and much legal reasoning) may actually impede good decision making

[192] Discussed in Chap. 5 at Sect. 5.2.4.

[193] Menkel-Meadow (1996), p. 24.

[194] See, for example, in the UK context, Genn (2009); Brooker and Lavers (2001), p. 1338. In the US setting, Welsh (2001), pp. 812–816. It is arguable, however, that this lack of creativity is at least in part due to lawyer co-option of mediation.

[195] "Many business people who find themselves in dispute are experienced negotiators and understandably believe that if they have not been able to negotiate a settlement, then a mediator is unlikely to be able to assist"—Genn (2009), p. 110.

[196] Sela (2009).

[197] Riskin (1982), p. 42;Wissler (2002); Wissler, (2004b).

[198] Not always of course. In many contexts lawyers may use mediation as a 'space' to practice their adversarial negotiations.

[199] Ross (1999), pp. 38–42.

[200] Goodman-Delahunty et al. (2010) Malsch (1990); Loftus and Wagenaar (1987–1988).

by limiting what we can hear from the other side and how we can process important information... Mediators who are neutral offerors of proposals and information can correct reactive evaluation and reduce waste in informational distortions".[201] By contrast, lawyers may also value mediators for their ability to deflate their own clients' over-optimistic, dogmatic positions (something that lawyers themselves may have difficulty achieving given their status as client 'champions').[202]

2.6.1 *Parties' Costs in Mediation*

While hyperbolic, anecdotal claims as to the cheapness of mediation abound, the empirical evidence on the issue of cost-effectiveness is more mixed. Discernable cost benefits for parties may vary wildly of course depending on context. Mediation fees may deviate hugely from in-court services provided on a *gratis* basis to the extravagant hourly rates charged at the higher echelons of the commercial market. Add to such outlays, the costs of attendance and preparation of lawyers (perhaps including Counsel) and potentially, the fees of other experts. Mediation thus does not always represent a cheap option for disputing parties. One particular difficulty in proving the cost-effectiveness of mediation in many contexts is the issue of what to compare the costs of mediation to. While it may be tempting to compare costs in mediation to parties' potential costs at trial, very often in the course of on-going litigation cases will settle anyway absent mediation. When parties mediate, it may be very difficult to ascertain at what point such settlement might taken place. Nevertheless, evidence that mediation generally leads to earlier settlement than non-mediated settlement suggests that costs savings may occur as a result.[203]

The findings of a number of early court-annexed ADR studies in the USA have been reviewed by Thomas Stipanovich, which in terms of providing evidence of the cost effectiveness of mediation (and other forms of ADR) in this context, represent a mixed bag.[204] One of the most famous (or infamous) studies of this kind was that conducted by the RAND corporation in 6 US districts in which court annexed ADR was deployed.[205] That study found "no strong statistical evidence" that in court-mediation schemes led to significant costs savings for disputing parties. The somewhat negative findings of the RAND research kicked up a significant storm of protest and the methodology behind that study was cogently critiqued by a number of commentators.[206] Other US research into court-annexed ADR

[201] Menkel-Meadow (2000), p. 34 (internal citations omitted).

[202] See discussion in Chap. 4 at Sect. 4.3.5.

[203] Wissler (2004b).

[204] Stipanowich (2004), pp. 849–866. Some of the well evaluated programmes concerned arbitration and 'early neutral assessment' rather than mediation, however.

[205] Kakalik et al. (1996).

[206] Stipanowich (2004), p. 852.

undertaken at around the same time as the RAND study provided more positive results as regards the costs effectiveness of the process for clients.[207] Nonetheless, writing in 2003 Deborah Hensler suggested that "the [US] evidence to date indicates that [court mediation programmes]... produce little in the way of time or costs savings".[208]

Research evidence from other jurisdictions also sounds cautionary notes regarding mediation's cost-effectiveness for parties. Shortly after the reforms introduced by the 1998 Civil Procedural Rules in England and Wales started to prompt the increased use of mediation, it was suggested that given early case preparation requirements in mediation, the process in fact involved a front loading of costs so that although resolution may be speedier than litigation, mediated settlement would be no cheaper.[209] Increased costs are, of course, most likely to occur where the mediation does not settle and thereafter the case continues along the litigation path. The recent research by Genn *et al.* in the London County Court pilots, found that although parties that settled cases often believed that mediation saved them costs, when cases did not settle, parties found that they added on average between £1,000 and £2,000 to their costs.[210] A study into a German mandatory small-claims mediation scheme found no evidence of costs or time savings for participating parties.[211] The issue of non-settlement and potentially wasted party costs[212] is more likely to arise in mandatory mediation environments, where settlement rates may more often be lower.[213]

On the other hand, international surveys of lawyers reveal that they often believe that recourse to mediation saves their clients money. Mediation participants also often also believe that the process is cost-effective. My work into Scottish commercial litigators' attitudes to ADR found that the vast majority of lawyer respondents believed that mediation would save costs and time for their clients. Around 80% of respondents[214] suggested that a reduction in legal costs for their clients was either "always relevant" or "often relevant" in suggesting mediation to their clients with some 85% of respondents suggested that saving clients' time[215]

---

[207] See the discussion in Stipanowich (2004), pp. 852–874.

[208] Hensler (2003), p. 188.

[209] Fortham (2001).

[210] Genn et al. (2007). The research by Gould et al. (2010), p. 60 into construction mediation in England found 25% of those who had been involved in mediation citing that mediation was a 'waste of money'. Nonetheless, some 40% of respondents involved in failed mediation cited benefits of having participated in the process, including improving mutual party understanding, narrowing of issues and partial settlement.

[211] Discussed in Alexander et al (2006), fn 45.

[212] Although partial settlement or 'narrowing the issues' may occur as a result of unsuccessful mediation.

[213] The evidence is mixed, however. See the discussion in Chap. 5 at Sect. 5.2.3.2.

[214] Including many who had never mediated.

[215] And hence, hidden 'executive' costs.

was similarly a relevant factor.[216] Scottish construction lawyers general share these views.[217] Evidence gleaned from participants in Small Claims mediation schemes in Scotland similarly suggests that clients save costs when compared to adjudicating the matter.[218] Penny Brooker and Anthony Lavers' research into construction lawyers' experiences with mediation in England and Wales also revealed that most respondents felt that mediation did entail cost savings for clients, but few lawyers were able to quantify their extent. Importantly, however, it was generally considered that fewer cost gains were to be garnered, the further the case had travelled along the procedural track of litigation.[219] Additionally, given the fact that engaging a mediator was itself potentially expensive, savings would be most likely to occur in the larger cases rather than those of a more modest nature.[220] Again in the realm of the English construction sector, "substantial" client cost savings generated by participation in mediation have been cited by Gould *et al.*[221] Such findings have been echoed in New Zealand, where research revealed that lawyers, mediators and disputing parties all generally believed that participation in mediation led to costs savings.[222] A report by the Ontario government in Canada into a mandatory mediation scheme also concluded that participation in the process led to a reduction in legal costs for clients.[223] Canadian lawyers mirrored this conclusion in an earlier study of mediation in Ontario.[224] Their American counterparts have often expressed similar views. For instance, Bobbie McAdoo's research into lawyers' responses to mediation in Minnesota revealed that 70% believed that mediation would save their clients litigation costs.[225]

2.6.2 Tactical Use

Non-settlement and the efficiency of the mediation process in general may be influenced by tactical use (or abuse, depending on one's viewpoint) of the process. Tactical use might involve disingenuous engagement in which a party (or their lawyer) might have no intention of seeking resolution to the impasse through

---

[216] Clark and Dawson (2007), pp. 232–233.

[217] Agapoui and Clark (2011), p. 167.

[218] Ross and Bain (2010), Chap. 6.

[219] Nonetheless, clients and their lawyers may perceive mediation a more risky prospect at an early stage in proceedings where little is known about the respective strengths of litigants' cases.

[220] Brooker and Lavers, (2002).

[221] Gould (2010) et al., p. 53. 76% of respondents reportedly saved more than £25,000 while 9% of respondents cited cost savings in excess of £300,000.

[222] Saville-Smith and Fraser (2004), para 4.1–4.2.

[223] Hann and Baar (2001).

[224] Macfarlane (1995).

[225] McAdoo and Hinshaw (2002).

mediation. Rather, recourse to mediation may be used as some sort of 'fishing expedition' to ascertain as much as information as possible about an opponent's case, or simply to waste the time and resources of one's foe. There is also evidence, particularly from the USA, suggesting that some lawyers routinely lie in mediation's to better their own client's cause in the ongoing negotiations.[226] While generally, it might be said that evidence of such tactical use in practice is in fact relatively low,[227] it may be that lawyers will be reluctant to engage in the process fearing tactical ambushing by their opponents, particularly when their own practical experience of mediation is limited.[228] Fearing another's tactical use of mediation may of course be a reflection of the ill-informed lawyer's own intentions for use of the process. Evidence suggests, however, that often lawyers' mindsets can be changed within the mediation process itself from cynicism and adversarialism to genuine engagement and collaboration.[229]

2.7 Quality Objections

Intrinsically linked to any doubts over its efficiency, is the idea that mediation may be resisted by lawyers because of concerns as to the quality of mediators. Empirical research has suggested that at times this is a reason why lawyers are reluctant to advise their clients to mediate. Similarly, lawyers may generally hold doubts as to the quality of mediators available in the field.[230] Again it can be argued that such views may often be linked to an ignorance of, and hostility towards mediation. In particular, negativity regarding the quality of providers may relate to the 'otherness' of mediation and the mediators who populate the field, as opposed to the familiar practice norms and players in traditional legal fields that lawyers can more easily relate to. Participation may be enough to dispel many quality concerns of lawyers. Survey research often finds lawyers reporting satisfaction *ex post* with the

[226] Peters (2007).

[227] Clark and Dawson (2007); Brooker and Lavers (2002).

[228] In Wissler's study of Arizona lawyers' attitudes to ADR, some 26% viewed mediation as an opportunity for the opponent to gain 'free discovery'—Wissler (2004b), p. 485.

[229] See the discussion at Sect. 2.5.3.

[230] For a summary of evidence of lawyers' concerns over lawyer quality in the family field, see Melville and Laing (2010), p. 170. See also Hoffman (2007), pp. 339–540 (a third of German lawyers and 42% of American lawyers surveyed surveyed expressed quality concerns regarding mediators); Vindelov (2006), p. 131 (Danish lawyers' reluctance to embrace mediation justified on basis of quality concerns). For a sophisticated discussion about the issue of regulation of mediators see Boon et al. (2007).

performance of mediators.[231] Nevertheless, quality concerns may have substance. Studies find lawyers sometimes dissatisfied with the performance of mediators.[232] Poor mediators are at times blamed for scuppering settlement opportunities. On the other hand, mediators are also criticised as being overly pushy in their relentless pursuit of settlement raising ethical issues regarding mediators' conduct.[233]

It must be remembered that mediation remains an emerging field of activity in many contexts. The extent that mediators are subject to regulation varies significantly across different jurisdictions and dispute fields. Despite being slower off the blocks in embracing mediation than their common law counterparts, many civil law countries have moved quickly towards stricter regulation of both the process and those that would offer mediation services.[234] Common law jurisdictions have generally been more cautious and, displaying more *laizez faire* attitudes, allowed the market to dictate requisite standards and fostered light-touch self-regulation. Across parts of the common law world there may be no legal requirements as to who may offer mediation services, save in particular institutionalised contexts, where for example, courts will approve rosters of mediators provided for court-annexed services. Requisite training, education and professional development activities for mediators is also markedly mixed.[235]

Arguments over regulation engage the debate between ensuring standardisation and quality assurance to help establish the process and instil confidence in users on the one hand, against fostering innovation and pluralism in the field on the other.[236] The fact that in many spheres mediation may still not be seen as a profession in its own right but rather a 'bolt-on' to mediators' existing professional backgrounds additionally does not assist attempts to produce a standard map for mediation practice. Significant disagreement also exists regarding the appropriate skills and competencies requisite for mediation practice. Lawyers, for example, may be less prone to harbour misgivings about the quality of prospective mediators when the same are drawn from the legal profession or offer their wares as evaluative, directive types. Such matters, as well as the general attempt by lawyers to claim mediation as a legitimate part of legal practice, are discussed in Chap. 3.

---

[231] Agapiou and Clark (2011), p. 166; Relis (2009). Also see the studies cited at footnote one above.

[232] For example, Agapiou and Clark (2011), p. 167 (a minority of respondents blamed mediators for failed mediations in the Scottish construction sector).

[233] Pollack (2007), p. 20; Genn (2009), p. 124.

[234] See Alexander (2001).

[235] Writing in the context of American court-annexed mediation, Deborah Hensler has suggested that, "legislatures and courts display a breezy indifference to the qualifications of those who act as third-party neutrals": Hensler (2003), p. 95.

[236] See Boule and Nesic (2001), p. 465; Boon et al. (2007).

2.8 Conclusion

This chapter has explored some of the reasons why lawyers may have resisted use of mediation as well as the evidence that exists in this respect. The above analysis has concentrated on broad themes. In practice, the various strands of rationale are often intertwined with each other. Sometimes reasons for resistance are explicitly articulated by lawyers. At other times they remain unspoken. In some instances resistance may emanate from subconscious barriers that lawyers erect. Some barriers are clearly more relevant than others in particular dispute contexts or jurisdictions. Furthermore, in practice, when handling individual cases, there may be a whole range of detailed reasons why lawyers will not see fit to encourage mediation, or will actively resist recourse to mediation in respect of the dispute at hand. As I have already noted in this chapter, across the globe, lawyers' barriers to mediation in a wide range of dispute contexts have begun to be dismantled, often forcibly by courts and legislators, but also at the behest of lawyers themselves who have increasingly turned to sample mediation's wares on a voluntary basis. In fact, in more mature jurisdictions relative to mediation's development the debate has largely moved on from the issue of lawyers' resistance to mediation to an examination of the motives of lawyers that have begun to populate the mediation field. It is to this issue that I now turn to in the subsequent chapter.

References

Abbott A (1988) The system of the professions: an essay on the division of expert labour. The University of Chicago Press, Chicago

Abel R (1988a) England and Wales: a comparison of the professional projects of barristers and solicitors. In: Abel R, Lewis PS (eds) Lawyers in society, volume one, the common law World. University of California Press, Berkley

Abel R (1988b) United States: the contradictions of professionalism. In: Abel R, Lewis PS (eds) Lawyers in society, volume one, the common law World. University of California Press, Berkley

Abel R (1999) American lawyers. Oxford University Press, New York

ADR Center (2010) The cost of non ADR - surveying and showing the actual cost of intra-community commercial litigation. European Union, Rome

Agapiou A, Clark B (2011b) A study of scottish construction contractors and sub-contractors' views and experiences relative to mediation (Unpublished, on file with the author)

Agapiou A, Clark B (2011b) Scottish construction lawyers and mediation: an investigation into attitudes and experience. Int J Law Built Environ 3(2):159–181

Alexander N (2001) What's law got to do with it? mapping modern mediation movements in civil and common law jurisdictions. Bond Law Rev 15(2):1–29

Alexander N et al (2006) Mediation in Germany: the long and winding road. In: Alexander N (ed) Global trends in mediation, 2nd edn. Kluwer International, Alphen aan den Rijn

Alleweldt F et al (2009) Study on the use of alternative dispute resolution in the European Union. Final report. Civic Consulting of the Consumer Policy Evaluation Consortium (CPEC), Berlin 16 October 2009. http://ec.europa.eu/consumers/redress_cons/adr_study.pdf. Accessed 1 Nov 2011

Ameer Ali NAN (2010) Mediation in the Malaysian construction industry. In: Brooker P, Wilkinson S (eds) Mediation in the construction industry: an international review. Spon Press, London

Armes J (2010a) Paradiso perso. Eur Lawyer 94:21–30

Armes J (2010b) All eyes on budgets. Eur Lawyer 94:11–12

Armes J (2010c) Shifting sands. Eur Lawyer 94:16–20

Ashenfelter O, Bloom D (1993) Lawyers as agents of the devil in a prisoner's dilemma game. National bureau of economic research, working paper No 4447. MA, Cambridge

Bohlander M (1998) Lawyers and the media: German experience. Leg Ethics 1(2):126–129

Bok F (1983) A flawed system of law practice and training. Harvard Mag 38–44 (May/June)

Boon A et al (2007) Regulation mediators? Leg Ethics 10(1):26–50

Borbély A (2011) Agency in conflict resolution as a manager-lawyer issue: theory and implications for research. Negot Conflict Manag Res 4(2):129–144

Boule L, Nesic M (2001) Mediation: principles. Process and Practice, Butterworths

Brooker P (2001) Commercial and construction ADR: lawyers' attitudes and experience. Civ Justice Q 20:327–347

Brooker P, Lavers R (2002) Commercial lawyers' attitudes and experiences with mediation. Web J Curr Leg Issues 4:2

Burrage M (1988) Revolution in the collective action of the French, American and english legal professions. Law Soc Inq 13:225–277

Campbell C (1976) Lawyers and their public. In: MacCormick D.N (ed) Lawyers in their social setting. W. Green, Edinburgh

Cappelletti M et al (1967) The italian legal system: an introduction. Stanford University Press, Stanford

ADR Centre et al (2010) Showing the actual costs of intra-community commercial litigation: survey data report. http://www.adrcenter.com/jamsinternational/civil-justice/Survey_Data_Report.pdf. Accessed 1 Nov 2011

Chase A (1986) Lawyers and popular culture: a review of mass media portrayals of American attorneys. Am Bar Found Res J 11(2):281–300

Cioff JW (2009) Adversarialism versus legalism: juridification and litigation in corporate governance reform. Regul Govern 3:235–258

Clark B, Dawson C (2007) Scottish commercial litigators and ADR: a study of attitudes and experience. Civ Justice Q 26:228–249

Coope S, Morris S (2002) Personal injury. Negotiation and settlement. Scottish Executive, Edinburgh

Daicoff S (1997) Lawyer know thyself: a review of empirical research on attorney attributes bearing on professionalism. Am Univ Law Rev 46:1337–1427

de los Angeles D (2011) Perceptions on court-annexed mediation in the philippines. Paper presented to 2nd Asian Mediation conference, Kuala Lumpar (On file with the author)

De Palo G, Cominelli L (2006) Mediation in Italy: waiting for the big bang. In: Alexander N (ed) Global trends in mediation, 2nd edn. Kluwer International, Alphen aan den Rijn

De Palo G, Harley P (2005) Mediation in Italy: exploring the contradictions. Negot J 21:469–479

de Roo A, Jagtenberg R (2003) The practice of mediation in eleven countries neighbouring the Netherlands. Dutch ministry of justice. http://www.civilmediation.org/downloads-get?id=133. Accessed 1 Nov 2011

Dezalay Y (1991) Territorial battles and tribal disputes. Mod Law Rev 54:792–809

Doyle M (2006) Evaluation of the small claims mediation service at manchester county court. Dept of Constitutional Affairs, London

Dzienkowski JS (1996) Lawyering in a hybrid adversary system. William Mary law Rev 38:45–61

European Union. Final report. Civic Consulting of the Consumer Policy Evaluation Consortium (CPEC), Berlin 16 October 2009. http://ec.europa.eu/consumers/redress_cons/adr_study.pdf. Accessed 1 Nov 2011

Felstiner W, Sarat A (1980–1981) The emergence and transformation of disputes: naming, blaming, claiming. Law Soc Rev 15(3–4):631–654
Felstiner W, Sarat A (1992) Enactments of power: negotiating reality and responsibility in lawyer-client interactions. Cornell Law Rev 77:1447–1498
Fortham J (2001) Settlement under the CPR: quicker but no cheaper. IHL 89:27
Freeman-Greene S (2001) Mediation: can we ignore it? http://www.leadr.co.nz/db/index.php/articles-mainmenu-162/78-mediation-can-we-ignore-it. Accessed 1 Nov 2011
Gage Educational Publishing Company (1997). Gage Education, Toronto Ontario
Galanter M (1984) Worlds of deals: using negotiation to teach about legal process. J Leg Educ 34:268–276
Galanter M (1994) Predators and parasites: lawyer-bashing and civil justice. Ga Law Rev 28 (3):633–681
Galanter M (2005) Lowering the bar: lawyer jokes and legal culture. University of Wisconsin Press, Madison, Wisconsin
Geertz C (1973) The interpretation of cultures. Basic Books, New York
Genn H (1998) The central London county court pilot mediation scheme evaluation report. Lord Chancellor's Department, London
Genn H (1999) Paths to justice: what people do and think about going to law. Hart Publishing, Oxford
Genn H (2009) Judging civil justice: the 2008 Hamlyn lectures. Cambridge University Press, Cambridge
Genn H, Paterson A (2001) Paths to justice Scotland: what people in Scotland do and think about going to law. Hart Publishing, Oxford
Genn H et al (2007) Twisting arms: court referred and court linked mediation under judicial pressure. Ministry of Justice Research Series 1/07, Ministry of Justice, London
Gibson RJ, Mnookin RH (1994) Disputing through agents: cooperation and conflict between lawyers in litigation. Columbia Law Rev 94:509–566
Goodman-Delahunty J et al (2010) Insightful or wishful: lawyers' ability to predict case outcomes psychology. Publ Pol Law 16(2):133–157
Gould N et al (2010) Mediating construction disputes: an evaluation of existing practice. Centre for Construction Law, Kings College, London
Gross LE (1999) The pubic hates lawyers: why should we care? Seton Hall Law Rev 29:1405
Guardian Newspaper. Compulsory mediation angers lawyers working in Italy's unwieldy legal system. http://www.guardian.co.uk/law/butterworth-and-bowcott-on-law/2011/may/23/italian-lawyers-strike-mandatory-mediation. Accessed 1 Nov 2011
Handler J (1978) Social movements and the legal system: a theory of law reform and social change. Academic, New York
Hann G, Baar C (2001) Evaluation of the Ontario Mandatory Mediation Programme (Rule 24.1): Final Report – The First 23 Months. Ontario Ministry of the Attorney General
Hedeen T, Salem P (2006) What should family lawyers know? results of a survey of practitioners and students. Fam Court Rev 44:601–611
Heinz J et al (1976) Diversity, representation and leadership in an urban bar: a first report on a survey of the Chicago bar. Am Bar Found Res J 2:717–785
Hensler DR (2003) Our courts, ourselves: how the alternative dispute resolution movement is reshaping our legal system. Penn St L Rev 108:165–197
Hoffman, A (2007) Mediation in Germany and the United States. European Journal of Law Reform 9:505–551
Ilter D, Dikbas A (2010) Construction mediation in Turkey. In: Brooker P, Wilkinson S (eds) Mediation in the construction industry: an international review. Spon Press, London
Irvine C (2010) The future of legal education: what's ADR got to do with it? Scots Law Times 25:139–142
Johnson T (1972) Professions and power. Macmillan, London
Kagan RA (1991) Adversarial legalism and American government. J Pol Anal Manag 10:369–406
Kagan RA, Rosen RE (1985) On the social significance of large law firm practice. Stanford Law Rev 37:399–443

Kakalik J et al (1996) An evaluation of mediation and early neutral evaluation under the civil justice reform act ("The RAND Report") RAND, ICJ

Kelemen RD, Sibbitt EC (2004) The globalization of American law. Int Organ 58(1):103–136

Kelly M (1994) Lives of lawyers: journeys in the organization of practice. University of Michegan Press, Ann Arbor

Kotz H (2003) Civil justice systems in Europe and the United States. Duke J Comp Int Law 13:61–79

Kritzer H (2001/2002) Lawyer fees and lawyer behavior in litigation: what does the empirical literature really say. Tex Law Rev 80:1943–1983

Krizter H (1998) Contingent-fee lawyers and their clients: settlement expectations, settlement realities, and issues of control in the lawyer-client relationship. Law Soc Inq 23:795–821

Kronman AT (1993) The lost lawyer: the falling ideals of the legal profession. Harvard University Press, Cambridge

LaFontaine Y (1985) Are lawyers a vivid contradiction. In: Gibson D, Baldwin J (eds) Law in a cynical society? opinion and law in the 1980's. Caswell Legal Publications, Calgary

Lande J (2000) Getting the faith: why business lawyers and executives believe in mediation. Harv Negot Law Rev 5:137–227

Larson MS (1977) The rise of professionalism. University of California Press, Berkeley

Lasserre B (2003) Optimising the management of your international disputes. Thanks for mediation: the French experience. BETRIEBSBERATER 26: 22–24

Lempereur A (1998) Negotiation and mediation in france: the challenge of skill-based learning and interdisciplinary research in legal education. Harv Negot Law Rev 3:151–174

Loftus EF, Wagenaar WA (1987–1988) Lawyers' predictions of success. Jurimetrics J 28:437

MacDonald R (2005) Legal culture. Discussion paper for civil justice reform group. http://www.bcjusticereview.org/working_groups/civil_justice/cjrwg_paper_02_23_05.pdf. Accessed 1 Nov 2011

Macfarlane J (1995) Court-based mediation for civil cases: an evaluation of the Ontario court (general division) ADR center. University of Windsor, Windsor

Macfarlane J (2001) Culture change? Commercial litigators and the Ontario mandatory mediation programme. http://dsp-psd.pwgsc.gc.ca/collection_2008/lcc-cdc/JL2-70-2001E.pdf. Accessed 1 Nov 2011

Macfarlane J (2002) Culture Change? A tale of two cities and mandatory court-connected mediation. J Dispute Resolut 2:241–366

Macfarlane J (2008) The new lawyer: how settlement is transforming the practice of law. UBS Press, Toronto

Malsch M (1990) Advocaten voorspellen de uitkomst van hun zaken Lawyers' predictions of judicial decisions: a study on calibration of experts. Swets & Zeitlinger, Lisse

Mather L (2003) What do clients want? what do lawyers do? Emory Law J 52:1065–1086

Mays R, Clark B (1996) Alternative dispute resolution in Scotland. Scottish Office Central Research Unit, Edinburgh

Mayson SW (1992) The future of the legal profession. Nottingham Law J 1:1–8

McAdoo B, Hinshaw A (2002) The challenge of institutionalizing alternative dispute resolution: attorney perspectives on the effect of rule 17 on civil litigation in Missouri. Mo Law Rev 67:473

McIlwaine L (2004) Tort reform and the compensation culture. JPI 4:239

Meiser I (2006) Mediation and conciliation in Switzerland. In: Alexander N (ed) Global trends in mediation, 2nd edn. Kluwer International, Alphen aan den Rijn

Melville A, Laing K (2010) Closing the gate: family lawyers as gatekeepers to a holistic service. Int J Law Context 6(2):167–189

Menkel-Meadow C (1996) The trouble with the adversary system in the post-mod multi cultural world. William Mary Law Rev 38:5–44

Menkel-Meadow C (2000) Mothers and fathers of invention: the intellectual founders of ADR. Ohio State J Dispute Resolut 16:1–37

Merry S (1990) Getting justice and getting even: legal consciousness among working-class Americans. University of Chicago Press, Chicago
Merry S, Sibley S (1984) (1984) What do plaintiff's want? Re-examining the concept of a dispute. Justice Syst J 9:151–178
Nedic M (2008) Mediation & lawyers: prejudice or interest? Paper presented at European Mediation conference, 10th April 2008, Belfast (On-file with the author)
Neuberger L (2010) Education mediators. Paper presented to the fourth annual Civil Mediation Council conference, London (On file with the author)
Niemeijer B, Pel P (2005–2006) Court-based mediation in the Netherlands: research, evaluations and future expectations. Penn State Law Rev 110:345–379
Ooi CSS (2005) The role of lawyers in mediation: what the future holds. http://www.malaysianbar.org.my/adr_arbitration_mediation/the_role_of_lawyers_in_mediation_what_the_future_holds.html. Accessed 1 Nov 2011
Osiel MJ (1989) Lawyers as monopolists, aristocrats and entrepreneurs. Harv Law Rev 103:2009
Parker C (1999) Just lawyers. Oxford University Press, Oxford
Paterson A (1988) The legal profession in Scotland – an endangered species or a problem case for market theory? In: Abel R, Lewis PS (eds) Lawyers in society, volume one, the common law world. University of California Press, Berkley
Pears G (1983) Beyond dispute: alternative dispute resolution in Australia. Corporate Impacts Publications, Edgecliff
Peters D (2007) When lawyers move their lips: attorney truthfulness in mediation and a modest proposal. J Dispute Resolut 1:119–142
Peters D (2010) It takes two to tango, and two to mediate: legal, cultural and other factors influencing United States and latin American lawyers; resistance to mediating commercial disputes rich. J Global L Bus 9:381–429
Peters D (2011) Understanding why lawyers resist mediation. Paper presented at 2nd AMA conference, Kuala Lumpur, Malaysia, 24–25 Feb 2011
Peters RJ, Mastin DB (2007) To mediate or not to mediate: that is the question. Dispute Resolut J 62(2):14–21
Pollack C (2007) The role of the mediation advocate: a user's guide to mediation. Arbitration 73 (1):20–23
Post RC (1987) On the popular image of the lawyer: reflections in a dark glass. Calif Law Rev 75:379–389
Prince S (2004) Court based mediation: a preliminary analysis of the small claims mediation scheme at exeter county court. University of Exeter, Exeter
Prujiner A (2006) Recent developments in mediation in Canada. In: Alexander N (ed) Global trends in mediation, 2nd edn. Kluwer International, Alphen aan den Rijn
Relis T (2009) Perceptions in litigation and mediation: lawyers, defendants, plaintiffs, and gendered parties. Cambridge University Press, New York
Riskin L (1982) Mediation and lawyers. Ohio State Law J 43:29–60
Rogers N, McEwen C (1998) Employing the law to increase the use of mediation and to encourage direct and early negotiations. Ohio State J Dispute Resolut 13:831–41
Rosenthal D (1974) Lawyer and client: who's in charge? Russell Sage, New York
Ross L (1999) Reactive devaluation in negotiation and conflict resolution. In: Arrow KJ et al (eds) Barriers to conflict resolution. W.W Norton, New York
Ross M (2004) Mediating in the shadow of civil procedural law in Scotland: 'nursing wrath' towards 'nurturing choice. Paper delivered to American Bar Association Dispute Resolution conference, New York, 2004 (On file with the author)
Ross M, Bain D (2010) In court mediation pilots: report on evaluation of in court mediation schemes in Glasgow and Aberdeen Sheriff courts. Scottish government, courts and constitution analytical team. http://www.scotland.gov.uk/Resource/Doc/310104/0097858.pdf
Russell C (2007) Mediation in England and Wales: a very English revolution. http://nt4992.vs.netbenefit.com/articles/viewarticle.asp?articleid=1805. Accessed 1 Nov 2011

Samuel E (2002) Supporting court users: the in-court advice and mediation projects at Edinburgh Sheriff court phase 2. Scottish Executive Central Research Unit, Edinburgh
Sander F (2000) The future of ADR. J Dispute Resolut 2000:3
Sarat A, Felstiner W (1989) Lawyers and legal consciousness: law talk in the divorce lawyer's office. Yale Law J 98:1663–1668
Saville-Smith K, Fraser R (2004) Alternative dispute resolution: general civil cases. New Zealand Ministry of Justice, Wellington
Scottish Consumer Council (2001) Consensus without going to court: encouraging mediation in non-family civil disputes in Scotland. Scottish Consumer Council, Edinburgh
Sela A (2009) Attorneys' perspectives of mediation: an empirical analysis of attorneys' mediation referral practices, barriers and potential agency problems, and their effect on mediation in Israel. Unpublished MSc thesis, Stanford Law School (On file with the author)
Sharma A (1997) Professional as agent: Knowledge asymmetry in agency exchange. Acad Manag Rev 22(3):758–798
Shestack JJ (2001) Introduction: a volume paving a path forward. In: Van Winkle JR (ed) Mediation: a path back for the lost lawyer. American Bar Association, Chicago
Sidoli del Ceno J (2011) An investigation into lawyer attitudes towards the use of mediation in commercial property disputes in England and Wales. Int J Law Built Environ 3(2):182–198
Smith H (2007) The inside track: how the blue chips are using ADR. http://geoffsharp.atomicrobot.co.nz/wp-content/uploads/2010/03/6398ADRreportD4.pdf. Accessed 1 Nov 2011
Spangler E (1986) Lawyers for hire: salaried professionals at work. Yale University Press, New Haven
Stipanowich T (2004) ADR and the 'Vanishing Trial': the growth and impact of 'alternative dispute resolution'. J Empir Leg Stud 1(3):843–912
Subrin S (2002) A traditionalist looks at mediation: it's here to stay and much better than I thought. Nevada Law J 3:196–227
Sugarman D (1995) Who colonized whom? Historical reflections on the intersection between law, lawyers and accountants in England. In: Dezalay Y, Sugarman D (eds) Professional competition and professional power. Routledge, London
Susskind R (2010) The end of lawyers? Rethinking the nature of legal services. Oxford University Press, Oxford
Tidwell A (1999) It's the process that counts: professionalising mediation in New South Wales. Murdoch J Electron Law 6(2)
Tromans R (2007) Challenging the conflict culture: mediations' struggle for acceptance in Europe. Eur Lawyer 68:19–23
Van Winkle J (2001) Mediation: a path back for the lost lawyer. American Bar Association, Chicago
Vindelov V (2006) Mediation in Danish law: in retrospect and perspective. In: Alexander N (ed) Global trends in mediation, 2nd edn. Kluwer International, Alphen aan den Rijn
Voegeli W (1992) (1992) Alternative dispute resolution in divorce disputes. Civ Justice Q 11:283–300
Wall C (2009) The framework for mediation in Hong Kong. Arbitration 75(1):78–85
Welsh NA (2001) Making Deals in Court-Connected Mediation: What's Justice Got to Do With It? Wash Univ Law Q 79:786–865
Welsh N (2004) Stepping back through the looking glass: real conversations with real disputants about institutionalized mediation and its values. Ohio State J Dispute Resolut 19:573–678
Wissler R (2002) When does familiarity breed content? a study of the role of different forms of ADR education and experience in attorneys' ADR recommendations. Pepperdine Dispute Resolut Law J 2:199
Wissler R (2004a) The effectiveness of court-connected dispute resolution in civil cases. Conflict Resolut Q 22:55–88

Wissler R (2004b) Barriers to attorneys' discussions and use of ADR". Ohio State J Dispute Resolut 19:459–508

Yu. H. (2009) Court Annexed Mediation. Civil Justice Quarterely 28(4):515–550

Zariski A (1997) Lawyers and dispute resolution: what do they think and know (and think they know)? - finding out through survey research. Murdoch Univ Electron J Law 4(2)

Zariski A (2000) Disputing culture: lawyers and ADR. Murdoch Univ Electron J Law 7(2)

Zariski A (2011) The new old lawyer: how lawyers have adapted to mediation to preserve their power, income, and identity. Paper presented to 2nd Asian Mediation conference, Kuala Lumpur (On file with the author)

Chapter 3
Lawyer Involvement in Mediation and the Co-Option Thesis

3.1 Introduction

While Chap. 2 examined the issue of lawyer resistance to mediation and the rationale behind such intransigence that does exist, an equally important matter in the mix of lawyers and mediation, particularly in those jurisdictions where developments lie at a more advanced stage, is an exploration of the motives of lawyers who have seen fit to engage with the process. This is especially so in view of the chorus of protests voicing the fear that the lawyer's dalliance with mediation may often represent a largely opportunistic manoeuvre designed to gain control of the field and usurp the role of other professionals in the process. In this chapter I will hence focus on an examination of why increasing ranks of lawyers globally have sought to set foot on the mediation terrain. I will also examine some of the tactics that lawyers have resorted to in gaining a foothold in the field. Lawyers have been especially adept at deploying this armoury in the professional skirmishes or 'turf wars' that, given its consensual, harmonious nature, paradoxically blight the mediation field.[1]

A desire to co-opt the field is of course but one of an array of reasons why lawyers may have sought to become involved in mediation. Aside from the simple fact that mandatory mediation rules may have removed any semblance of choice for lawyers in many contexts, as I discussed at the outset of this book, lawyers can in many senses be seen as pioneers of the modern ADR movement and champions of its cause. Lawyers may thus be true believers in mediation's worth. Indeed, lawyers often harbour genuine reasons for their promotion and use of mediation, including: responding to the call of their clients; a genuine belief that mediation may produce superior outcomes and more client-friendly disputing processes; and a desire to increase levels of satisfaction with, and more enriching experiences in their own

[1] The mediation field generally has been characterised by much internal squabbling by competitors trying to establish a power base in the field—for a potted discussion see Parkinson (2010).

B. Clark, *Lawyers and Mediation*, DOI 10.1007/978-3-642-23474-3_3,

work. With regard to the latter issue, it has been suggested that mediation activity represents an antidote of sorts to a decline in lawyers' professionalism, offers some kind of redemption or 'path back' for the lost lawyer,[2] or is reflective of a paradigm shift in legal practice from zealous advocate to problem-solving professional.

Simply put, lawyers may naturally see mediation as a legitimate commercial opportunity, falling within their existing sphere of practice and expertise, to offer services in a new and growing market. This aim should not be conflated with more cynical endeavours to 'milk' the mediation process for selfish aims and exclude others from practice. There is, of course, a fine line between these two goals. Legitimate pursuance of the first may creep incrementally towards fulfilment of the second without necessarily any conscious and determinative attempt to achieve this.[3] Whether mediation represents natural terrain for lawyers also depends on its normative form which varies significantly by context. Skirmishes between competing professionals over their respective roles in mediation thus also often represent disputes over the normative make-up of mediation itself. This is important because in terms of how different professions compete for a sphere of practice, each tries to establish a normative basis for their presence in that field. According to Yves Dezalay, "[d]ifferent professions endeavour to construct or, more exactly, to 'reduce' complex, polymorphous and changing social problems into a 'need' which, precisely, calls for the kind of treatment that they alone can provide because they control the know-how on which it is based".[4] Similarly, in the words of Andrew Abbot: "[a] profession's work is made up of problems that require service, problems that can belong to individuals or groups, that can be difficulties to be overcome or to be improved. These problems have two kinds of properties. First, there are objective properties—those given the nature of the problem itself. They can be natural facts, cultural facts, technical facts, or organizational facts. But professional work... is shaped also by the constructive act of professional work...Professions don't just find things laid out for them; they construct their problems as they work with them".[5]

Lawyers traditionally have transformed occurring social phenomenon into legal problems, of which they profess to alone have the tools to fix.[6] While mediators, in their grass roots, facilitative personae, may have sought to reframe disputes in a more nuanced, multi-faceted sense, in which the legal aspect of the problem is one of but a wide range of a matters germane to the dispute at hand,[7] lawyer involvement in mediation can be seen, either in design or by effect, to have reasserted the primacy of the legal dimension to disputes within mediation itself. 'Quality'

[2] Van Winkle (2001); Kronman (1993).

[3] We should also remember that the motives of individual lawyers in this regard may also deviate sharply from those of professional bodies.

[4] Dezalay (1991), p. 795.

[5] Abbot (1986), p. 190.

[6] Felstiner and Sarat (1980–1981).

[7] Or even completely irrelevant.

proponents[8] advanced ideas of ADR truly as an alternative to the law and legal processes and the lawyers who inhabited that system. Thus lawyer infiltration has been particularly galling for those with 'purist' notions of what the process of mediation denotes.

The uncertain nature of the mediation process itself also renders it a natural battle ground for competing professionals. The practice of mediation is to some extent clothed in mystique. It is not an easily discernible process. It is sometimes referred to as an 'art'. Moreover, there are many forms of mediation. Mediation's normative flexibility allows it to be moulded in such a fashion to suit the traditional offerings of different would-be practitioners. So, for lawyers, "mediation" may become a legal-centric, evaluative process, even the 'practice of law'[9]; for psychologists it may become a form of therapy; for other professionals, perhaps expertise in the subject matter becomes an important characteristic or 'selling point' of those seeking to practice this activity.

3.2 The Co-Option Thesis

The cooption thesis posits that facing up to the stark reality of trenchant promotion of mediation by courts and policy-makers and the resultant potential threat to their traditional business of litigation-based dispute resolution practices, lawyers have moved from a position of resistance to tactical embracement of the process. Lawyers further stand accused of seeking to normatively reshape the mediation process into one that better fits their own interests and comports more naturally with their own practice and cultural norms, perhaps to the detriment of participants who might use it. In the process, this juridification of mediation helps keep the mediation prize out of reach of other professionals seeking to gain a foothold in the market. Simple 'economic' and 'market control' professional theories—positing that professionals such as lawyers seek rationally to pursue financial goals and/or control the markets that they populate respectively—lend succour to such suspicions.[10] Portents of the future for mediation activity worldwide may be gleaned from experience in more established mediation jurisdictions. In the USA,[11] for example, lawyers can be seen to have made concerted efforts to lay a claim to the field with a real measure of success, at least in contexts in which there is money to be made. Those involved in developing mediation in less mature environments may fear that like ripples on a pond, lawyer co-option will spread

---

[8] See Chap. 1 at Sect. 1.1.2.

[9] See Sect. 3.4.3.

[10] See generally Abel (1989a).

[11] Nolan-Handley 2002.

to their own jurisdictions, as legal professionals learn the lessons handed down by their American counterparts.

To determine the extent that lawyers have purposely attempted to dominate mediation is no easy task. In the ensuing section I will seek to shed light on the issue by an analysis of empirical evidence relating to lawyers' engagement with mediation, as well as an examination of the behaviour of lawyers and their professional bodies relative to the process. The discussion will begin with an overview of general professional behaviour which may fuel belief that lawyers have sought to co-opt the field.

3.2.1 The Seeking of New Markets

That lawyers should seek out new markets (such as mediation) is no surprise. All professions are involved in a constant process of change in which they must adapt to an ever-shifting environment to sustain existing, and seek out new professional goals. In this sense, "[i]f lawyers want to preserve their hegemony and social power they must be able to evolve. If not, they risk finding themselves rapidly overtaken by history, or more concretely, by their immediate competitors..."[12] New markets or potential fields of practice can be considered disputed terrain, with different professional explorers seeking to plant their flags in the virgin territory first. There are particular reasons that lawyers in particular may be interested, and feel legitimised in laying claim to mediation, including that: lawyers are key players in related fields of traditional dispute resolution; in recent years, mediation has grown stronger bonds with traditional disputing practices and in some contexts been located within the same (e.g. through court-annexed mediation schemes); lawyers' traditional markets and monopolies are on the wane; mediation may seem a natural environment for new breeds of 'problem-solving' lawyers.

3.2.2 The History of Lawyers and Professional Skirmishes

Lawyers enjoy, if that is the correct word, a fierce reputation for putting their rivals to the sword. This in itself may add fuel to the arguments around lawyer co-option of the mediation field.[13] It is true that lawyers, akin to many professional groupings of course, have a history of skirmishes and jurisdictional turf battles with others in respect of various market activities. Winners and losers are inevitably produced.

[12] Dezalay 1991, p. 801.

[13] Their general reputation may also add fuel to such suspicions, see Chap. 2 at Sect. 2.2.

As Abbot notes, "professsions' histories are littered with splinter groups and faltering competitors. . .occasionally recalled as precursors, charlatans or worse."[14] The truth of the matter is perhaps more nuanced than folklore pertaining to lawyers suggests, however. While historically, American lawyers have blazed a trail in competitive jousting with other professionals, protecting their traditional jurisdictional turfs, pursuing unauthorised practitioners of their art, and blithely encroaching on to ground of others, the same may not be said of other legal professions across the globe.[15] History tells us that lawyers have not in fact always fought and won in their jurisdictional battles with other professionals. In the UK, for example, from the period 1850 to 1950, lawyers ceded work to accountants and found their status relative to their professional counterparts diminished.[16] Pursuance of the 'professional project'[17]—primarily concerned with improving a profession's social status[18]—by rendering entry demanding and thus limiting the supply of professionals, may in fact lead to jurisdictional encroachments by others as demand for services begins to outstrip supply.[19] By such means lawyers have thus opened up competition rather than suppressed it. Some potentially lucrative work is simply seen as of insufficient importance to be undertaken by lawyers and hence ceded to others.[20] There also exists evidence of interdependence between lawyers and other professionals, borne out by lawyers seeing the need to work with others on a *quid pro quo* basis. For example, despite moves designed by English lawyers to quash the intrusion of 'folk devil' accountants onto their turf, history suggests a legal profession subsequently channelling business to, and working alongside accountants.[21] In the mediation field this can commonly be seen, for example, in the co-mediation of family disputes involving lawyers and psychology professionals found in certain civil law countries across Europe.[22] Despite the prevalence of lawyers in certain mediation contexts, the seemingly easy co-existence of lawyers and other professionals in the mediation field is in fact a feature of many settings internationally.

---

[14] Abbot (1998), p. 247.

[15] Dezalay (1991); Abbot (1998).

[16] Sugarman (1995).

[17] Larson (1997).

[18] And not originally concerned with the pursuance of financial aims –see Chap. 2 at Sect. 2.4.2.

[19] Burrage (1988).

[20] See Chap. 2 at Sect. 2.4.2.

[21] Sugarman (1995), pp 229–230. He also argues that complacency and strong traditional markets may have led to the ceding of power to accountants in perceived fringe areas. The 'gentlemanly' nature of the English legal profession may also have militated against too much involvement at the coal face of business.

[22] See, for example, de Roo and Jagtenberg (2006).

3.2.3 Demand Creation and New Markets

In many jurisdictions, entry to the legal profession, for so long an exclusive club with prohibitive admission requirements, has widened markedly, leading to over-supply in some cases.[23] When a profession begins to lose control over the extent of production and its own supply of producers, it may naturally shift to demand creation for its wares.[24] Professions may hence begin to innovate, expand their knowledge base and bend their professional norms to encompass new practices and techniques.[25] Mediation may hence represent such an innovation for lawyers.

This need for new markets may be especially acute in an era when lawyers have ceded traditional monopolies to others.[26] Allied to this is the fact that in many countries traditional markets and traditional legal ways of working are diminishing; a process it has been argued is set to continue, not least because of increasing commoditisation and expansion of IT services and expanding consumerism and 'self-help' trends.[27] Writing recently, Richard Susskind has sounded alarm bells for the future of the legal profession: "[t]here are "profound forces at play, forces that are lessening the need for the traditional 'black letter" lawyer. When it becomes possible to standardise, systematise, package and even commoditise the law, the need for the traditional bespoke handling by the conventional lawyer lessons considerably".[28] While Susskind, painted as a harbinger of doom for the profession, has been accused of hyperbolism in such matters,[29] the commoditisation of legal information has been steadily increasing over recent decades. In Germany, for example, the need for specialised legal services has reduced because qualified non-lawyer business clerks have gained access to legal data banks. The requirement for bespoke, specialised knowledge in the area has hence been reduced.[30] This made it impossible for lawyers to "create and secure an exclusive professional jurisdiction in the insurance industry."[31] The increasing global development of 'self-help' legal information generally on the internet may be diminishing the need for recourse to specialised legal service.

---

[23] See Macfarlane 1998, p. 3 reporting that the numbers of American and Canadian lawyers have almost doubled since the 1970's. The shift from entry by apprenticeship to entry by University degree can be seen as one way in which numbers have swelled.

[24] Abel (1982).

[25] Abel (1989b), p. 123.

[26] Glasser (1990), pp 3-4 (lawyers in England and Wales); Dezalay (1991) (American and European lawyers).

[27] See generally, Susskind 2010, Chaps. 3 and 4.

[28] Susskind (2007).

[29] As he admits himself—Susskind 2010, pp xvii-xix.

[30] Hartman (1993).

[31] Hartman (1993), p. 422. It was also reported that insurance companies continued to recruit lawyers over insurance clerks to meet any contingent demand for legal services, because the over-supply of lawyers made them cheaper to recruit.

Other professionals have pushed at the margins of legal practice for centuries, heaping pressure on lawyers to defend their borders. Examples of lawyers' traditional work being lost to others can be found worldwide. In the UK, for example, the lawyer's traditional conveyancing monopoly has long been lost. Encroachment in the core spheres of succession and trusts by hybrid executries professionals and 'will-writers' has also seen such markets diminish. In my own jurisdiction of Scotland, new breeds of hybrid professionals such as 'commercial attorneys', with both legal and technical/commercial expertise, have sought to gain a foothold in the area of construction disputes, both in tendering advice on contracting and dispute resolution and additionally, appearing as party representatives in the Scottish civil courts.[32] Audit firms have successfully competed for the provision of legal services with established legal professionals in Spain, particularly in the area of tax advice work.[33] Such competition reflects the complex nature of business problems, in which the legal dimension is only but one of a smorgasbord of different arising issues. The promise of a 'one-stop-shop' for resolution of business, technical and legal issues thus may become irresistible. Given the historical limitation on lawyers working internally with other professionals that have existed in many jurisdictions, non-lawyers, not hidebound by such restrictions may find it easier to offer desired joined-up services.[34] Generally, the ascendancy of the 'consumer' movement in many jurisdictions, urging legislators to open up competition in legal services further, presents a further threat to traditional markets.[35] The legal profession thus faces an uncertain and unsettled future. This is especially troubling not least because at this juncture lawyers' professional standing has arguably already reduced and been in decline for some time.[36]

3.2.4 *Evidence of Lawyer Accommodation in Other Fields*

In terms of determining lawyers' rationale for involvement in mediation, insights can also be gleaned by analysing the profession's responses to other potential 'threats' in the past. Historical evidence of this activity can arguably be found in the expansion of legal aid work and the inception of law centres in countries such as the UK, the USA and New Zealand. In the same vein as mediation perhaps,

---

[32] Commercial Attorneys are construction professionals such as surveyors, architects and engineers who have also undertaken post graduate legal qualifications.

[33] Marcos (2000).

[34] In recent years Multi Disciplinary Practices where lawyers and other professionals may work together in the same firm have become possible in many jurisdictions.

[35] The leading international consumer organisation is Consumers International—see http://www.consumersinternational.org/.

[36] Kronman (1993); Burger (1995); Dezalay (1991), p. 804 (suggesting that as early as 1991 the decline in the status of European lawyers significantly exceeded that of their American counterparts).

although lawyers first resisted these developments as an unpalatable encroachment on their turf, when it became clear that they had failed to stem the tide, the profession resorted "to its more successful tactic of cooptation".[37]

Arbitration, as one of the precursors to mediation in the modern ADR movement, is a particularly striking example of successful lawyer infiltration. In the English context, John Flood and Andrew Caiger have charted the rise of involvement of English lawyers in arbitration towards a position of domination. English lawyers were able to mobilise effectively, infiltrate arbitration institutions and infuse the process with the accoutrements of law.[38] In the context of the USA, Bruce Benson has argued that the commonly held view that the business community sought out statutes providing legal enforceability of arbitral awards was a myth perpetrated by lawyers.[39] Rather, he contends that faced with increasing competition from arbitration, lawyers cast aside their distaste for the process. They became its champions in the name of legalising arbitration and ensuring their place within it.[40] As he explains "[w]hile many lawyers may have preferred to squelch the competitive threat posed by arbitration, others apparently recognized that its rapid development and widespread use suggested that its elimination was not possible... if an alternative forum to the public courts was to be used, trial lawyers wanted a forum that they might be able to influence and perhaps even dominate.... lawyers hoped to initiate arbitration statutes written in a way that would lead to a role for lawyers in the arbitration process, and they sought such statutes by lobbying through their bar association."[41] Their encroachment into the process continued unabated. Attorney representation in American arbitration rose exponentially.[42] American lawyers were also quick to gain prominence as arbitrators at the expense of non-lawyers.[43] Professional bodies soon became overrun with legal types.[44] In the modern context, arbitration systems globally have often been pillared, not least because lawyer involvement has formalised and legalised the process thus ramping up the complexity, time and costs involved[45] Against this backdrop, it holds few

---

[37] Paterson (1988), p. 101.

[38] Flood and Caiger, (1993) pp 425–440.

[39] Benson (1995), pp 490–497.

[40] For a discussion of early lawyer resistance to arbitration see Grossman 1939–1940.

[41] Benson (1995), p 492. See also Auerbach 1983, chpt 4 for a stimulating review of the early 20th Century spats between lawyers and businessmen in the context of arbitration.

[42] From 36% of American Arbitration Association cases in 1927 to 91% in 1947: Auerbach 1983, p. 111.

[43] Meason and Smith (1991), p 26.

[44] Auerbach (1983), chpt 4.

[45] For a critique of the escalating legalities and costs of international commercial arbitration see Durcan (2008); Seidenberg (2010); For arbitration in Eastern Europe, see Salpius (2006), p. 46. See also Cheung (1999) for a discussion of related matters in Hong Kong. My own research in the Scottish construction and commercial sectors has revealed that lawyers themselves are vocal about the escalating costs of arbitration—Agapiou and Clark (2011); Clark and Dawson (2007).

surprises that similar fears would be voiced over mediation's prospects when set against the tactical nous of lawyers to convert potential threats into opportunities.

Such examples, as well as musings on theories of professional behaviour, are useful in the sense that they offer insights into the general behaviour of lawyers in like scenarios. They thus offer glimpses of potential future occurrences within mediation. More instructive, however, is the evidence to date of lawyers' inroads into mediation itself. There now follows an analysis of some of the reasons that lawyers have engaged in mediation, including evidence as to lawyers' own attitudes towards involvement, and a depiction of some of the strategies that lawyers can be seen to have deployed in gaining a foothold in the field.

3.3 The Roots of Lawyer Engagement with Mediation

3.3.1 Introduction

As charted in Chap. 1, lawyers may truly be considered pioneers of modern mediation in many contexts. True, it may be the case that judges and policy makers have often espoused 'efficiency' motives for their promotion of mediation and been mainly concerned with alleviating court dockets and producing savings for the public purse. By contrast, early lawyer aficionados could often be described as 'quality proponents' or 'true believers' in mediation, seeing the worth of the process *per se*, quite apart from any benefits that its harvesting would reap for civil court systems.[46] Nonetheless, the early standard bearers for mediation within legal ranks typically amounted to a fringe minority at best, unrepresentative of the general attitudes and posturing of their peers or professional bodies towards mediation. As I explored in Chap. 2, hostility and ambivalence within the legal profession often was, and may typically remain, the norm. In practice, many lawyers have been dragged kicking and screaming into mediation through rules dictating compulsory engagement or financial imperatives encouraging use. Nevertheless, even in such cases where there has been little initial choice but to engage with the process, it does not necessarily follow that once lawyers enter the field that they do not consequently develop a professional agenda for their participation in it and/or become converted to the ways of mediation. Aside from their mandatory yoking to mediation, as I shall discuss below there is also significant evidence of widening, voluntary engagement by lawyers either as mediators or party representatives.

[46] See Chap. 1, Sect. 1.1.1.

3.3.2 Commercial Imperatives

Surveys of lawyers do not, of course, find them lining up to shout from the rooftops about their intension to cynically manipulate the mediation field. Amongst other reasons for seeking involvement, lawyers often do draw attention, however, to the commercial benefits accruing from such engagement. My own work in Scotland has over the years, detected a strong commercial bent to lawyer involvement in the field. My 1996 research found a significant number of fledgling lawyer-mediators stating that mediation represented an opportunity to gain a foothold in an emerging market and add another string to their professional bows.[47] Although with the benefit of hindsight, we can see that many such respondents were in fact labouring under a misconception as to how lucrative mediation work would transpire to be, my later research a decade on found Scottish commercial litigation lawyers similarly anticipating the commercial boon resulting from engagement in mediation. A significant majority of lawyers surveyed in that work suspected that mediation presented an opportunity to offer new services to clients. The vast majority did not perceive that mediation developments would dry up their existing income streams.[48] Cognate evidence was revealed in my subsequent study of Scottish construction lawyers.[49] Reflecting the commercial possibilities of mediation for the lawyer, legions of articles in the legal press in particular have highlighted the resulting business opportunities and how these might be exploited by lawyers.[50] Training courses in mediation practice or mediation party representation tailored for lawyers have also developed exponentially. 'How to' books on establishing mediation practices for lawyers also abound.[51]

3.3.3 Belief in the Process

Research also uncovers lawyer engagement because of a genuine commitment to the process and the benefits that may accrue for their clients. Julie Macfarlane, in her 2001 study of Ontario lawyers' involvement with court-connected mediation,[52] famously depicted such enthusiasts as "true believers" holding deep-seated

[47] Mays and Clark (1996).

[48] Clark and Dawson (2007), pp 239–240. Although see the discussion in Chap. 2 at Sect. 2.4.3 regarding lawyers' reported fears over the potentially negative financial implications of mediation development.

[49] Agapiou and Clark (2011), p 175.

[50] See for example, Clark (2003) (my own somewhat premature call to arms for lawyers in Scotland to embrace the commercial opportunities it would afford them); Mercer (2006); Seamone (2000).

[51] Such as Mantle (2011); Van Winkle (2001); Mosten (2001); Partridge (2009).

[52] Macfarlane (2001), chpt. III.

personal commitments to mediation and acting as zealous preachers for the process.[53] Other studies also indicate that lawyers enter the mediation field (or at least claim to) because they believe in the value of mediation rather than their own financial rewards.[54] As I noted in Chap. 2, many surveys of lawyers find respondents espousing positive views on the perceived merits of mediation and regaling tales of positive, and at times, unexpected, eye-opening experiences in the process, which may lead them to seek repeat experiences.[55] Clearly many lawyers are genuine proponents of mediation and their involvement stems from the same. On a more prosaic level perhaps, lawyers often seem to favour mediation because of their own belief that it will save their clients time and money.[56]

3.3.4 *Better Professional Experiences*

There is also evidence of lawyers turning to mediation in the quest for a more personally fulfilling professional experience. Craig McEwen's study into mediation and divorce lawyers in Maine revealed that many respondents supported mediation because its problem-solving ethos assuaged their own desires to perform professional tasks and serve their clients well.[57] It may seem natural for such views to be held in the family field where lawyers may often become immersed in the waters of acrimony and ill-feeling that may subsist between disputing couples. Moreover, such bitterness may be exacerbated by litigation and traditional, adversarial disputing practices.

The seeking out by lawyers of more fulfilling professional experiences may be found in other dispute areas too. Deborah Hensler has articulated that the acute juxtaposition between mediation and the unsatisfactory process of litigation is a marked attraction of the process: "[w]hatever their specialism, some lawyers see in mediation an opportunity to do something that they themselves find more personally fulfilling than litigation. Seemingly, for some lawyers, mediation is a transformative experience. Some mediators talk about the 'magic' of resolving disputes. Other talk of their experience. . .saying that they have a feeling of being 'in the zone' when a mediation session is progressing satisfactorily. Still others talk of the connection between mediation and spirituality".[58] In a similar vein, Julie Macfarlane has charted the rise of the 'New Lawyer' who eschews traditional,

[53] Others in favour of the process uncovered in the research were more pragmatic and balanced in their attitudes towards mediation, while yet others who were mandated to participate in the programme were manipulative, dismissive or oppositionalist in their outlook—Macfarlane (2001), chpt. III.

[54] Such as Goffield et al (1999), p 231; Lande 2000, Sect. 5.

[55] At Sect. 2.5.3.

[56] See the discussion in Chap. 2 at Sect. 2.6.1.

[57] McEwen et al (1994), pp 156–163.

[58] Hensler 2003, pp 190–192.

zealous adversarialism, in favour of a more client-centred, collaborative, inclusive approach to lawyering.[59] For lawyers within this camp, mediation may represent a natural playing field.

Linked to the pursuit of a more fulfilling professional experience is the notion that mediation represents some kind of pathway back for the "lost lawyer".[60] The detrimental impact of traditional practice norms (such as, long hours, prevalence of competitive behaviours, pressure to run up 'billable hours' and adversarial climate) on the health and psyche of lawyers has been well documented. Reported stress, substance abuse and relationship breakdown levels are higher within the legal profession than most other fields.[61] Tales of mediators describing themselves as 'recovering lawyers' abound. There is significant empirical evidence suggesting that many lawyers have become disillusioned with general practice, and are seeking more enriching work.[62] Mediation may be one of a number of ways in which more palatable experiences can be found. By contrast to the drudgery of standard legal practice, mediation may seem 'fun' by comparison and hence sought out on this basis. Allied to this is the notion that lawyers may seek out 'friendlier' activity such as mediation to present a better face to society and improve their own, often poor, publically perceived levels of professionalism.[63] Legal professional bodies may seek to align themselves with mediation in an effort to rebrand lawyers in a more palatable manner as softer, problem-solving professionals. Sometimes this desire is made explicit: for example, the 1989 Canadian Bar Association Task Force on Alternative Dispute served up a rallying cry for practitioners to see ADR "as a strong expression of the legal profession's continuing commitment to fair and effective dispute resolution".[64]

3.3.5 Assisting Negotiations

Stephen Subrin has theorised that American lawyers like mediation to a great extent because lacking confidence and experience in advocacy, they seek to avoid trials and crave settlement.[65] Similarly Marc Galanter stated that "[l]awyers find trials

---

[59] See generally Macfarlane (2008).

[60] Kronman (1993); Van Winkle (2001).

[61] For a review of evidence see Daicoff (1997), pp 1345–1349; Riskin (2002), part I. The issue of mental health has received significant attention of late in the USA, with organisations established specifically for members of the legal profession suffering from depression—see http://lawyerswithdepression.com/depressionstatistics.asp Accessed 1 November 2011. A recent survey of Australian lawyers suggested that some 15% suffered moderate to extreme levels of depression—see Collings (2009). Such problems may be exacerbated by the inclement financial climate that lawyers may often be working in currently.

[62] See, for example, Seligman et al (2001); Stefancic and Delgado (2004).

[63] Lande (2000), p. 158.

[64] Canadian Bar Association (1989), p. 4.

[65] Subrin (2002/2003).

distasteful: they may bring little financial gain, they disrupt one's practice, they require extensive preparations, and they expose one to risks of losing or revealing lack of expertise".[66] While there is significant evidence that some lawyers dismiss mediation as an unnecessary accoutrement given their own abilities to negotiate disputes,[67] it is clear that mediation is often seen by lawyers as a way to help expedite settlement, particularly by utilising the mediator to pressure their clients into accepting reasonable compromises. Research by Tamara Relis in the Canadian context as well as a study by Machteld Pel and Lia Combrink in the Netherlands setting, for example, found that lawyers typically espoused tactical, settlement-orientated reasons for attempting mediation and viewed mediation primarily as a vehicle for expediting standard lawyer negotiations.[68] In fact, in the following chapter I will discuss the way that mediation has come to be deployed by lawyers essentially as a measure by which mediators assist them to negotiate more effectively. Many practice norms of mediation are in fact based around this lawyer-centric need, rather than supporting the parties themselves in the resolution of their dispute.[69]

3.3.6 Responding to Client Demand

Those who suspect foul play with respect to lawyer involvement in mediation may also underestimate the extent that their presence in the process has been driven by client desires. Traditionally it can be said that lawyers dominate the lawyer-client relationship and wield more influence in how disputes are resolved. Particularly in sectors involving sophisticated repeat players, however, clients may be more in control and directive in terms of the conduct of their lawyers.[70] In the aftermath of the promotion of collaborative problem solving pioneered by Fisher and Ury's *Getting to Yes*, as Deborah Hensler has suggested in the context of 1980s USA, "[b]usiness decision makers and their advisors... urged lawyers to make more use of mediation in resolving legal disputes".[71] Clients in many contexts may also seek

---

[66] Galanter (1985), p. 12.

[67] See Chap. 2 at Sect. 2.6.1.

[68] Relis (2009); Pel and Combrink (2011). It has also been suggested that participation in mediation may also be seen as less of a risk for lawyers than in standard adjudicatory processes because a poorer result in mediation may not, in the client's mind, emanate from a lawyers' substandard professional performance, as would perhaps be the case where perceived poor outcomes result from advocacy in court—Hensler (1999), p. 17.

[69] An associated point here is the fact that given the significant reduction in civil trials in many jurisdictions, mediation may in fact provide a rare opportunity for lawyers to practice their advocacy skills.

[70] See the discussion in Chap. 2 at Sect. 2.3.3.

[71] Hensler (2003), p. 183.

out the support and layer of protection they assume lawyers representing them in the mediation process may provide.[72] The market for specialised mediation-advocates is increasing. In the Austrian context, for example, increasing client demand for lawyers who are specifically able to support clients through the mediation process has recently been noted.[73] Specialised mediation advocates are creating niches for themselves and being recruited by firms other than their own to represent business clients in mediation.[74]

3.4 Strategies Used to Gain a Foothold in the Field

Clearly lawyers then may hold a multitude of reasons for their involvement in mediation. Often such motives seem legitimate. An examination of the behaviour of legal professional bodies and individual lawyers globally suggests, however, that they have taken certain strategic steps designed to ensure lawyers' prominence in any expediting of mediation. Indeed, lawyers now densely populate the mediation field in many contexts. As I discussed in Chap. 1, globally there is significant evidence of lawyer domination in certain dispute areas, with those drawn from other professions struggling to gain a foothold. Evidence tells us that lawyers have increasingly mined the rich vein of opportunity arising from mediation practice, particularly across the common law world in jurisdictions such as the USA, Australia, Canada and England & Wales, in which the process has become more embedded.[75] Strategic tactics undertaken by professional bodies include defensive marketing, claiming 'ownership' of the discipline, mobilising to capture pilot schemes, lobbying policy makers to formulate rules that favour lawyer-mediators, and pursuing 'unauthorized practice of law' cases against non-lawyer mediators. Individual lawyers may also perpetrate lawyer domination of mediation by 'shopping' exclusively for lawyer-mediators and influencing their clients in their engagement of the same.

While in the ensuing section I provide a snap-shot of the above activities and the effect that they have had on perpetrating domination of mediation practice by lawyers, it is, however, worth first providing a little context to the attempts made by lawyers to populate the mediation field. First, it is hardly surprising that American lawyers were quick to lay claim to mediation given the speed at which, in the post-Pound era, mediation and other ADR programmes were institutionalised and brought firmly into the confines of traditional justice systems in the USA. In the court-connected setting, the pioneering efforts of grassroots communitarian

[72] See the discussion in Chap. 4 at Sect. 4.3.2.2.

[73] Matti et al (2006).

[74] Something reportedly increasingly common in Scotland—discussion with John Sturrock of Core Mediation, 2010.

[75] See the discussion in Chap. 1 in Sect. 1.2.

enthusiasts may quickly have been forgotten. Given that modern lawyers' virgin experiences with mediation often took place within the shadow of formal legal processes (although I accept that lawyers have since taken additional steps purposely to gain primacy in the field) a natural inclination to see mediation as their own may have transpired as a result of mediation's location within the traditional legal domain. The courts and traditional legal dispute resolution, represents lawyers' turf, their terrain and woe betide others who dare step on it. As mediation has become more aligned with the traditional justice system, it hence may have taken on a natural infinity with those who inhabit that system: namely, lawyers.[76] Lay mediators thus become the 'other', finding it difficult to encroach upon legal ground rather than the other way around.

The views of lawyers in other jurisdictions as to their place within mediation have doubtless been fuelled by observation of lawyer dominated processes in the USA. Even if at the time of such claims over mediation by lawyers in other jurisdictions, mediation developments, not rooted in the sphere of traditional legal disputing had already taken place, legal professional bodies may have had scant awareness of them. To be fair to the lawyers, the general scope and success of grassroots mediation developments have often been barely visible,[77] so it is perhaps not surprising that lawyers would have overlooked them.

3.4.1 *Asserting Ownership and Defensive Marketing*

Laying claim to mediation as a potential sphere of practice is one way in which lawyers may seek to strike a pre-emptory blow in the field and institute an insurance policy to be activated in the event of practical developments. Two examples in my own and neighbouring jurisdiction are cited below.

I shall begin with evidence from my own research in the field seeking to ascertain the state of ADR (including mediation) in Scotland in 1996. Despite the fact that at the time of my study, the Law Society of Scotland (LSS)[78] had hitherto established an ADR Committee and begun to accredit lawyer-mediators, in the course of undertaking my research it became evident that the LSS was concerned less with developing mediation *per se* and more with adroit manoeuvring to ensure that lawyers were at the forefront of any growth in mediation, if indeed such a growth were to occur.[79] Defensive marketing was afoot. It seemed that the ADR Committee was expending little in the way of effort in promoting mediation but represented more of a strategic, symbolic sop towards the process. As my fellow

[76] Nolan-Handley (2002), p. 242.

[77] See Chap. 1 at Sects. 1.1.1 and 1.1.2.

[78] The representative body for Scottish solicitors.

[79] Clark and Mays (1996), p. 33.

researcher and I noted soberly at the time, the majority of the ADR Committee (including its convenor) failed to respond to our repeated requests for an interview or questionnaire responses for our government-sponsored research, perhaps illustrating an absence of any real interest in the subject.[80] Bolstering our suspicions, respondents to the study (including lawyers themselves) often lamented the lack of engagement from the professional bodies in seeking to propagate mediation.

Across the border in England and Wales, a similar picture had already emerged. Writing in the early 1990s, Simon Roberts noted that "both [the English] Bar and Law Society,[81] after a period of caution, have begun to show an active, proprietary interest in ADR".[82] He pointed to two reports commissioned by the English Bar and Law Society[83] respectfully that with, scant evidence of debate or justification, anticipated an expansion of ADR (principally mediation) within the civil justice sphere with commercial litigation lawyers acting as mediators. The professional bodies clearly viewed that mediation, if it were to develop, ought to form part of mainstream legal practice. A strategic position of sorts then ensued. The Bedlam Report for example, in a fit of what Roberts termed "breathtaking arrogance"[84] stipulated, with little attempt at any justification, that mediators should be lawyers or magistrates of at least five years' standing.

3.4.2 *Lobbying and Regulatory Capture*

The above examples represent of course but two illustrations of a phenomenon that is common across the globe. Such early claims to ownership may represent a first step on a journey for lawyers with the desired destination a "capture" of mediation. One method by which the aims of capture can be furthered by lawyers is by seeking the promulgation of laws and regulations affirming their primary role in the process. In many countries lawyers have a significant impact on legislative processes. First, many who walk the corridors in the higher echelons of power are lawyers or former lawyers. In particular, lawyers are legion within the legislative and executive branches of many governments. Legal professional bodies are also powerful players in the legislative systems of many countries and exert great lobbying influence as 'insider' interest groups.[85] In this light, lawyers' ability to 'capture' regulatory

---

[80] Clark and Mays (1996), p. 33. The research was sponsored by the Scottish Office of the UK government.

[81] The professional bodies respectively for English barristers and English solicitors.

[82] Robert (1992), p 258. But see Mistelis (2006) suggesting that the earliest developments in English mediation emanated from lawyers.

[83] Bedlam Report (2001); Brown Report (2001).

[84] Roberts (1992), p.258.

[85] Heinz (1983); Scheingold (2004). Although their political clout may be dwindling in some jurisdictions in line with perceived reductions in professional status.

processes, in particular those which lap the shores of their core business, should not be underestimated. Particularly in those jurisdictions that have moved into a 'regulatory' phase as regards mediation, fresh provisions governing mediation activity have often had the effect to exclude non-lawyers from certain practice areas. Such developments can be seen across continental Europe in particular and other civil law jurisdictions that have moved swiftly after the birth of mediation to the regulation of its practice.[86] Recent legislation in Greece, for example, dictates that mediation may only be offered by suitably qualified legal professionals and that training and regulatory functions and accreditation activities are vested in legal professional bodies.[87] Similarly, in Germany some states have legislated to mandate that mediators be drawn solely from the legal profession.[88] South Africa too has passed legislation which has had the effect that mediators require to be appropriately qualified and experienced lawyers.[89] Lawyers have been actively lobbying governments for recognition of their rights to appear as mediators in other jurisdictions too in which mediation is gaining ground and seeking the restriction of others' liberty to practice with varying levels of success.[90]

It is of course true that in many countries, particularly across the common law world, both the mediation process and professionals seeking to engage within it generally remain largely unregulated by law. The establishment of desired professional standards, appropriate practice norms or requisite training and experience for mediators is generally left to the vagaries of the market or through self-regulatory, professional bodies—many of which are interdisciplinary in nature.[91]

Nonetheless, on a more micro level, lawyers have been adept at mobilising to ensure that they dominate particular pockets of mediation activity. One key way to ensure this is by the controlling of approved rosters of mediators set forth for mediation practice in particular programmes. Such rosters are particularly relevant in the court-connected context. In the USA, for example, although generally there

[86] See the discussion in Chap. 1 at Sect. 1.2.3.

[87] Law on mediation for both domestic and cross-border disputes on Dec. 16, Law 3898/2010.

[88] Under the terms of Section 15a of the German Introductory Code to the Code of Civil Procedure (EGZPO). It should be noted though that under the Draft Law to implement the recent EU Directive on Mediation, it has been proposed that lawyer representation of parties in mediation only be allowed with the consent of the other party—an issue that has generated significant lawyer disquiet—see Duve (2011).

[89] Act 103 of 1991, s2(1).

[90] For example for Switzerland, see Meiser (2006), p386 (lawyers lobbying government in favour of mediation to secure their position within it) and for Turkey, see Ilter and Dikbas (2010), pp 141 and 145 (bar associations demanding that proposed new laws on mediation limit participation to lawyers).

[91] In the UK, for example, under such bodies as the Civil Mediation Council (for England and Wales) and the Scottish Mediation Network (for Scotland).

exists no prohibition on who may hang a shingle outside their office advertising their wares as a mediator, State judicial departments often keep rosters of approved mediators, which parties may have recourse to in the context of civil disputes. While few States preclude disputing parties from exercising an unfettered freedom of choice in their selection of mediators,[92] at least until after case-filing in court,[93] appearing on an official roster is important as it provides an official badge of approval of sorts and may also open the door to public subsidies for mediation practice. Furthermore, in-court schemes, in which the provision of mediation is provided in-house and/or by way of state subsidy, generally require that any mediators used by disputing parties are drawn from approved rosters. Lawyers, who may have been instrumental in the drafting of guidelines for inclusion on such rosters, are often favoured by the requirements imposed. So, for example, in the Alabaman roster for general civil practice, aside from other provisions such as being of good character and requisite mediation training, one of the requirements for inclusion on the roster is to be an attorney of at least four years' standing or have performed as a mediator ten times in the preceding two years. So attorneys do not require any previous mediation experience to gain access to the roster but those drawn from other professional backgrounds do. Similarly, the Office of Dispute Resolution in Colorado recommends that mediators that they contract with to provide state-sponsored mediation services *inter alia* have substantive knowledge of the law. In Connecticut approved rosters are dominated by retired judges. Inclusion on Idaho's Civil Mediation Roster requires membership of the Idaho State Bar. Rules favouring lawyers to varying degree for approved roster inclusion exist in many other States such as Delaware, Florida, Louisiana, Mississippi, New Hampshire, South Carolina and Washington.[94] Given that 'where the action is' as regards mediation practice is often found in the shadow of court litigation, the shaping of rosters favouring lawyers, which provide a seal of approval in such settings, has contributed greatly to the domination of American lawyers in mediation.[95] Such lawyer domination is both aided by and helps propagate a self-perpetuating system in which lawyer-centric, evaluative mediation is the norm.[96] Non-lawyers may find themselves looking in, envious, from the outside.

Similar patterns of lawyer mobilisation can be found in other jurisdictions. In her research into the 1995 mediation pilot scheme in English medical negligence cases operated by the (then) Department of Health, Linda Mulcahy pointed to the marked

---

[92] The District of Columbia is one exception.

[93] Once a case is listed, some states stipulate that only mediators on the roster may be used—e.g. the State of Georgia.

[94] Information on the various US State roster requirements was sourced from the Institute of Government, College of Professional Studies at the University of Arkansas 2010.

[95] A recent survey by the American Arbitration Association found that 63% companies surveyed and 73% percent of *Fortune* companies attributed their use of mediation to court referral, American Arbitration Association 2006, pp 19 and 28.

[96] See discussion in Chap. 4 at Sect. 4.2.3.

ability of lawyers to respond to mediation's potential threat to their portfolio in taking control of the process of both design and implementation of the scheme to the exclusion of others. She noted that

> [l]egal activists… minimised the challenge posed by mediation by mobilising during the planning stage of the pilot scheme. By helping to frame its parameters medical negligence specialists secured their inclusion in it. The majority came to understand and give meaning to mediation as an off-shoot of the civil justice system which could be used in the rare cases in which solicitors are not able to achieve settlement through bi-lateral negotiations. In this way mediation became an adjunct of the courts and litigation system rather than an alternative to it.[97]

In addition, in a spate of pilot, judge-led mediation schemes in England and Wales, such as those in Exeter and Guildford county courts, it also appears that lawyers have been instrumental in the design and delivery of such initiatives and ensured their place on the approved mediation panels.[98]

Other common law examples abound. As noted in Chap. 1, family court mediation schemes in New Zealand prescribe recourse either to lawyer-mediators or judicial mediation.[99] Around 40% of those accredited on the general panel of mediators held by the Hong Kong International Arbitration Centre are lawyers.[100] Across the civil law world lawyers may also dominate approved rosters of mediators in various contexts. For example, the "Panel of Members of Mediators Conducting Mediation Process at the Chamber of Commerce and Industry of the Russian Federation" comprises a majority of lawyers.[101] In Slovenia the majority of recent mediators in recently established court-annexed schemes are drawn from those with legal backgrounds.[102] In German court-connected mediation, judges typically refer disputing parties to lawyer-mediators appearing on registered panels held by local Chambers of Lawyers.[103] In Italy, lawyers (and economics professionals) are treated preferentially in approved rosters in respect of the requisite training and background of mediators seeking inclusion therein.[104] International organisations too may encompass panels of mediators that are dominated by lawyers.[105]

---

[97] Mulcahy (2001), p. 205. See also pp 209–211.

[98] Prince and Belcher (2006), pp 30–34.

[99] See Chap. 1 at Sect. 1.2.2.5.

[100] Cheung (2010), p. 69.

[101] Available at http://www.tpprf-arb.ru/en/documents/list-of-members Accessed 1 November 2011.

[102] Ristin 2010.

[103] Hillig and Huhn (2010), p 49.

[104] Article 4.4 of the decree no 222 of 2004.

[105] See, for example, the dominance of lawyers in the World Intellectual Property Organization, Domain Name Dispute Panel (this panel includes mediators, arbitrators and experts).

In the European context it may be argued that the terms of the recent European Mediation Directive[106] may lend support to the notion that the mediation role is naturally one for lawyers. At the time of writing, in another move which may have the effect to cement lawyer domination in the field, the Italian Tribunale di Palermo has, *inter alia*, recently referred the question as to whether articles 3 and 4 of the Directive should be interpreted as requiring that mediators should be equipped with legal skills to the European Court of Justice.[107]

3.4.3 *Mediation and the Unauthorized Practice of Law*

Aside from discreet regulation of mediation activity itself and domination and control of approved rosters, in some jurisdictions, lawyers have sought to assert their primacy in the field by recourse to "unauthorized practice of law" doctrines.[108] Such an approach paints mediation activity, or at least certain facets of it, as falling within the confines of legal practice, to which lawyers may hold monopolised rights over. The most extensive experience of this issue arising in the mediation context has been in the USA. In keeping with their aggressive stereotype, American lawyers have generally sought to enforce their exclusivity in respect of the practice of law and doggedly pursued those who have arguably infringed upon their turf. This has occurred particularly with regard to the general area of provision of legal advice—a key point of controversy arising within mediation practice.[109] It should be noted at the outset of this discussion that in some jurisdictions assertion of monopoly rights of lawyers to engage in 'legal' activity are not so strongly felt. In certain jurisdictions the exclusive rights of professional lawyers in such matters may in fact be quite limited. To an extent this emanates from the fact that lawyers have often singularly failed over the years to press home rights to exclusivity, to the extent that such rights may have ever existed. So for example, unlike their American counterparts, "[w]hile the British believed [legal] advice to be an important legal function, they never attempted a dominant settlement in the area".[110] Hence, in the UK, reported pursuit of non-lawyer mediators engaging in legal practice within mediation is unheard of. The doctrine has arisen with regard to mediation in

[106] Directive 2008/52/EC.

[107] September 7, 2011 (case C-464/11).

[108] The issue is also important in the sense of determining whether lawyer-mediators should be governed by their own professional rules while engaged in mediation. This also raises questions as to the appropriateness of existing lawyer professional rules and ethical guidelines to deal with mediation practice. These matters are dealt with in Chap. 6.

[109] For a potted discussion of the history of unauthorized practice of law in the USA see Nolan Handley 2002.

[110] Abbot (1998), p. 250.

other jurisdictions beyond the USA, however, including in Canada[111] and Germany.[112]

3.4.3.1 Is Mediation the Practice of Law?

Is mediation the practice of law? This is a debate with a pungent whiff of schism. The answer to this question hinges both on one's perspective as to what mediation entails and also what the practice of law actually involves. So, while this assertion may appear particularly curious to the purist who views mediation as a non-legal process that sits quite apart from legal activity, it is more understandable in the context of court initiated or institutionalised mediation, which has by design or circumstance morphed into a more evaluative, legal-centric species of the process. In its classic, facilitative mould where legal issues may be seen as of little relevance, the role of the mediator can be contrasted sharply with that of the lawyer or judge. According to this paradigm, mediators are mere facilitators of parties' own endeavours to resolve their disputes. Mediators do not advise parties or proffer evaluations of their legal positions. Nor do they express views on likely court outcomes. Such activity hence entails no 'legal practice' on the part of the neutral. At first blush then, it may seem surprising that Carrie Menkel-Meadow, one of the most sophisticated scholars in the area, has suggested that mediation amounts to the practice of law.[113] While the description of facilitative mediation I outline above act reflects most officially sanctioned discourse on the mediation process, as Menkel-Meadow, has pointed out, "to the extent that mediators, especially those who work within court programs or by court referral, 'predict' court results or 'evaluate' the merits of the case (on either factual or legal grounds), they are giving legal advice".[114] If lawyers hold a monopoly on the exercise of such activities, then a non-lawyer mediator's involvement with the same may amount to the unauthorized practice of law. Another key aspect of mediator activity that may encroach upon the lawyer's borders is the drafting of agreements to legally capture any settlements crafted by the parties. Of course, when mediating parties are represented by their own lawyers then the legal agents may undertake this activity. An important 'justice' issue when dealing with *pro se* disputants in the court-connected context in particular,[115] however, may be ensuring that they produce legally binding settlements. In the absence of legal representative or the availability of *post hoc* legal advice, such a task may be seen as an important role of the mediator.

---

[111] Burnet (2007) (paralegal found to have committed unauthorized practice of law, *inter alia*, for activities in context of family mediation).

[112] Such as in Germany—see Alexander et al (2006).

[113] Menkel-Meadow (1996), p. 57.

[114] Menkel-Meadow (1996), p. 57.

[115] See the discussion in Chap. 5 at Sect. 5.3.2.

3.4.3.2 Blanket Exceptions for Mediators

While clearly in some contexts then mediators will in practice carry out functions of a legal colour, it is questionable whether this *per se* is enough to paint such activities as "legal practice". In particular, the absence of a client-lawyer relationship between mediator and disputants is arguably a striking omission in any analysis depicting mediation activity as the practice of law. In this sense, the American Bar Association section on Dispute Resolution espoused principles to govern the area in 2002.[116] Central to their position was the general notion that mediation did not amount to the practice of law. A major plank of the analysis focused on the fact that mediators do not represent the parties to the mediation in the same way that a lawyer does. Given the absence of any pervading client-attorney relationship between the mediator and the parties, even if arising legal issues were discussed between them, such discussions would not amount to the tendering of legal advice (even if the mediator is an attorney). This general position has been supported in emphatic terms by John Cooley suggesting that by dint of the nature of their relationship with mediating parties, mediators cannot be seen to be practising law. In response to assertions that tendering advice relative to legal issues of relevance within mediation and the drafting of settlement agreements may amount to the practice of law, he asks such questions as, "Where is the representative relationship?... What is the fiduciary duty owed by whom and to whom?... How can the mediator receive confidential information from two parties with adverse interests and be practicing law with respect to either of them – or both of them? How can a mediator accept a service fee from two people with adverse interests, yet be practicing law with respect to both of them? If a lawyer were practicing law in such a situation, would not he or she be in a classic conflict of interest situation?"[117]

Nonetheless, while the lack of a lawyer-client relationship provides a clear and determinative method of handling the situation other approaches to the issue unauthorized practice of law within mediation eschew such a blanket, 'carve-out' exception. Some writers have contended that the more important issue in determining whether legal advice tendered amounts to the practice of law depends on the issue of party reliance. When mediation parties seek out and rely upon legal advice, then *ipso facto*, the provision of the same must amount to the practice of law.[118] With this in mind, other espoused approaches to the issue of the practice of law within mediation require a more nuanced, micro-analysis of the conduct of mediators. The question then is not so much "is mediation the practice of law" but "when is mediation the practice of law"? In particular, such approaches may require a distinguishing between conduct on the one hand which although clearly engaging the legal activity, does not amount to the practice of law, and on the other

[116] American Bar Association (2002).

[117] Cooley (2000).

[118] Menkel-Meadow (1996).

hand, that which does. This is no easy task. I will now discuss below some approaches in respect of the tendering of legal advice within mediation and the drafting of legal agreements.

3.4.3.3 The Schism Between Legal Information and Legal Advice

One common approach found in various US state rules for dealing with the practice of law within mediation is to draw a line in the sand between the provision by the mediator of legal advice (amounting to the practice of law) and legal information (not amounting to the practice of law). So for example, the Virginia Guidelines on Mediation and the Unauthorized Practice of Law,[119] stipulate that "a mediator may provide the parties with legal information but may not give legal advice". Legal advice in this context amounts to the applying of law to the facts of the case in such a way as to (a) predict the outcome of the case or an issue in the case, or (b) recommend a course of action based on the mediator's analysis. Mediators may, however, issue general, legal procedural information and legal resources and ask reality testing questions that engage legal issues germane to the dispute. This approach echoes that put forward by various writers in the field as a suitable demarcation between legal information and advice.[120]

Such an approach is not without its drawbacks, however. While recognising that the prescriptive nature of Virginia State's definitions of the practice of law may have dictated such an approach to legal practice within mediation, the American Bar Association (ABA) noted that "[w]here a particular state's definition of the practice of law would permit a mediator to discuss legal issues with the parties, including offering a neutral perspective on strengths and weaknesses in a case, the parties and mediators would be ill-served by rules similar to those adopted in Virginia..."[121] As the ABA note in their guidance, it is incredibly difficult to determine within the midst of a mediation session when a mediator may be proffering advice and when she may be simply providing information. The ability for mediators to provide neutral, generic 'legal information' which does not encroach upon the borders of legal advice is highly questionable. For example, mediators may ask reality testing questions in such a way as to have the effect of imparting legal advice. Furthermore, on a practical note, problems are compounded by the fact that mediation proceedings are generally private, and not recorded, which would render a regulator's task in enforcing provisions very difficult.[122]

[119] Drafted by the Department of Dispute Resolution Services of the Supreme Court of Virginia, and the North Carolina Guidelines for the Ethical Practice of Mediation and to Prevent the Unauthorized Practice of Law, adopted by the North Carolina Bar in 1999.

[120] See, for example, Schwartz (1999), p. 1737.

[121] American Bar Association (2002), para 5.

[122] American Bar Association (2002), para 6.

Despite the practical problems with such an approach, the model set out in the Virginia guidelines is similar to that which currently exists in Germany. In recent times, German lawyers have sought to assert their primary rights as mediators at the expense of others. Legal professional bodies have litigated against non-lawyer mediators seeking to restrict their right to practice and curtail their advertising activities.[123] After a period of uncertainty the matter has been clarified by recent legislation. Currently the right to provide legal services in Germany is tightly governed by the Legal Services Act 2008 ("Rechtsdienstleistungsgesetz"). Save for some limited exceptions, only lawyers are allowed to provide legal services. While the legislation provides that the process of mediation itself does not amount to the provision of legal services,[124] non-lawyer mediators are explicitly precluded from indulging in activity deemed to amount to legal practice within mediation such as proposing legal solutions, evaluating underpinning legal issues or drafting legal agreements.

3.4.3.4 Drafting Legal Agreements

Capturing agreements reached in a legally binding form may often (but not always[125]) be an important aspect of the mediation process. The ABA guidelines set out various provisions seeking to draw a line between permissible and non-permissible behaviour in this regard. According to the Guidelines: "When an agreement is reached in a mediation, the parties often request assistance from the mediator in memorializing their agreement. The preparation of a memorandum of understanding or settlement agreement by a mediator, incorporating the terms of settlement specified by the parties, does not constitute the practice of law. If the mediator drafts an agreement that goes beyond the terms specified by the parties, he or she may be engaged in the practice of law. However, in such a case, a mediator shall not be engaged in the practice of law if(a) all parties are represented by counsel and(b) the mediator discloses that any proposal that he or she makes with respect to the terms of settlement is informational as opposed to the practice of law, and that the parties should not view or rely upon such proposals as advice of counsel, but merely consider them in consultation with their own attorneys."[126]

This approach hence draws a line between capturing the parties' agreed terms in a draft agreement and going beyond that. Even in the latter scenario, practice of law is avoided if the parties have their own attorneys present and a claim is made by the mediator that the settlement is for information only. This echoes the point made by Menkel Meadow above regarding reliance by clients. Where parties have their own

[123] Alexander et al (2006), p. 33.

[124] S 2 Abs. 3 Nr. 4.

[125] It should be noted that in some contexts mediation results in 'principled' but legally non-enforceable agreements.

[126] American Bar Association (2002), section headed, "drafting legal agreements".

lawyers present, even if a mediator goes beyond the parties' own espoused terms in the settlement agreement, it seems proper that clients should take advice from their own legal advisors as to the appropriateness of the new provisions.

3.4.3.5 Summary of Unauthorized Practice of Law and Mediation

While recourse to unauthorized practice of law doctrines to prohibit non-lawyers from mediation practice seems like the barest form of cynical, lawyer capturing of the field and an affront to the non-legal origins of the process, it becomes more understandable in the context of modern, institutionalised mediation. The reality is that mediation has in many contexts become more infused with the law, legal norms and practices. No more is this true than in the court-connected context, where the process has thrived. Particularly where the parties themselves are not legally represented and the need for lawyers to respond to the parties' legal requirements becomes compelling, arguments that those who engage in such behaviour to be regulated legal professionals hold more legitimacy. This may be true, not least because there may be limited redress within the mediation process itself against mediators who may have provided erroneous legal advice to parties. At the very least, within the court-connected context, it may be contended that, just as lawyers require training in mediation techniques, non-lawyers should receive some education in law.[127]

3.4.4 Lawyer 'Shopping' for Lawyer-Mediators

One of the most pertinent reasons why lawyers dominate the field in certain settings may lie in the manner that mediators are selected. Consistent with the important role that lawyers often play as gatekeepers to mediation in many contexts and the power they wield over their clients generally,[128] it is likely that they will also be influential in determining the choice of mediator.[129] Surveys of lawyers internationally often find lawyers favouring lawyer-mediators.[130] Being in control of selection processes, experience hence suggests that lawyers often 'shop' for lawyer-mediators. They may also enter into agreements for repeat business with lawyer-mediators who prove successful in terms of settlements.[131] Writing in

[127] See the discussion in Chap. 5 at Sect. 5.3.

[128] See the discussion in Chap. 2 at Sect. 2.3.

[129] See Goldfien and Robbennolt (2007), pp 285–286.

[130] The many reasons why lawyers often prefer lawyer-mediators are explored in Chap. 4 at Sect. 4.3.5.

[131] This can be termed the practice of 'settlement brokering' a long recognised practice in which law firms reward mediators who settle cases swiftly, increasing settlement stats for the firm, Kovach 1997, p. 26.

the US context, John Lande has noted that "[i]n a large, diverse, and somewhat impersonal market of mediation services, buying those services considered appropriate for particular cases is an important and difficult task, which is often performed by the principals' lawyers. The lawyers are repeat players who become familiar with the disputing practices and practitioners in their community and thus are usually in a better position than their clients to serve as expert shoppers for mediation services".[132] That this has become the norm in many settings in the USA is undisputable.[133] Similar evidence exists in other jurisdictions. It has been noted, for example, that English lawyers are increasingly seeking to circumvent established mediation organisations (which are typically multi-disciplinary in nature) in the engagement of mediators by selecting lawyer-mediators through established legal contacts.[134] Similarly, English construction mediation research has found that mediators are typically recruited directly from the market. In such a market the buyers are lawyers and the mediators selected, generally also lawyers.[135]

3.5 Conclusion

At first blush it does seem both surprising and unseemly that lawyers have been able to gain a primacy in the mediation field at the expense of others. This is so, particularly because of the "alternative" nature of classic mediation. Moreover, some of the tactics that they have consciously deployed such as lobbying for exclusive rights to practice, defensive marketing, commandeering approved rosters and pursuing unauthorized practice of law claims, have an unsavoury tinge to them and are redolent of the opportunistic, ruthless lawyer stereotype. Cognate activity by lawyers competing with professional opponents in other fields also lends succour to suspicions that lawyers seek to milk mediation. Nonetheless, as noted above, lawyers were often true pioneers of mediation and harbour genuine motives for their involvement. There is also evidence of their peaceful co-existence with mediators drawn from other professional backgrounds.

What is equally clear is that as mediation processes have often shifted in their location from outside to within court processes, the lawyer—as mediator or representative—becomes a more natural participant within it than may hitherto have been the case. Yes, mediation practice models have arguably been developed and honed by lawyers to better fit their professional cultural and practice norms, but such new models have also developed because of the court-connected location within which mediation exists and different process requirements that this entails.

132 Lande (1997), p 847.

133 See generally Welsh (2001a); Welsh (2001b).

134 Russell (2007).

135 Gould (2010), pp 10–11.

As I elaborate in the next chapter, both within and outside of the court-connected setting, mediation participants often seek out engagement by lawyers, both as mediators and party representatives, and it is natural that lawyers would seek to respond to that demand. A natural follow-on from this issue is whether or not lawyers are appropriate participants in mediation and it is this matter that the following chapter addresses.

References

Abbot A (1986) Jurisdictional conflicts: a new approach to the development of the legal professions. Law Soc Inq 11:187–224

Abbott A (1988) The System of the professions: an essay on the division of expert labour. The University of Chicago Press, Chicago

Abel R (1982) The politics of the market for legal services. In: Thomas P (ed) Law in balance. Martin Robertson, Oxford

Abel R (1989a) Comparative sociology of legal professions. In: Abel R, Lewis P (eds) Lawyers in society comparative theories. University of California Press, Berkeley

Abel R (1989b) American lawyers. In: Abel R, Lewis P (eds) Lawyers in society comparative theories. University of California Press, Berkeley

Alexander N et al (2006) Mediation in Germany: the long and winding road. In: Alexander N (ed) Global trends in mediation, 2nd edn. Kluwer International, Alphen aan den Rijn

American Arbitration Association (2006) Dispute-wise business management: improving economic and non-economic outcomes in managing business conflicts. http://www.adr.org/si.asp?id=4124. Accessed 1 Nov 2011

Bedlam LJ (2001) Committee on ADR. General Counsel of the Bar, London

Benson B (1995) An exploration of the impact of modern arbitration statutes on the development of arbitration in the United States. J Law Econ Organ 11(2):479–501

Brown H (2001) ADR report. The Law Society, Courts and Legal Services Committee, London

Burger WE (1995) Remark:the decline in professionalism. Fordham Law Rev 63:949

Burnet H (2007) Paralegal gets four months house arrest. Law Times, 15 October 2007

Burrage M (1988) Revolution in the collective action of the French, American and English legal professions. Law Soc Inq 13:225–277

Canadian Bar Association Task Force on Alternative Dispute Resolution (1989) Alternative dispute resolution: a Canadian perspective. Canadian Bar Association, Ottawa

Cheung O (1999) Critical factors affecting the use of alternative dispute resolution processes in construction". Int J Conflict Manag 17(3):189–194

Cheung SO (2010) Construction mediation in Hong Kong. In: Brooker P, Wilkinson S (eds) Mediation in the construction industry: an international review. Spon Press, London

Clark B (2003) A time for change? The development of commercial ADR in Scotland 20. Scots Law Times 169–172

Clark B, Dawson C (2007) Scottish commercial litigators and ADR: a study of attitudes and experience. Civ Justice Q 26:228–249

Clark B, Mays R (1996) The development of ADR in Scotland. Civ Justice Q 16:26–37

Collings O (2009) Depression strikes as lawyers struggle in downturn. The New Lawyer, 6th May. http://www.thenewlawyer.com.au/article/Depression-spikes-as-lawyers-struggle-in-downturn/479923.aspx. Accessed 1 Nov 2011

Cooley J (2000) Shifting paradigms: the unauthorized practice of law or the authorized practice Of ADR. http://www.mediate.com/cooley2.cfm#bio. Accessed 1 Nov 2011

Daicoff S (1997) Lawyer know thyself: a review of empirical research on attorney attributes bearing on professionalism. Am U L Rev 46:1337–1427

de Roo A, Jagtenberg R (2003) The practice of mediation in eleven countries neighbouring the Netherlands. Dutch ministry of justice. http://www.civilmediation.org/downloads-get?id=133. Accessed 1 Nov 2011

Dezalay Y (1991) Territorial battles and tribal disputes. Mod Law Rev 54:792–809

American Bar Association Section on Dispute Resolution (2002) Guidelines on mediation and practice of law. http://www.mediate.com/articles/abaupl.cfm. Accessed 1 Nov 2011

Durcan K (2008) International arbitration: Getting pricier but still growing. Law Society Gazette, 16th October 2008. http://www.lawgazette.co.uk/features/international-arbitration-getting-pricier-still-growing. Accessed 1 Nov 2011

Duve C (2011) Lessons learnt by from the implantation of the EU mediation directive in Germany: the point of view of lawyers. Directorate-General for Internal Policies. http://www.europarl.europa.eu/document/activities/cont/201105/20110518ATT19590/20110518ATT19590EN.pdf. Accessed 1 Nov 2011

Felstiner W, Sarat A (1980–1981) The emergence and transformation of disputes: naming, blaming, claiming. Law Soc Rev 15(3–4)):631–654

Flood J, Caiger A (1993) Lawyers and arbitration: the juridification of construction disputes. Mod Law Rev 56:412–440

Galanter M (1985) A settlement judge is not a trial judge: judicial mediation in the United States. J Law Soc 12:1–18

Glasser C (1990) The legal profession in the 1990s – images of change. Leg Stud 10:1–11

Goffield DE et al (1999) Background characteristics and incentives of mediators in Georgia: exploring differences in public, private, and government agency mediators. Mediation Q 16:221–233

Goldfien J, Robbennolt J (2007) What if lawyers have their way? An empirical assessment of conflict strategies and attitudes towards mediation styles. Ohio State J Dispute Resolut 22:277–319

Gould N et al (2010) Mediating construction disputes: an evaluation of existing practice. Centre for Construction Law, Kings College, London

Grossman MH (1939–1940) Arbitration and the lawyer. New York Univ Law Q Rev 17:511

Hartman C (1993) Legal data banks, the glut of lawyers, and the German legal profession. Law Soc Rev 27:421–441

Heinz JP (1983) The power of lawyers. Ga Law Rev 17:891–911

Hensler D (1999) A research agenda, what we need to know about court- connected ADR. Dispute Resolut Mag 6:15–17

Hensler DR (2003) Our courts, ourselves: how the alternative dispute resolution movement is reshaping our legal system. Penn St L Rev 108:165–197

Hillig J, Huhn M (2010) Construction mediation in Germany. In: Brooker P, Wilkinson S (eds) Mediation in the construction industry: an international review. Spon Press, London

Ilter D, Dikbas A (2010) Construction mediation in Turkey. In: Brooker P, Wilkinson S (eds) Mediation in the construction industry: an international review. Spon Press, London

Institute of government, college of professional studies at the university of Arkansas (2010) State requirements for mediators. http://www.mediationworks.com/medcert3/staterequirements.htm. Accessed1 Nov 2011

Kovach K (1997) Cost of mediation: whose responsibility? Conflict Resolut Q 15(1):13–27

Kronman AT (1993) The lost lawyer: the falling ideals of the legal profession. Harvard University Press, Cambridge

Lande J (1997) How will lawyering and mediation practices transform each other? Fla State Univ Law Rev 24:839–901

Larson MS (1977) The rise of professionalism. University of California Press, Berkeley

Macfarlane J (2001) Culture change? Commercial Litigators and the Ontario Mandatory Mediation Programme. http://dsp-psd.pwgsc.gc.ca/collection_2008/lcc-cdc/JL2-70-2001E.pdf. Accessed 1 Nov 2011

Macfarlane J (2008) The new lawyer: how settlement is transforming the practice of law. UBS Press, Toronto

Mantle M (2011) Mediation: a practical guide for lawyers. Dundee University Press, Dundee

Marcos F (2000) The storm over our heads: the rendering of legal services by audit firms in Spain. Int J Leg Profession 7:7–39

Matti S et al (2006) Mediation in Austria. In: Alexander N (ed) Global trends in mediation, 2nd edn. Kluwer International, Alphen aan den Rijn

Mays R, Clark B (1996) Alternative dispute resolution in scotland. Scottish Office Central Research Unit, Edinburgh

McEwen C et al (1994) Lawyers, mediation, and the management of divorce practice. Law Soc Rev 28:149–186

Meason JE, Smith AG (1991) Non-lawyers in international commercial arbitration: gathering splinters on the bench. N West J Int Law Bus 12:24–48

Meiser I (2006) Mediation and conciliation in Switzerland. In: Alexander N (ed) Global trends in mediation, 2nd edn. Kluwer International, Alphen aan den Rijn

Menkel-Meadow C (1996) Is mediation the practice of law? Alternatives High Costs Litigat 14(5):55–61

Mercer D (2006) How do i become a mediator? Resources for Attorneys. http://www.resourcesforattorneys.com/becomeamediatorarticle.html. Accessed 1 Nov 2011

Mistelis L (2006) ADR in England and Wales: a successful case of public private partnership. In: Alexander N (ed) Global trends in mediation, 2nd edn. Kluwer International, Alphen aan den Rijn

Mosten FS (2001) Mediation career guide: a strategic approach to building a successful practice. Jossey Bass, San Francisco

Mulcahy L (2001) Can leopards change their spots? An evaluation of the role of lawyers in medical negligence cases. Int J Leg Profession 8(3):203–224

Nolan-Handley J (2002) Lawyers, non-lawyers and mediation: rethinking the professional monopoly from a problem-solving perspective. Harv Negot Law Rev 7:235–286

Parkinson L (2010) Competition betwcen professionals and fields. Mediate.com video. http://www.youtube.com/watch?v=6xzpAnO2Ny4. Accessed 1 Nov 2011

Partridge M (2009) Alternative dispute resolution: an essential competency for lawyers: how to use ADR to Achieve better results and lower costs. OUP, New York

Paterson A (1988) The legal profession in Scotland – an endangered species or a problem case for market theory? In: Abel R, Lewis PS (eds) Lawyers in society, volume one, the common law world. University of California Press, Berkley

Pel M, Combrink L (2011) Referral to mediation by the Netherlands judiciary. Justice Q 25–65

Prince S, Belcher S (2006) An evaluation of the effectiveness of court-based mediation processes in non-family civil proceedings at exeter and guilford county courts. Department of Constitutional Affairs, London

Relis T (2009) Perceptions in litigation and mediation: lawyers, defendants, plaintiffs, and gendered parties. Cambridge University Press, New York

Riskin L (2002) The contemplative lawyer: on the potential contributions of mindfulness meditation to law students, lawyers and their clients. Harv Negot Law Rev 7(2):1–66

Ristin G (2010) New legislation on alternative dispute resolution in the republic of Slovenia. www.mediationeurope.net/eng/documents/Rstin_Gordana-Newlegislation2.tmp.doc. Accessed 1 Nov 2011

Roberts S (1992) Mediation in the lawyer's embrace. Mod Law Rev 55:258–264

Russell C (2007) Mediation in England and Wales: a very english revolution. http://nt4992.vs.netbenefit.com/articles/viewarticle.asp?articleid=1805. Accessed 1 Nov 2011

Salpius E (2006) Arbitration in eastern Europe. Arbitration 72(1):45–48

Scheingold S (2004) The politics of rights: lawyers, public policy and political change, 2nd edn. University of Michigan Press, Michigan

Schwartz J (1999) Laymen cannot lawyer but is mediation the practice of law? Cardoza Law Rev 20:1715

Seamone ER (2000) Bringing a smile to mediation's two faces: how aspiring mediators might jump start careers immediately following law school. University of Iowa, College of Law. http://www.uiowa.edu/~cyberlaw/elp00/Evan/mediation/. Accessed 1 Nov 2011

Seidenberg S (2010) International arbitration loses its grip: are U.S. Lawyers to blame? Am Bar Assoc J 50–51

Seligman MEP et al (2001) Why lawyers are unhappy. Cardoza Law Rev 23:33–53

Stefancic J, Delgado R (2004) How lawyers lose their way: a profession fails its creative minds. Duke University Press, Durham

Subrin S (2002/2003) A traditionalist looks at mediation: it's here to stay and much better than I thought. Nevada Law J 3:196–227

Sugarman D (1995) Who colonized whom? Historical relations on the intersection between law, lawyers and accountants in England. In: Dezalay Y, Sugarman D (eds) Lawyers, accountants and the social construction of markets. Routledge, London

Susskind R (2007) How the traditional role of lawyers will change. Times Online, November 5, 2007. http://www.thetimes.co.uk/tto/law/article/2210094.ece. Accessed 1 Nov 2011

Susskind R (2010) The end of lawyers? Rethinking the nature of legal services. Oxford University Press, New York

Van Winkle J (2001) Mediation: a path back for the lost lawyer. American Bar Association, Chicago

Welsh NA (2001a) Making deals in court-connected mediation: What's justice got to do with it? Wash Univ Law Q 79:786–865

Welsh N (2001b) The thinning vision of self-determination: the inevitable price of institutionalization? Harv Negot Law Rev 6:1–96

Chapter 4
Mediation and Lawyers: Does the Cap Fit?

4.1 Introduction

This chapter tackles the vexed issue of the appropriateness of lawyers populating the mediation field both as party representatives and also as mediators. My own first forays into the ADR field quickly dispelled me of the notion that the mediation community was in any sense united about the merits of lawyer involvement in the process. The issue is hotly contested. Views are often sharply divided. Concerns voiced have often focused on the notion that the traditional background, education, training and professional role of lawyers is anathema to mediation practice. It is thus ironic perhaps that in turn these very same perceived deficiencies are highly prized by proponents of lawyer-mediators and lawyer party-advocates. Of course, to a great extent this debate may turn on the particular normative form of mediation that lawyer involvement occurs within. While a jarring between lawyers and mediation in its classic, facilitative, interests-based mould may seem obvious to some, lawyers appear an altogether more comfortable proposition within evaluative or settlement-orientated guises of the process.[1] Indeed, perceived illegitimate or damaging behaviours by lawyers in one mediation model may seem natural, useful and even essential in another.

Aside from the general position of lawyers in mediation, further complications may arise when sitting judges take on the mediation role. Judges may share many of the traits of lawyers generally that critics have suggested may blight their involvement in the mediation process, but the special status that judicial officers enjoy as public adjudicators entails further complications (or potential benefits) that deserve a distinct treatment.

[1] For definitions of evaluative and facilitative forms of mediation see Sect. 4.3.6.

B. Clark, *Lawyers and Mediation*, DOI 10.1007/978-3-642-23474-3_4,

4.1.1 *The Risk of Lawyer Involvement*

Len Riskin's classic work, "Mediation and Lawyers"[2] can perhaps be seen as the launch pad for numerous other more contemporary critiques of lawyers' involvement in mediation.[3] The main concern voiced by Riskin regarded the suitability of lawyers' general involvement within mediation in light of their training, on-going professional activities and typical personality traits which he argued might be at odds with the consensual, problem-solving nature of mediation. There was an inclination,[4] he mused, on the part of lawyers to "put people and events into categories that are legally meaningful," to "think in terms of rights and duties established by rules," to "focus on acts more than persons," and to suffer from an "under-cultivation of emotional faculties"—all of which are arguably anathema to the key features of consensus-building, focus on underlying disputant interests, and party-empowerment inherent in mediation.[5] In short, he argued, that mediation may not be, to use the now memorable phrase, on the lawyer's "standard philosophical map."

Despite this somewhat bleak outlook, it should be remembered that Riskin was at pains to highlight the value that lawyers could add to the mediation process.[6] Some of these benefits are articulated below.[7] His view, however, was that if lawyers were to become comfortable wearing the skin of the mediator or mediation advocate, *inter alia* this would require a fundamental shift in their traditional rights-based mindset and adversarial bent.[8] He argued that such a *volte face* could be achieved for example, through education and training in mediation, and in particular, through practical exposure. Running through the ensuing analysis, it shall hence be important to bear in mind to what extent such a transformation has occurred within legal professions since the days of Riskin's work. Riskin was also referring primarily to American lawyers in his work. In this regard there may be fundamental differences between lawyers in different jurisdictions, which will impact upon their suitability for involvement in mediation.

Before discussing evidence regarding the specific merits or otherwise of lawyers acting as mediators or party representatives, I will begin by briefly exploring two important underlying issues that impact upon the ensuing analysis: legal education and lawyer personality types.

---

[2] Riskin (1982).

[3] Including in the UK context, Roberts (1992).

[4] In his later work, Riskin admits that this is a broad brush depiction—see Riskin (2002), pp. 14–16.

[5] Riskin (1982), p. 45.

[6] Riskin (1982), particularly at part IV.

[7] At Sect. 4.2 for lawyer representatives and Sect. 4.3 for lawyer-mediators.

[8] See discussion of lawyers' cultural norms in Chap. 2 at Sect. 2.5.

4.1.2 Legal Education

The general issue of legal education was examined in Chap. 2 in the context of resistance to mediation and I will not repeat that here.[9] Suffice to say that many of the arguments presented there also hold significant resonance in the context of participation within mediation. As noted in the former discussion, the general premise of legal education across the common law and civil law world is one in which the traditional, narrow, adversarial role of the lawyer as 'zealous advocate' has been prevalent with scant focus on the development of negotiation and mediation skills, problem solving approaches or a more holistic approach to client's problems. Furthermore, the standard depiction of lawyer-client relationships in law school also suggests the lawyer firmly in control of decisions relative to the disposal of clients' disputes in a way that may be inconsistent with classic, facilitative models of mediation. As I noted in Chap. 2, progress has been made in law schools globally in better embedding mediation and collaborative negotiation topics within their curricula, but more often than not such endeavours remain optional, 'bolt-on' subjects rather than integrated within a core that typically remains steeped in the standard Langellian approach.

4.1.3 Lawyer Personalities

Law school experience and immersion within traditional legal practice communities doubtless contribute to shaping the normative form of the lawyer's role. Nevertheless, it can be argued that many of the traditional traits of lawyers that Riskin referred to, which may militate against effective lawyer engagement with mediation, are inherent personality types commonly found in those with a predisposition to study law. Significant empirical evidence lending support to this assertion has been comprehensively reviewed by Susan Daicoff.[10] Surveying the available data, Daicoff has highlighted a number of key differences in personality traits, values and ways of thinking inherent in lawyers. In particular, she mines evidence suggesting that compared to others in society, law students are more dominant, self-confident and less 'afilliative' in their outlook; desire leadership to a greater extent; rely more on rationality within decision-making; and place less of an emphasis upon feelings and emotions.[11] The main thrust of her argument is that these characteristics are set in stone at an early stage of the fledgling lawyer's personal development and cannot

[9] See Chap. 2 at Sect. 2.5.1.3.

[10] Daicoff (1997).

[11] Daicoff (1997), p. 1349.

easily be altered.[12] While such personality traits may in fact be beneficial for many aspects of a lawyer's workload and feed the demands of clients, she argues, *inter alia*, that they have led to unbridled, zealous advocacy, given rise to unethical, aggressive and ultra-competitive behaviour as well as the unshackled pursuit of financial gain and thus contributed to a current crisis in professionalisation within the legal field.[13] Equally, many such traits can be seen to render lawyers somewhat unsuitable for mediation activity with its emphasis on feelings, creativity, collaboration and exploring mutual interests. In a like fashion, the mediator's need to exhibit tact and sensitivity with participants as well as ration their own authority in the mediation[14] may sit uneasily with typical lawyer traits.

Daicoff's work has been subject to voluble criticism. In particular, assaults have been levied against her assertion that lawyer personality traits are largely immutable and cannot be easily altered through education and skills training. Critics have pointed to significant evidence suggesting that legal education and skills training can alter certain mindsets and values that law students may typically hold.[15] In short, their thesis is that leopards can change their spots. This holds important repercussions for lawyer involvement in mediation and suggests that appropriate training and education in law school and whilst in practice may render lawyers more commensurate with mediation environments. While specific evidence on the impact of training and education on altering lawyers' suitability for, and predisposition towards mediation is in fact mixed,[16] an abiding feature of research into lawyers' interactions with mediation is the notion that mediation practice, in particular, may have a profound impact upon lawyers' appreciation and suitability for the process.[17]

It is also worth noting at this juncture that many jurisdictions have seen a shift over recent years in the general demographic of entrants to the legal field. In particular, increasing numbers of women, ethnic minorities and students drawn from poorer socio-demographic groups have begun to enter the legal profession globally.[18] Such shifts in the make-up of new legal professionals may lead to

---

[12] The competitive nature of Law School experience as well as the adversarial focus of much traditional law learning may of course amplify many of these characteristics—see Chap. 2 at Sect. 2.5.1.3.

[13] Daicoff (1997), p. 1344.

[14] The paradox of the mediator role is that mediators exercise their authority while concurrently rationing its use.

[15] Particularly through the medium of ethics training. See Brown et al. (2005–2006).

[16] Although my own work (Clark and Dawson 2007, p. 245) has found a link between training and mediation practice (at least in terms of proclivity to engage in mediation practice), it has been argued that mediation training may not per se be sufficient to engender increased and appropriate engagement with the process—see Riskin (1982), p. 42.

[17] Riskin (1982), p. 42; Peters (2011). See the discussion in Chap. 2 at Sect. 2.5.3.

[18] See, for example, Brusegard (2004) (Canada); Sommerlad et al. (2010) (England and Wales); Maharg et al. (2003) (Scotland). Increases in non-traditional ethic and socio-demographic groups entering the profession remain modest in many jurisdictions, however—see Wilder (2003) (USA);

changes in typical lawyer, psychological composition, impacting upon the general suitability of lawyers for mediation. It has been contended that increasing numbers of women entering the profession may, in particular, create a more conducive environment within which mediation may flourish.[19] As is explored further below,[20] there is some evidence that women are naturally better predisposed towards professional participation in mediation, at least in its classic, facilitative mode. In many jurisdictions, however, non-traditional groups often face 'glass ceilings', in which the higher echelons of practice remain out of reach. For the time being then, domination of powerful positions within the legal profession often remains in the hands of traditional socio-demographic groups. To the extent that senior members of a profession shape acceptable practice norms and attitudes within that profession, which rub off on subordinates, the continued, elevated presence of traditional types may lead to a suppression of personality and attitudes commensurate with mediation practice.

4.2 Representing Clients in Mediation

Although lawyer representation of clients is common in certain dispute settings, such party advocacy is discouraged or proscribed in other contexts.[21] Some commentators have viewed lawyer attendance in mediation in a purely negative light. My own research revealed that such a jaundiced perception was prominent in the minds of many early Scottish pioneers. A family mediator interviewee in my 1996 study, exemplifying commonly held views on the matter, suggested that lawyers would "wreak havoc" in the process.[22] While this seems somewhat hyperbolic, it is worth considering in what manner might lawyers "wreak havoc" in mediation? In this sense, it has been argued, for example, that lawyers are "likely to become a dysfunctional element in the [mediation] process, not only jealous of its

---

Maharg et al. (2003) (Scotland). The http://www.lsac.org/lsacresources/data/vs-ethnic-gender-admits-archive.asp (accessed 1 November 2011) record increases in accepted ethnic minority applicants for US and Canadian Law Schools of only 5.1% between the period from 2000 to 2009.

[19] See for example, Carrie Menkel-Meadow's assertion that increasing numbers of women entering the profession may lead, *inter alia*, to more co-operative and less confrontational behaviour, more client participation in dispute settlement and a shift from the assertion of individualism to pursuit of collectivism—see Menkel-Meadow (1985).

[20] See Sect. 4.3.9.

[21] Equally in other contexts where lawyers are typically absent, such absence may reflect the limited importance or value of the dispute in hard terms and resulting unavailability of lawyers rather than any process design which aims to exclude their presence.

[22] Mays and Clark (1996), p. 90. Although the practice in family mediation in Scotland is for participants to take legal advice regarding any settlements produced in mediation.

intrusion into their domain of competence, but also unable to adapt professionally to a situation of controlled and defused, rather than polarized and contentious, conflict."[23] In Chap. 2 I examined the issue of lawyers' potential disdain for mediation resulting from its unwanted encroachment on their professional borders.[24] What is interesting in the context of this chapter is the idea that lawyers may not be able to adapt to mediation's rather different ethos of dispute resolution that is not fundamental to traditional, legal routes. While in Chap. 2 I examined the traditional cultural norms and adversarial practices of lawyers that may militate against lawyer embracement of mediation, equally the same shall doubtless impact upon the way that lawyers behave in mediation as party representatives.

One preliminary point here is that it can be speculated that civil lawyers may have more general difficulty adapting to the nuanced role of party advocate in mediation than their common law counterparts. This may emanate from the fact that the civil lawyer is traditionally trained as a 'legal scientist' with detailed knowledge of the law and unrivalled technical know-how in legal practice, whereas the common lawyer in general business practice has developed more of a rounded, trusted advisor status, proffering general business advice as well that of a legal nature.[25] This multifaceted role may be more suited to assisting in mediation, where the law is one of a spectrum of issues germane to resolving the dispute, than the traditional, pure nature of the civil lawyer's function.

4.2.1 *Lawyer Negotiations*

While evidence of how lawyers actually behave as party representatives in mediation can offer compelling insights into the merits of their role, what we know about lawyer negotiations in the general sense is a useful place to begin any analysis of this issue. In terms of the latter issue, the empirical evidence is surprisingly sparse. Historically speaking, standard instructional material on 'how to negotiate' for lawyers, often reflected, and no doubt perpetrated, the hard-nosed, adversarial stereotype. The utilisation of such techniques can be seen to represent some kind of race to the bottom. Summarising the typically espoused US approaches to lawyer negotiation skills in the 1970s, such as 'pitching it high',[26] tactically claiming a lack of authority to settle, appearing irrational and 'good-cop/bad-cop' behaviours, Hoffman has noted that "[t]he unspoken assumption in these suggestions is that the opponent is willing to take advantage of the negotiator–fairly or unfairly–and

---

[23] Rosenberg (1991), pp. 487–491.

[24] See Chap. 2 at Sects. 2.4 and 2.5.

[25] See for example, Rosen (2002).

[26] Holding an inflated initial position.

therefore success requires using competitive negotiation techniques, and using them more effectively than the opponent."[27]

Classic (American) studies of lawyer negotiations suggest, however, that lawyers' negotiating techniques may not be quite so adversarial and hard-bargaining orientated as 'folk-conceptions' (and traditional educational approaches) might indicate. Far from unearthing a plethora of aggressive, adversarial litigators, Gerald Williams' seminal 1970s research into Arizona lawyers revealed that respondents commonly believed at least that their colleagues acted in a cooperative, consensual fashion in their negotiations.[28] The same work was later repeated with some modification by Andrea Schneider. She uncovered generally similar findings, although a slight upsurge in overly aggressive lawyer behaviour in negotiations was detected. It is also interesting that in both pieces of work, lawyers were generally more likely to view the cooperative or problem-solving techniques of their peers as more effective than competitive or adversarial approaches thus dispelling the worth of clichéd negotiating practices.[29] These findings were broadly replicated in research into the negotiation styles of law students enrolled in negotiation classes in the Law Schools at Hastings, Boalt and Stanford in the USA, in which the majority of participants were found to exhibit 'compromising' negotiation styles.[30] In the UK personal injury context, Hazel Genn similarly found that lawyers preferred cooperative styles of negotiation.[31] Nonetheless other American research into the negotiating styles of law students has found them more prone than other types of students to engaging in what might be deemed unethical negotiating behaviour.[32]

With regard to whether traditional lawyer negotiations are beneficial for clients, more recent work into the negotiation styles of Australian lawyers by Rosemary Howell has found that although lawyers were committed to obtaining good outcomes, their clients often viewed that their lawyers' behaviour impeded rather than promoted positive outcomes. Her findings also suggest that lawyers are "task focused rather than relationship focused; concerned with detail, precision and form rather than strategic outcomes; focused on the present rather than the future; and reflective of an acceptance of and reliance on rules, systems and processes which encourage linear thinking and which discourage creative problem solving outside established precedent".[33] Such traits may not gel particularly well with a process

---

[27] Hoffman (2003), p. 3.

[28] Williams (1983); repeated by Schneider (2002).

[29] The two general approaches delineated by Williams were 'cooperative' and 'competitive'. Schneider preferred the terms 'problem-solving' and 'adversarial'. It is worth noting that lawyers may use positional bargaining out of habit even though they may express a preference for a problem-solving approach, see Heumann and Hyman (1997).

[30] Nelken (2005).

[31] Genn (1987), pp. 131–132, 166.

[32] Menkel-Meadow (2004), pp. 107–108.

[33] Howell (2005).

such as mediation that seeks to generate solutions which are forward thinking, creative and satisfy mutual interests.

In a similar vein, Julie Macfarlane has painted a damning picture of the typical negotiation strategies of lawyers in Canada and the USA by pointing, *inter alia*, to the fact that lawyers typically see negotiation as an adjunct to litigation, proceed from a rights-based, bargaining approach and that relatively little time is spent on actual negotiations but is rather devoted to navigating the procedural path of the dispute—all practice norms arguably not conducive to effective client advocacy in mediation.[34] Even if lawyers generally do perceive that they act in a co-operative fashion with their fellow lawyers, such cooperation may take place within a traditional, procedural and substantive legal paradigm. Macfarlane reveals the schism which exists between the normative function of a lawyer in standard client negotiations and the role required in mediation. In constructing a case from which to barter in general practice, positions are also taken rigidly, with confidence and bluster,[35] and clung on to for dear life. Furthermore, lawyers typically generate information to present as fact. Such information is not generated for the disclosure or sharing with the other side, nor for creating options for settlement, which are essential attributes of problem solving in mediation.[36] Cooperation between lawyers may often be self-serving and occur at a time suited to lawyers rather than clients.

Research into negotiation and settlement in personal injury actions in Scotland found that although the vast majority of actions settled extra-judicially, adversarial negotiation traits were strong in which a blatantly 'inflated' quantum of damages was commonly sought by pursuers and late, financial compromise settlement seemed to be the norm. The bulk of settlements were reportedly reached only after setting of a date for proof or trial, which appeared to focus parties' minds on reaching a settlement.[37]

In sum, much of the available evidence regarding traditional approaches to lawyer negotiations is at least suggestive of incompatibility with effective mediation practice. Nonetheless, in certain contexts there is evidence of shifting approaches to negotiation practice in many contexts, suggestive of a better compatibility with mediation engagement.

4.2.2 Evidence of Shifts in Negotiation Approaches

In the family dispute setting, Austin Sarat and William Felstiner's classic study demonstrated that far from driving combative behaviours, American divorce

[34] Macfarlane (2008), pp. 69–72. See the discussion in Chap. 2 at Sect. 2.5.2.

[35] Adversarial lawyers may be wrong but they are never in doubt!.

[36] Macfarlane (2008), Chaps. 3 and 4.

[37] Coope and Morris (2002).

lawyers often sought to dampen the adversarialism of their client.[38] Research elsewhere has suggested that the negotiation practices of family lawyers are in fact more consensual and potentially commensurate with mediation practice than in other areas.[39] This is of little surprise. Family law, in particular, has long been characterised by a stronger 'harmony' ethic within dispute resolution, not least because of the requirement to protect the interests of children, presumptions of two-party parenthood and mutual parental contact and the ensuing need to foster a continuing relationship between former spouses. Lawyers' roles in resolving family disputes have thus evolved from a traditional, adversarial, partisan approach to a more conciliatory, welfare based stance. Family lawyers often perceive their role as more complex than merely providing legal advice and include the proffering of general guidance and emotional support.[40] Collaborative norms are ingrained within the family law systems of many nations[41] and reflected in the growth of 'collaborative law'[42] practiced by many family lawyers. Many family lawyer associations globally espouse commitment to collaborative, non-adversarial practices—fundamental characteristics of the mediation. Nonetheless, as a caveat to such assertions, it should be noted that Schneider's work into lawyer negotiation styles found that the family law practice area harboured the highest percentage of "unethically, adversarial lawyers" and lowest percentage of problem solvers when compared to other practice areas.[43] Moreover, even in the family context, lawyers may typically remain in control of decision-making regarding how disputes are handled and resolved, which may be problematic in the context of mediation.[44] It should also be remembered that in many jurisdictions, voluntary referral by family lawyers to mediation remains low. It has been suggested that this reluctance may to some extent stem from a disinclination on the part of lawyers to allow their clients to dwell on emotional issues (for which mediation may provide an outlet), but rather a desire to persuade clients to 'move-on' and find a resolution to the dispute.[45]

Of course, as has been previously noted,[46] lawyers generally across many environments may be shifting into more cooperative forms of dispute resolution

[38] Sarat and Felstiner (1997).

[39] Myers and Wasoff (2000).

[40] See, for example, Eekelaar et al. (2000).

[41] Through, for example, legal rules regarding the interests of children that must be reflected in any settlement reached.

[42] Collaborative law dictates that party representatives promise to seek resolution of the dispute with the opponent in a consensual manner and generally precludes litigation of the dispute (by that lawyer).

[43] Given the view that family practice may be considered fertile ground for the development of mediation, the authors note, "[f]or those of us from outside the family law field, this [prevalence of adversarial lawyering] seems shocking"—Schneider and Mills (2006), p. 617.

[44] See the discussion in Chap. 2 at Sect. 2.3.1.

[45] See Melville and Laing (2010), p. 170.

[46] See Chap. 2 at Sect. 2.5.3.

rendering them more amenable to mediatory approaches. To some extent this can be seen to have been caused by the marked shift in formal civil justice mechanisms globally towards an acceptance of settlement as a legitimate aim of the system and encouragement of early resolution of disputes. Cultural shifts at the fringes of legal professions may also indicate that changes are afoot—witness, for example, the fact that law firms globally have relabelled their litigation departments as hubs of "conflict resolution". This rebranding exercise is suggestive of a wider range of practices beyond traditional dispute resolution routes. Increased exposure to mediation for lawyers through formal education and discreet training courses will also potentially lead to a growing cadre of lawyers comfortable in the mediation role.[47] While training and education in mediation may not, *per se*, always be sufficient to precipitate a growth in use of the process itself, nonetheless the spill over effects trickling down from educational exposure may begin to pervade on lawyers' general practice and increase their suitability for the mediation role.

4.2.3 Lawyers in Mediation

In Chap. 2, I suggested that lawyers' unfamiliarity with mediation may lead to resistance and discomfort in the prospect of engagement with the process. Equally in the above paragraphs we have seen that traditional legal education, cultural norms and negotiation practices may render lawyers unnatural inhabitants of mediation even if there are some indications that lawyers have begun to shift towards the adoption of norms that may better comport with mediation. What then can empirical evidence tell us about lawyers' activities within mediation? What beliefs do they hold about their role in the process? Various empirical research studies across different jurisdictions, through, for example, survey research, interviews or observation, have sought to address the issue of the role of the lawyer within mediation. Some of the key findings of this work are discussed here.

4.2.3.1 Standard Adversarial Lawyering in Mediation

One issue central to the ethos of mediation relates to the nexus of control over any settlement reached. Mediation's official discourse generally contemplates that the client shall be heavily involved in the process and responsible for creating the norms upon which the dispute is resolved. It may be speculated that lawyers, traditionally the producers of their clients' agreements, will struggle to accept the shift in settlement 'ownership' that mediation posits. Indeed, evidence of this can be

[47] But see Sect. 4.2.3 below regarding lawyer behaviour in the process.

detected in research conducted in a raft of different jurisdictions. A study by Olivia Rundle into the views of Tasmanian lawyers involved in court-connected mediation suggests that many do not place a significant emphasis upon the notion of direct disputant participation in the process.[48] The bulk did not support uncontrolled client participation and were more concerned with the potential problems emanating from client participation than any benefits that might accrue from such a client-centred approach.[49] A study of New Zealand lawyers' attitudes towards ADR in 2004 found that less than half of respondents (42%) viewed that increasing client control was a benefit of mediation.[50] Similarly, evidence from a study of Israeli lawyers also suggests that lawyers tend to retain control over dispute resolution within mediation.[51] Cognate findings can be gleaned from a study of Minnesota lawyers' interaction with mediation.[52] Roselle Wissler's research into US court-connected mediation found that lawyers often talked more than their clients within mediation sessions.[53] In fact there is substantial evidence from US studies of mediation in court-connected contexts in particular suggesting that lawyer control over the process and limited client participation therein has become the norm.[54]

That this is so can at least in part be attributed to the fact that mediation has been swallowed up and spat out merely as part of the general disputing practices of lawyers. As early as 1998 in the USA, it was reported that "in some places, it is taken for granted that mediation is the normal way to end litigation".[55] Such mediation, which has become a prominent feature of litigation systems has been termed "liti-mediation".[56] John Lande has pointed to the resultant weakening of the client's central role in mediation and missed opportunities for integrative, interest-based bargaining, as the process becomes one in which mediators essentially assist lawyers to negotiate more effectively.[57] Lawyers' general patterns of disputing behaviour may continue unabated in mediation. So for example, levels of evidential discovery undertaken by lawyers may remain stable irrespective of whether mediation is used or not.[58]

---

[48] Rundle (2008).

[49] Rundle (2008), p. 82.

[50] Saville-Smith and Fraser (2004), Table 4.2. Interestingly, however, clients were less likely (a mere 16%) to view control as a benefit, see Table 4.6.

[51] At least in the sense that they do not envisage that mediation leads to an increase of the time that clients spend in reaching a resolution—Sela (2009), p. 52.

[52] McAdoo (2002), p. 473.

[53] Wissler (2002), p. 658.

[54] For a classic treatment see Welsh (2001).

[55] Lande (1998).

[56] Lande (1998).

[57] See also Kuhner (2005) (finding that lawyers typically dominated court-connected mediation sessions at the expense of their clients in USA and Argentina).

[58] See, for example, McAdoo (2002), pp. 472–473. This issue ties in with the timing of mediation. When mediation is attempted at an earlier stage in legal proceedings (or indeed before they have

Tamara Relis's groundbreaking work into mediation in court-connected medical negligence matters in Canada also found evidence of lawyer domination of the process, with clients and their interests often side-lined. Lawyers were typically in charge of proceedings with non-attendance by defendants, commonplace. The impact of lawyers was also found generally to lead to a reduced participative element for clients in the mediation process.[59] As Relis noted, the diminished place for clients in this model of mediation may negatively affect perceptions of procedural justice, which are instead positively influenced by disputants' perceptions of having 'voice'.[60] Lawyer domination is also important not least in the sense that Relis's study also revealed that there often exists a mismatch between the respective aims, expectations, understandings and experiences of lawyers and lay participants in mediation. In particular, the lawyer-centric form of mediation deployed "frequently fail[ed] to address parties' extralegal needs, aims and plans for the process."[61] Her research found lawyers often commonly seeking to use mediation as a way to pursue traditional legal (monetary) aims, when clients often sought, other non-monetary aims such as apologies, explanations and the opportunity to vent in front of the other party. Such client interests did not dissipate as the dispute resolution journey progressed or were 'reframed' in legal terms, leaving the prospect thus of lawyer dominated mediation failing to meet parties' needs.[62]

Writing in 2001, Julie Macfarlane's research revealed five 'ideal types' of lawyers who participated in court-connected mediation in Ontario.[63] Some lawyers—the "true believers"—had clearly bought into the original, classic vision of mediation as a forum in which client empowerment and self-determination was fundamental, while others were dismissive or openly opposed mediation developments. Two groups, identified by Macfarlane, however, represent lawyers who, although keen to make use of the process, either continue to see a dominant role for themselves relative to their clients and perceive that their traditional lawyers' role should continue unabated in the process,[64] or see mediation as something to be 'captured' and transformed into an vehicle in which to drive competitive, adversarial lawyer behaviours.[65] Such tactical deployment of

commenced) then discovery levels are likely to be reduced. Lawyers may baulk at pre-discovery scheduling of mediation, however, on the basis that the case is not yet ripe and negotiations at mediation ill-informed by the legal dimension to the dispute.

[59] With lawyers often agreeing to "not invite" defendants to the mediation: Relis (2009), Sect. 1.2.

[60] Relis (2009), p. 14. It can be argued that the appropriate deployment of lawyers in mediation may enhance users' procedural justice, however. For a discussion of this issue and procedural justice in mediation see Chap. 5 at Sect. 5.2.4.5.

[61] Relis (2009), p. 11.

[62] Relis (2009), pp. 15–17.

[63] Macfarlane (2001), Chap. III.

[64] The "pragmatists".

[65] The "instrumentalists".

mediation is redolent of criticism of lawyer involvement in arbitration systems as their presence in the process has become the norm.[66]

Other empirical work in the field has shown that mediation may arguably become tainted as lawyers are apt to use mediation in a tactical manner as 'fishing expeditions'. In Penny Brooker's study into construction lawyers' experience with mediation in England and Wales, around half of those lawyers interviewed revealed strategic, arguably cynical reasons for deployment of mediation and averred that some parties did not mediate in good faith.[67] My own research has revealed that Scottish commercial litigators were not immune to such temptations either.[68] Similarly, Linda Mulcahy's research into English lawyers' interaction with a medical negligence pilot mediation scheme, generated the interesting finding that, while away from the gaze of their clients, medical negligence lawyers were likely to operate in a co-operative fashion with their adversaries,[69] their unfamiliarity with the mediation process and their perception of how their clients expected them to behave in the mediation made them apt to act in a *more* adversarial fashion within the mediation.[70] She also observed that while lawyers may enter the mediation process with good intentions, their natural instinct to take control of settlement on behalf of their clients often overrode their purpose.[71]

4.2.3.2 The Worth of Lawyer Advocacy

It would be misleading to suggest that their common presence in mediation is purely a result of some kind of tactical grab by lawyers to ensure a share of the spoils. As I have already noted, there is significant client demand in this regard.[72] Moreover, it can be argued that lawyer involvement as client advocates in mediation sessions is useful and at times, essential.

To begin with, it is clear that experienced mediation advocates may assist mediators in expediting settlement in mediation and aid their clients in effective participation. Neimeijer and Pel's research into court-connected mediation in the Netherlands, for example, uncovered many mediators espousing positivity about

[66] See for example, Flood and Caiger (1993), p. 430 referring to the infamous debate in the UK Chartered Institute of Arbitrators over whether lawyers were killing arbitration. For further discussion of lawyers' tactical infiltration into arbitration see Chap. 3 at Sect. 3.2.4.

[67] Brooker (2005), pp. 37–38.

[68] Clark and Dawson (2007), p. 234.

[69] Generally because of a small, specialised legal community and the need to foster good working relationships with professional colleagues.

[70] Mulcahy (2001), pp. 212–213.

[71] Mulcahy (2001), pp. 214–217. In Mulcahy's view, the passing of control of settlement discussions to the client represented the biggest challenge for lawyers in mediation.

[72] See the discussion in Chap. 3 at Sect. 3.3.6. Although to what extent such demand may have been created by lawyers themselves is debatable.

the role of lawyers in helping their clients expedite settlement in mediation.[73] In this sense, it is argued, for instance, that lawyers may be useful in that they may influence their clients to moderate extreme demands.[74] Furthermore, while I have already alluded to substantial evidence suggesting that lawyer participation in mediation may undermine the concept of active client participation in mediation, lawyers may in fact provide encouragement for their clients, and inject them with confidence to actively participate in the process. Research in the family field in particular has revealed that the presence of lawyers generally encouraged direct client participation.[75] This is none too surprising. As has been noted above, family lawyers may be generally more familiar with client-centred approaches to conflict resolution than in other fields.[76] Outside of the family field, Macfarlane's research into Ontario lawyers' relationship with mediation also found some lawyer representatives keen to embrace the original vision of mediation and support their clients in procuring settlement and generally in the fulfilment of their empowered role in the process.[77] Doubtless other, more experienced lawyer-advocates who have experienced the potentially profound impact of mediation upon clients in dispute may do the same and encourage their clients to take a central role in the process.[78]

A second aspect to lawyer involvement in mediation is that some of the supposed goods that lawyer-advocates bring to the table can be seen to counteract perceived weaknesses of the mediation process. In this sense, lawyers may be considered standard bearers for the protection afforded by the law striking out against the 'dangers' of non-legal, informalism. For example, in the context of family matters, Craig McEwen *et al* argue that lawyer participation in mediation is necessary to protect clients from the pressures to settle exercised by the mediator.[79] In a similar vein, Craig Pollack, cocking a snook at evangelistic fervour for mediation, has gone so far as to argue that mediators are "settlement junkies" prepared to "feed their habit by any means". He argues that lawyers are needed to protect clients from mediators' voracious appetite in this regard, which may swallow up the client's interests in the process.[80] Such views perhaps smack of headline-grabbing provocation. Nevertheless, in a competitive market, where supply may often outstrip demand, mediators trade upon their reputation. A high settlement rate is the most obvious, albeit, perhaps unsophisticated, way for potential users to determine a mediator's effectiveness *ex ante*. Aside from operation of the market, it is also

---

[73] Niemeijer and Pel (2005), pp. 368–369.

[74] McEwen et al. (1995).

[75] McEwen et al. (1995), p. 1375.

[76] See the discussion at Sect. 4.2.2.

[77] Macfarlane (2001), Chap. III.

[78] Legions of lawyers I have spoken to in my own country and in other jurisdictions have spoken of the benefits that have accrued for their clients from their active participation in mediation.

[79] McEwen et al. (1995), p. 1394.

[80] Pollack (2007), p. 20.

important to recognise that, in many contexts, mediation is in an embryonic state and those at the forefront of practice in these areas may be significantly driven by self-preservation. Particularly in circumstances in which the mediation process must show that it can 'wipe its feet' in monetary terms, for example, to attract state subsidies or judicial support, then proving that mediation works—primarily through producing settlements—is absolutely crucial. Against a backdrop of such pressures, settlement-heavy approaches to mediation and the practice of the mediator are likely to flourish.[81] Lawyers, if they are present, may thus act as a bulwark against such pressures.

Where a marked power imbalance exists between the disputing parties, for example, through stark discrepancies between their respective levels of intelligence, eloquence, confidence and knowledge of the legal parameters of the dispute, the presence of lawyers may help to redress the balance in this sense.[82] As Tina Grillo, in her classic critique of family mediation practices noted, "[i]n evaluating whether [lawyers'] exclusion actually furthers client empowerment, it is useful to consider the reasons why a person engaged in a divorce might want the services of a lawyer".[83] In this sense, she notes that lawyers are hired to protect client's rights and act as a buffer or layer of 'insulation' between the client and their opponent. As a client's mouthpiece, a lawyer may be able to more effectively voice a client's position in the mediation session.[84] This approach need not amount to domination or control of the client, but rather a partnership approach with the client, with the lawyer articulating more eloquently and forcibly the arguments the client seeks to advance. It is worth noting here though that clients may not always seek empowerment in the sense of active participation in the mediation or control over framing any settlement reached. Clients may be happy to cede significant control to their lawyers. What entails empowerment for some clients may only be found in the efforts of a champion acting on their behalf. Grillo put it succinctly: "'[d]on't call me, call my lawyer' are sometimes the most empowering words imaginable."[85]

[81] Such settlement heavy forms of mediation are of course often presided over by lawyers or judges. For a discussion see Sect. 4.3.

[82] The argument that power imbalances may not be alleviated and may even be exacerbated within mediation is a fundamental and longstanding critique of the process (Rueben 2000; Grillo 1991). Equally, of course the presence of lawyers on one side and absence from the other may exacerbate and create imbalances between the disputing parties. Japanese research, for example, has suggested that lawyer representation led to better financial settlements for parties in divorce mediations, particularly where the other party was not represented—Murayama (1999), pp. 66–72. The issues of handling power imbalances and achieving 'justice' in mediation are discussed in more detail in Chap. 5 at Sects. 5.2.4 and 5.2.5.

[83] Grillo (1991), p. 1597.

[84] Research into divorce mediation in Georgia, USA has revealed that a vast majority of participants found that having a lawyer present was beneficial—see Gordon (2002), Table 1.

[85] Grillo (1991), p. 1599. There is some empirical evidence suggesting that in practice women are not so disadvantaged as Grillo suggests, see the discussion in Chap. 5 at Sect. 5.2.5.

Corroborating such sentiments, in response to the argument that lawyers may take control over the process to the disadvantage of clients, in her study of the impact of lawyers on mediation settlement conferences in Australia, Jill Howieson has noted that even where lawyers demonstrably appear to compromise client control over both process and outcome, the presence of lawyers in mediation may in fact enhance their clients' perceptions of distributive justice,[86] and do not substantially interfere with client perceptions of procedural justice.[87] Furthermore, only 16% of disputants interviewed thought that 'more control' was a benefit of their participation within the mediation process, suggesting that many may be comfortable with the prospect of taking a back seat and letting lawyers assume control in mediation sessions.[88] Similarly, it is also notable that very few respondents to a recent survey of users of the Edinburgh sheriff court mediation service in Scotland stated that they attempted mediation because it gave them more control over the outcome.[89] Much depends upon context of course, but as I shall explore more fully in Chap. 5,[90] my contention is that in court-connected contexts, in particular, party empowerment within mediation should not always be seen as an overriding objective of mediation and may require to be sacrificed at the altar of other, more pressing aims.

Although in contexts in which lawyers are generally excluded from mediation clients are advised to consult with their representatives prior to adhering to agreements reached, it has been argued that this *per se* is not sufficient to ensure that a client's legal rights are protected. Grillo pointed to the possibility of privileged or unhelpful information being disclosed by the client in mediation, which could be exploited by the other party in the aftermath of a failed mediation. So in that sense, subsequent lawyer consultation may be tantamount to closing the door after the horse has bolted.[91] On a related point, she also viewed that lawyers may feel somewhat constrained in seeking any post-hoc variations to agreements reached on the basis that they would not want to be seen as saboteurs thus limiting their ability to protect clients from unfair agreements.

---

[86] I.e. how just clients view the outcome to be.

[87] Howieson (2002), para 75–85.

[88] Howieson (2002), Table 4.6.

[89] c.7% of respondents—Mantle (2008). The author of the report concedes, however, that the data set is too small for significant findings to be drawn from the survey.

[90] Chapter 5 at Sect. 5.3.

[91] Grillo (1991), p. 1598.

4.3 Lawyer-Mediators

4.3.1 General Points

Turning to the issue of lawyers acting as mediators, similar concerns to those alluded to above regarding lawyer advocates in mediation have been voiced. In this sense, the classic Riskinian view of lawyers suggests again that their traditional learning and training, partisanship, adversarialism and focus on rights-based, narrow advocacy may be anathema to the mediator's role. My early Scottish research suggested that non-lawyer participants in the mediation field were often extremely doubtful about the merits of lawyer-mediators.[92] As noted in Chap. 1, grass roots pioneers in mediation's early development often eschewed the role of the lawyer therein.[93] Commentators have joined hands to question the value of lawyers taking on the mediation role.[94] While being generally favourable regarding lawyer mediators, the issue is well summed up Currie: "too much substantive [legal] expertise can put the mediator's neutrality at risk by biasing them toward standard solutions and diverting their attention from underlying interests and needs".[95] Moreover, aside from being over-evaluative, lawyers-mediators, as traditional positional bargainers, may be prone to viewing the dispute as a zero-sum game and refuse to acknowledge the possibility of 'expanding the pie'.[96] The potential for creativity of settlement—a key potential benefit in mediation—may then be lost.

The traditional role of lawyers may often it seems bleed into their mediation practice in which lawyer-mediators struggle to throw off the shackles of their professional alter-ego, and engage in evaluative, directive behaviour.[97] So as Vindelov notes in respect of the Danish context, "[a]necdotal evidence suggests that the more that lawyers are involved as mediators... the more evaluative and settlement-orientated mediation tends to be... It appears to be difficult for lawyer-mediators to relinquish control of the dispute and trust in the capacity of the parties to reach a satisfactory solution to their problem."[98]

Despite the notion that the lawyer as mediator is a fish out of water, the issue is more nuanced than anti-lawyer sentiment might suggest. It is contended that lawyers, conversely, may be ideally suited to mediation practice. First, in terms of potentially important, fundamental skills and attributes that mediators should hold and exhibit, there is no reason why some lawyers should not hold them in

[92] Mays and Clark (1996), Chap. 5.

[93] See Chap. 1 at Sect. 1.1.2.

[94] Roberts (1992) (England and Wales); Guthrie (2001), Pt II (arguing that American lawyer-mediators compromise facilitative mediation).

[95] Currie (2000).

[96] Lande (1998), p. 5.

[97] Guthrie (2001), Pt II.

[98] Vindelov (2006), pp. 132–133.

spades, in the same way as mediators those drawn from other professions. The National Academy for Dispute Professionals (UK) suggests, for example, that "[s]ome lawyers are natural mediators."[99] The term 'natural' may be taken to refer to attributes or traits that cannot be learned but are rather innate, or at least honed over time from a wealth of professional experience. Some of the traits that experienced lawyers in particular may exhibit, which may be important in mediation, include authority, the ability to command the respect and gain the confidence of the parties and legal representatives at the mediation; the ability to remain calm in the eye of the storm; professionalism; keeping confidences; general standards of courtesy; an eye for fairness and even-handedness; active listening skills, and powers of analysis and distillation of the salient issues.[100]

4.3.2 Training and Education

Mediation training and education, along with learning through co-mediating, continuing professional development, mentoring and reflective practice systems may also hone the skills of lawyers (along, of course, with those drawn from other professional backgrounds) and render them more effective in the role.[101] While I have already discussed the limited educational exposure to mediation that lawyers in many jurisdictions experience in law school, there presently exists a glut of training and educational programmes in mediation theory and practice for lawyers and other professionals across the globe. Training and education in mediation varies significantly, however, across jurisdictions. To some extent there can be said to be a civil law/common law divide in terms of mediation training.[102] Traditionally, at least in general civil or commercial areas of practice,[103] standard mediation training for lawyers in common law nations has tended to take the form of predominantly skills-based, short-form courses, amounting typically to 30 or 40 hours in duration. The civil law world, however, which generally has moved quickly to more stringent regulation of the mediation process and the mediator's role within it, has tended to prescribe much more extensive educational and training programmes for mediators.

---

[99] See http://www.nadr.co.uk/background/medlawyer.php Accessed 1 November 2011.

[100] According to Goldberg and Shaw's research into what determines a successful mediator, the central conclusion to be drawn is that a—if not *the*—core element in mediator success is the mediator's ability to establish a relationship of trust and confidence with the disputing parties. Such factors seemed to outweigh any process skills that mediators may hold—Goldberg and Shaw (2007), p. 414. Other recent research has identified such traits as doggedness, patience, effective listening and the ability to be flexible in terms of thinking practically and what process skills to use in any particular case—for a summary see Lande (2008).

[101] Although practical experience may be the best proxy for expertise.

[102] See, for example, Alexander (2006).

[103] In other areas, such as family mediation, training has typically been more extensive.

Although they also encompass the development of relevant practical skills, such civil law programmes tend to be far more steeped in theoretical learning than their common law counterparts. Post-graduate university programmes have more recently begun to proliferate in common law jurisdictions, which seek to marry theory and practice.[104] It may still remain the exception currently, however, that lawyers in the common law world endeavouring to enter mediation practice would seek out such qualifications. Accrediting bodies rarely require attendance at such programmes and short, skill-based training remains the norm. The notion of mediation as a 'bolt-on' to existing legal experience is thus particularly strong in common law jurisdictions.

4.3.3 The Value-Added Nature of Lawyer-Mediators

While it can be argued then that some lawyers at least will be suitable neutrals in mediation, it can be posited that lawyers are in fact *superior* to non-lawyers in this regard. This is particularly so *because* of the traditional legal training and experience that lawyers possess, that is so decried by sceptics. Indeed, it is contended that lay-mediators will be found wanting compared to their lawyer counterparts in view of their lack of legal background and expertise. It is hence of no coincidence that mediators who are concurrently lawyers are quick to advertise their services as '"lawyer-mediators".[105] The premise here is that lawyers represent some kind of 'mediator-with-bells-on'. So aside from possession of certain generic mediation skills and desired character traits alluded to above,[106] lawyer-mediators may also have at their fingertips powers beyond the gift of the laity. In particular, an understanding of the legal issues germane to the matter being mediated, an appreciation of how the dispute might otherwise be handled in traditional adjudication and what legal remedies might be available, as well as an ability to interpret the nuances of the lawyer/client relationship and the workings of lawyers may be seen as powerful tools in the mediator's bag. It is argued that lawyers may also be able to get to the meat of the dispute quicker thus better expediting settlement.[107] As explored below, it can also be argued that mediating clients themselves often seek out the wares that lawyer-mediators are uniquely placed to offer.[108]

---

[104] Including an MSc in Mediation and Conflict Resolution I am involved in at Strathclyde University, set up in 2010, the first of its kind in Scotland.

[105] See, for example, in Scotland the CALM website at http://www.calmscotland.co.uk/plugins/faqmanager Accessed 1 November 2011.

[106] At Sect. 4.3.1.

[107] For example, in an evaluation of court-connected mediation in the Netherlands, lawyer mediators generally needed less contact time to reach an agreement than non-lawyers—Niemeijer and Pel (2005), p. 362.

[108] Notwithstanding that lawyers rather than their clients are often the true 'buyers' of mediation services—see Chap. 3 at Sect. 3.4.4.

4.3.4 Lawyer-Mediators and the 'Lawless' Nature of Mediation

I know mediators who claim that they can mediate anything. Some prefer not to read the case file, go in cold, and work with what they find in the room. Their focus is on managing the relationship between the parties and assisting them to reach an agreement—the parties' own agreement—which is mutually acceptable. Where legal issues are germane to the dispute at hand, then the approach of such mediators (and in fact general discourse in mediation) would normally dictate that these matters are for the parties (and their lawyers, if present) to determine themselves and weigh up in the matrix of issues relevant to any settlement reached. Generally, classic forms of mediation seek to suppress or downplay legal positions in favour of maximisation of mutual party interests, to which the law may have little or even no bearing. Hence, arguably mediators working within this framework have no need to comprehend the nuances and complexities of the legal parameters of disputes that fall before them. It is in fact this 'lawlessness' that fuels much of the criticism of lay mediators. A significant amount of the lambasting of non-lawyer mediators is in fact a reflection of the more fundamental critique of classic, facilitative, norm-generating mediation, in which it is contended the mediator has no interest in the objective fairness (far less legal fairness) of any agreements crafted by the parties. At the extreme end of the spectrum, this might result in mediators presiding over agreements which are non-enforceable at law. More subtly, agreements reached may not be commensurate at all with what may appear legally 'just' in the circumstances. One might riposte that such arguments are of little relevance if parties go home happy with the settlement they have crafted in their case. Issues of concern around 'unfair' agreements may arise, however, when mediation has involved *pro se* participants, parties who have had little choice but to mediate their dispute and/or in the court-connected context. In such settings the desire to illustrate that mediation outcomes comport with justice in the formal sense may be irresistible.[109]

4.3.5 What Do Lawyers Want from Mediators?

It will turn few heads that lawyers may have a predilection for legal evaluation in mediation and in practice often plump for lawyer-mediators. As I noted in Chap. 3, lawyers, as repeat players in mediation, have in many settings become the *de facto* buyers of mediation services, and often 'shop' for evaluative, lawyer-mediators.[110] There is also significant evidence of lawyers circumventing professional lists of mediators (which may often be multi-disciplinary in nature with mediators drawn

[109] See the discussion of such matters in Chap. 5 at Sects. 5.2.4 and 5.2.5.

[110] At Sect. 3.4.4.

from a range of professions) and engaging lawyer-mediators directly from the marketplace. Surveys of lawyers (and judges[111]) often reveal their preference for lawyer-mediators.[112] A multiplicity of reasons may be relevant in this assessment. Lawyers may feel a cultural 'pull' towards those mediators that reflect better their own professional personae. In this sense, Relis's research into Canadian medical negligence mediation found lawyer representatives valuing mediators mainly for the strategic, evaluative and legal skills that they brought to the table.[113] Lawyers may prefer mediation models which comport better with their own traditional legal skills and experience.

A related reason why lawyers may prefer lawyer-mediators is that they feel that their own efforts as mediation advocates will be better understood and supported by mediators with litigation experience. In this sense, lawyer-mediators may validate the presence of the lawyer advocate in mediation. As John Van Winkle, in the context of general civil mediation in the USA, put it: "[m]ediators who minimise or fail to recognize the important advocate role of lawyers in mediation will not only frustrate and perhaps alienate the lawyers, they will also do a disservice to the client who would benefit from negotiation and evaluation advice. Mediators with a broad base of trial experience are better equipped to understand and support the advocate's role. Mediators with trial experience are also better able to understand and appreciate how complex, important and sometimes fragile the relationships are between attorneys and clients".[114] It is also contended that lawyers who understand the legal parameters to a dispute are able to work better in partnership with lawyer advocates in expediting a settlement and influencing their parties to accept the same.[115] I should add that such an assumption is, of course, predicated on the basis that settlement is influenced primarily by legal norms and/or standard positional bargaining. Similarly, lawyers who take a narrow approach to the negotiation game to be played in mediation simply favour evaluative-mediators in the quest to get to the meat of the issue quickly.[116]

[111] See for example, McAdoo (2004), appendix A.7, finding that 70% of judges surveyed believed that "legal experience" and "substantive knowledge in area of case being litigated" were important mediator qualifications.

[112] Clark and Dawson (2007), p. 240 (Scottish lawyers); Brooker (2008), pp. 227–230 (English lawyers); McAdoo (2002), pp. 433–435 (American lawyers); Relis (2009) (Canadian lawyers); Sela (2009), table 4 (Israeli lawyers). Although research into the preferences of American law students found that a majority favoured mediators who were creative and elicitive in their approach rather than evaluative—see Goldfien and Robbennolt (2007), pp. 300–303.

[113] Relis (2009), p. 12 and Chap. 7.

[114] Van Winkle (2001), p. 41.

[115] Van Winkle (2001), p. 41.

[116] See for example, Stipanowich (1996), p. 105.

4.3.6 The Facilitative/Evaluative Divide

Evaluation within mediation is a highly contentious issue that runs to the heart of what mediation practice involves. Of course, not only lawyer-mediators evaluate in their practice and evaluation does not always relate to the legal parameters of disputes in mediation but may pertain to a wide spectrum of matters such as economic imperatives, the welfare of children, reputational issues, future relationships and business prospects. Given that the debate is often linked to the merits of lawyer-mediators, it is however, worth spending a little time here mining the rich vein of literature in the area. The initial debate over evaluation in mediation was sparked by the seminal work of Len Riskin who developed a "grid" of mediation styles differentiating between evaluative and facilitative approaches.[117] The ensuing hullaballoo across the evaluative/facilitative divide has since been played out between mediation purists, espousing a facilitative, norm-generating[118] approach within mediation and those who advocate an evaluative approach, where the mediator is typically more pro-active in attempting to broker settlement and the underlying law may play more of a prominent role in the mediation.[119] So whereas 'pure' mediators are mere facilitators of parties' communication and negotiation, in evaluative models of mediation it may be that, "a mediator focuses… on the legal claims, assesses [their] strengths and weaknesses… predicts the impact of not settling and pushes the parties to his/her evaluation of the appropriate settlement". Riskin later amended his grid and propounded the related distinction between 'directive' and 'elicitive' approaches to mediation.[120] This new distinction "focus [es] on the extent to which almost any conduct by the mediator directs the mediation process, or the participants, toward a particular procedure or perspective or outcome, on the one hand or, on the other, elicits the parties' perspectives and preferences-and then tries to honor or accommodate them."[121] Legal (and other types of) evaluation may clearly be an important tool by which the mediator attempts to direct the parties to particular settlements.

Evaluative or directive approaches to mediation have been heavily criticised. It is argued that being leaning too heavily on the provision of legal advice and leading parties towards 'legal solutions' may be problematic in that the wider benefits of mediation may hence go unfulfilled. In a survey of New Zealand ADR practitioners, respondents generally viewed that, "the full range of potential benefits, especially

---

[117] Riskin (1996).

[118] In the sense that the norms on the basis of which settlement is reached are created by the parties—see Waldman (1997).

[119] Riskin (1996), p. 25.

[120] Riskin (2003).

[121] Riskin (2003), p. 30.

those related to increased user satisfaction with outcomes and compliance with ADR resolutions, were less likely to be achieved where mediation focused on risk assessment, cost-benefit review, or evaluation of the likelihood of success in court rather than consensual solution development".[122] Evaluation may also, it is argued, detract from the possibility of creativity of settlement as it tends to narrow the settlement range to traditional outcomes found in court or lawyer-led negotiations.[123] One particularly pressing concern is that evaluation may damage the neutrality of the mediator. When the mediator expresses a view as to what she perceives to be an objectively fair outcome in the circumstances (a settlement evaluation) or passes judgement on the legal merits of the parties' cases (legal evaluation) then inevitably the impression may firmly be made that she is siding with one party over the other. In view of this potential blight on impartiality, many writers contend that while evaluation may be a useful device to eradicate a deadlock in negotiations,[124] it is a high risk manoeuvre. Evaluation may thus be seen as some kind of last throw of the dice. Another, particular matter of concern with a legal evaluation is that the view expressed may be debatable, or plainly wrong. This may especially be the case where the mediator is not a lawyer or legal specialist in the area of dispute. The issue may arise more generally given that the full gamut of fact and law that would be revealed in a judicial determination may not have surfaced in the mediation context and hence evaluations are made at least partially in the dark. Furthermore, unlike the remedies that may flow in negligence from negligent advice tendered from a lawyer, there may be limited scope for such redress from the mediator who tempts parties into particular settlements on the basis of a spurious evaluation.[125] Legal evaluations may be especially concerning where the parties to the mediation do not have recourse to their own lawyers to help form a view on the veracity of the evaluation tendered.[126]

Some have argued that given its departure from traditional notions of the process, evaluative mediation should simply not be labelled "mediation". The argument follows that although evaluative processes may have their place, they should be labelled differently to distinguish them from 'pure' mediation.[127] I would contend, however, that frankly this kind of comment is somewhat unhelpful. Mediation has evolved in a pluralistic sense to embody a multitude of normative forms. It is true that we should be wary of the prospect of certain forms developing

---

[122] Saville-Smith and Fraser (2004), para 4.2.

[123] See Love (1997), p. 944.

[124] Recent research by Stephen Goldberg and Margaret Shaw into what makes successful mediators has found that 33% of mediation advocates (mainly lawyers) valued evaluative behaviours, whereas only 10% of the mediators themselves referred to the value of such tactics—Goldberg and Shaw (2007), p. 393.

[125] Love (1997), p. 942.

[126] Albeit that I argue in Chap. 5 that mediators should provide such evaluations in the context of court-connected mediation when requested by pro se litigants—see Chap. 5 at Sect. 5.3.

[127] Kovach and Love (1998).

to comport better with the professional agendas of actors involved such as lawyers. In general, however, the choice of mediator and style of mediation process surely should belong to the parties themselves.[128] If parties desire a mediator who is a lawyer and who will express opinions on underpinning legal issues, suggest appropriate settlements and comment on objective levels of fairness of settlements reached, then surely that is the parties' prerogative.

Nonetheless, the stark schism between rhetoric and reality in mediation is more difficult to defend. Despite the primacy in mainstream mediation discourse sanctioning facilitative approaches, evidence suggests that mediators are in practice far more evaluative and directive than their rhetoric suggests.[129] There are of course settings in which evaluative behaviour is openly acknowledged[130] but often, it seems that evaluation is the great unspoken. If we are to gain the informed consent of parties to enter into mediation then a little honesty in this respect would not go amiss.

4.3.6.1 The False Dichotomy Between Facilitation and Evaluation

Some commentators have pointed to the fact that the schism between facilitative and evaluative mediation is a false one and that every mediator is evaluative to a certain extent whether this is a consciously deployed tactic or not.[131] It is argued, for example, that much reality testing—a key weapon in the armoury of the facilitative mediator—is often in fact laden with evaluation. Reality testing questions are often asked to prompt answers that the mediator has already considered and would like the party to arrive at 'be themselves'.[132] Equally, it is simplistic to describe mediators as either facilitative or evaluative, evidence suggests that many mediators do not subscribe to one fixed style but in fact are more likely to mix their approaches both across different mediations and within the same mediation to best handle the 'action in the room'.[133]

---

[128] Although lawyer domination of mediation may in effect remove party choice in this respect.

[129] As Kressel (2007), p. 275 notes, there is a "very tight grip in the ADR world on the idea that the proper mediator is a neutral, nondirective facilitator of parties' own search for solutions. Although it is often at striking odds with research evidence about mediator behaviour, this version of the role is pervasive in training programs and officially sanctioned discourse". Also see the UK family mediation research by Greatbatch and Dingwall (1990) suggesting that mediators have agendas and seek to move parties towards desired settlement ranges. Similarly, in the context of mediation practice in the context of French industrial disputes, "[e]ven though most [mediators] and mediation training make it an absolute rule not to intervene in core issues, both direct observation and several interviews actually revealed the mediator's will to be a participant in the discussion and not just act at a distance as in facilitation—Grima and Paille (2011), p. 442.

[130] For example, in the English homelessness mediation contexts—Ng (2011).

[131] See Stemple (2000), p. 379.

[132] Stemple notes that "[t]he reality testing of pointed questions is at least. partly evaluative and it is perfectly proper mediation"—Stemple (2000), fn 23.

[133] Golan (2000), p 61; Lande (2000), p. 321.

4.3.7 *What Do Clients Want from Mediators?*

Relis's recent work finds mediation participants expressing preferences for facilitative styles of mediation and praising the skills and abilities of mediators which are steeped in the facilitative model of practice while paying scant concern to evaluative techniques.[134] Other research in the sphere of employment disputes has also found clients favouring facilitative approaches to mediation.[135] Nonetheless, there is evidence from other studies of clients' attitudes on mediation, particularly, but not limited to the court-connected context, that parties may have a preference for lawyer mediators and other evaluative types. In an evaluation of the Exeter small claims mediation scheme in the UK, for example, a majority of clients viewed that legal skills and experience were essential for mediators.[136] Research into Dutch court connected mediation suggested that sometimes parties specifically sought out lawyer-mediators, particularly to ensure that agreements reached could be properly framed in legal terms.[137] There was also evidence from that research that parties sought evaluation from their mediators.[138] Research into the views of disputants who were involved in judicial mediation in the New Zealand Family Court suggested that they both expected and desired a firm, directive stance from the mediators.[139] Amanda Bucklow's recent research into the attitudes of repeat mediation users in the UK found that while 47% of respondents stated that a facilitative mediation approach was the most successful in their experience, another 47% viewed that a mix of facilitative and evaluative techniques was most desirable.[140] Empirical evidence from the USA has suggested that clients' perceptions of fairness in some mediation settings are enhanced when mediators provide legal evaluations.[141] Similarly in the context of German construction mediation there is some evidence that participants expect mediators to propose a solution to their dispute.[142] My own research in respect of the attitudes towards, and experiences of Scottish construction industry participants with mediation suggests that there may be an appetite for evaluative mediatory practices.[143] A recent American Bar

[134] Relis (2009), p. 12.

[135] McDermott and Obar (2004) (reflecting on a mediation programme in the US Equal Employment Opportunity Programme).

[136] Enterkin and Sefton (2006).

[137] Niemeijer and Pel (2005), p. 354.

[138] Niemeijer and Pel (2005), p. 367.

[139] Barry and Henaghan (1986).

[140] Bucklow (2007), p. 47.

[141] Wissler (2001) (summarising the findings of four American general civil and family mediation schemes).

[142] Duve (2008), p. 1540 cited in Hillig and Huhn (2010), p. 49.

[143] In the sense that respondents generally favoured mediators offering opinions of the merits of disputes. Many also viewed that settlements in mediations that they were involved in were often primarily crafted by the mediators—Agapiou and Clark (2011).

Association survey into the attitudes of mediation users in general civil and commercial disputes, found a significant number favouring evaluative, directive techniques in mediation.[144] Similar findings were uncovered in a recent survey of mediation users in Singapore.[145]

It is clear then that many parties in mediation want the mediator to be able to provide legal information and/or advice. If the ability to provide legal information/advice is seen to be a key attribute of the mediator then this clearly favours lawyers over those drawn from other professional fields.[146] This issue, which holds significant relevance in the context of court-connected mediation, shall be pursued further in Chap. 5.

4.3.8 *Evidence as to Differences Between Lawyer-Mediators and Non-Lawyer-mediators*

In terms of whether lawyer-mediators are generally distinguishable from non-lawyers in the role, recent US research has found that at least in terms of settlement rates, attorney mediators and non-attorney mediators could not generally be differentiated.[147] The same finding was reported by Neimeijer and Pel in the Dutch context.[148] Relis's recent research also found little discernable differences between lawyer and non-lawyer mediators. Explaining this, she noted that "something had changed within lawyer-mediators' understandings of ways of looking at disputes... frequently no discernable differences could be found when comparing the discourse of lawyer-mediators with non-lawyer-mediators [on such issues as to whether defendants should attend in person]."[149] She did, however, find a marked distinction between the discourse of lawyer-mediators and attorneys representing clients in mediation session despite their shared educational and cultural background. This could be explained on the basis that "[i]t was if experiencing mediations with disputants present sensitized lawyer mediators to the human realities of cases and perhaps changed their ways of perceiving disputes. This change seemed to be more than mediation training alone could achieve".[150] Relis's

[144] American Bar Association Section of Dispute Resolution (2008).

[145] Onn (2006).

[146] The differential between advice and information is hard to draw. While "information" in this context could be considered to be general information about the underlying legal norms to the type of dispute at hand, civil court process and available remedies, "advice" might include an analysis of the legal merits of the parties' respective cases and a view on the most likely adjudicative outcome to be proffered by court. See Chap. 3 at Sect. 3.4.3 for a discussion in the context of the unauthorized practice of law.

[147] Lingl (2011).

[148] Niemeijer and Pel (2005), p. 362.

[149] Relis (2009), p. 17.

[150] Relis (2009), pp. 103–104.

findings suggest then that garnering experience as a lawyer-mediator may be the best proxy for developing expertise. Much depends on the practice model, however, that the lawyer-mediator acts within. If the model deployed does not encourage lawyer-mediators to shed their well-worn legal gown, or indeed actively promotes the use of their traditional lawyering skills, then such transformation is unlikely to take place.

4.3.9 Gender Issues

I noted above[151] that given that increasing ranks of women have entered the legal profession over recent years in many jurisdictions this may have a bearing on developing a more conducive climate for mediation to flourish within. While studies of women's negotiating behaviour often reveal few differences in their typically styles compared to those of men, there is some evidence suggesting that women generally pursue more cooperative approaches in their negotiations than males.[152] Moreover, it has been theorised that women "are more likely to treat a negotiation as an event in a long-term relationship, one linked to a larger social context and concerned with fairness and sensitivity to others, while men see it as a one-time event with no direct consequences for future interactions", thus fuelling more co-operative behaviour by women.[153]

In terms of whether women (including women lawyers) are more adept in the mediation role, available research is inconclusive. Despite the idea that women may be naturally more inclined towards the consensual, relational and harmonious nature of mediation practice, Goldberg and Shaw's recent work into the traits of successful mediators, found that "[f]emale mediators were not cited [by mediation advocates] significantly more or less often for being friendly and empathic than were male mediators, nor were female mediators cited significantly more or less often for their process or evaluative skills than were their male counterparts."[154] Research into divorce mediation in Georgia, USA in fact found that participants of both genders were generally slightly more positive about male rather than female mediators.[155] Other research, however, has found that female mediators may comport better with the grassroots, facilitative nature of the process. It has been suggested that women are more ideological in their approach towards mediation than their male counterparts, favouring working "more vigorously towards integrative agreements... [and describing] mediation more philosophically and... more

---

[151] At Sect. 4.1.3.

[152] Waters et al. (1998).

[153] Kolb and Putnam (2005), p. 137 (internal citations omitted).

[154] Goldberg and Shaw (2007), p. 406.

[155] Gordon (2002), p. 139.

closely to peacemaking while male mediators tended to describe mediation as an efficient method for handling disputes".[156] Relis's research does provide some evidence that female lawyers are more suited to mediation than males, in the sense that "female attorneys' discourse... evinced greater sensitivity than males to disputants' extralegal needs within the diverse elements of mediation and related litigation."[157] Female attorneys were also more likely to utilise the process in less a tactical fashion than their male peers. Furthermore "female defence lawyers experienced mediation more extralegally than their male counterparts." Finally, plaintiffs tended to hold a higher regard for female defence lawyers compared to male defence lawyers, "remarking on their compassion and understanding".[158]

4.4 Judicial Mediation

Sitting[159] judges can commonly be found acting as mediators in different contexts. They perhaps remain most prominent in civil law jurisdictions in which judges have traditionally enjoyed a 'settlement-master' role within an inquisitorial system of civil justice. It may thus seem a natural progression from this starting point, that on the development of modern mediation schemes within their courts, judges may covet the mediation role. Indeed court-connected mediation in civil law countries often follows what can be termed a 'justice model'[160] in which the court provides litigants with a judge to mediate in-court at no cost. The common law world of court-connected mediation has by contrast been traditionally framed as a 'market model'[161] in which courts refer parties to mediation (with or without their consent), and direct them to an external mediator, perhaps drawn from a list of accredited professionals approved by the court or simply from the market, often at the parties' own cost. In more recent times, however, sitting judges have taken on the mediation role in the common law world too, particularly as initiatives in mediation within the central domain of their courtroom have begun to take root.[162] This development has followed hard on the heels of a rise of civil jurisdiction-style, judicial settlement conferences in the common law world.[163] So it can be said that across the civil law and common law divide, judges often engage in both judicial settlement conferences and also judicial mediation. Such advances in judicial dispute

[156] Gordon (2002), pp. 141–142.

[157] Relis (2009), p. 22.

[158] Relis (2009), p. 23.

[159] Or active (as opposed to retired judges, who densely populate some mediation environments).

[160] Alexander (2006), p. 23.

[161] Alexander (2006), p. 23.

[162] For a review of different judicial mediation schemes across the civil and common law world see Alexander (2009), Chap. 3, fn 13.

[163] See, for example, Galanter (1982); Resnick (1982).

resolution cannot be isolated from the general phenomenon of courts (and judges) wresting greater control from disputing parties in litigation systems in both the civil and common law worlds and the promotion of settlement as a legitimate function of the court.

As a preliminary point, it is useful to distinguish judicial mediation from the more traditional settlement conference role of the judge. Although the two processes may be similar (and in some contexts, in practice, indistinguishable from each other) settlement conferences entail judges leading litigants to a negotiated solution which is unashamedly based upon the legal issues germane to the dispute. That this is so is of little surprise—the conference takes place before an adjudicator of the law within the confines of the courtroom—the very locus from which justice in the formal sense is meted out. Judicial mediation, by contrast may allow for the fostering of wider, facilitative, interest-based resolution of disputes in the classic mould of the process. Unlike the case with settlement conferences, resolution of the legal issues need not necessarily be the focus of the discussions. Whether in practice more holistic approaches are in fact achieved in judicial mediation is a different question though and one discussed below.[164]

4.4.1 *Judges as Mediators*

Given their traditional training and cultural background, in common with lawyers generally, it may be speculated that there may exist a tendency for judge-mediators to be evaluative, directive and narrow in focus in their interpretation of potential settlements. From a mediation purist's position, however, the position of judge-mediator may be even more profoundly troubling than in respect of other legal professionals. While educational exposure may help eradicate unhelpful, lawyerly practises in mediation, it is arguably that the same will be insufficient to save the process when judges mediate. This is so, the argument follows, because whatever the adeptness of judges as mediators, their status may tarnish their role as mediator in the eyes of clients and their legal representatives. Judges' typical authority over others who come before them and general adjudicatory role may, in particular, skew participants' perceptions of the mediation process and the role of the mediator therein. Standard discourse in mediation suggests that although mediators should have authority, they should ration their use of such authority and pepper it with diplomacy and humility. Simon Roberts has eloquently written on the topic: "[t]he judge who attempts to mediate enjoys, whether he likes it or not, an authority which is in no way derived from his association with the values seen to underlie mediation. Courts are places where other people tell us what to do... judges are such people.

[164] The European Directive on Mediation (recital 12, article 3) recognises the distinction between judicial mediation and more traditional settlement functions, mainly on the basis that mediating judges are precluded from subsequently adjudicating the matter.

The adjudicator represents a neutral superior, seen to hand down an imposed decision... This in itself is going to colour the way in which mediatory intervention by... judges is perceived by disputants... The authority is inevitably going to make disputants more disposed than they might otherwise be to follow their suggestions and be receptive to their persuasion".[165]

To limit such "contamination" of the mediation process, in most (but not all) judicial mediation schemes a different judge will consequently adjudicate the matter if the case does not settle. It is contended that a system in which the same judge will both mediate and consequently adjudicate the same case is especially problematic both in the sense that it may stifle parties' candour in the mediation and, more worryingly, lead to judges consciously or subconsciously making use of information gleaned in the mediation at the consequent trial thus undermining the integrity of the court and basic rules of procedural justice.[166] Equally, it may raise further issues of procedural justice in that judges concurrently mediating and adjudicating cases may tarnish the court's obligation to determine the law in a fair objective manner and in accordance with due process. Nevertheless, while dictating that mediating judges should never consequently try the same case has merits,[167] it has been contended that, *per se*, this is insufficient to preserve the purity of the mediation process; by dint of the office of the judge, mediator contamination has already occurred.[168]

Not all commentators would see such 'contamination' in a negative light but rather view the judges' background, experience and standing as a boon for the process. Particularly in respect of in-court judicial mediation programmes, with their emphasis upon driving settlement and procuring efficiency,[169] the leverage judges are able to exercise is seen as positive element of their involvement in the process. Ross Cranston QC has pointed to the "advantages that the courtroom setting impresses upon the participants, most notably the clients, that they are involved in proceedings of some dignity, and, as importantly, that they will be subject to a full-blown trial if they do not settle; that the judge can express a greyer view of the matter than the optimistic advice of the lawyers; that the less confrontational setting of a mediation can give the parties a chance to explain themselves directly to a judge, who can help them find a graceful way to acknowledge the

---

[165] Roberts (1993), pp. 555–556.

[166] See for example, Cratsley (2005).

[167] For criticism of 'med-arb' schemes in which a judge or arbitrator will consequently adjudicate a dispute in the event that their attempts at mediation have not been successful, see Newman (1994), pp. 173–178. Some commentators believe that sitting judges who mediate should not necessarily be precluded from adjudicating the same case subsequently at trial, not least for reasons of efficiency, in particular if the parties consent—see for example, Polster (2007). Additionally, in the civil law world, judges, such as those in Germany, who engage in settlement practices often consequently adjudicate the dispute—see Alexander (2009), p. 6.

[168] Roberts (1993), p. 556.

[169] Not to mention the arguable need to procure settlements reflective of legal norms. See the discussion in Chap. 5 at Sect. 5.3.

wisdom of making some concession; and that because of judicial time is valuable, the judge-mediator necessarily demands that the parties prepare carefully for the mediation in advance and get to the point earlier than might be the case with a private mediator".[170] Of course, this view represents a very narrow and lawyerly view of mediating, with its emphasis upon judges expressing "greyer" views on the merits of disputes, and the 'precious time' of the judge prevailing upon parties to get to the nub of the issues, and hence towards settlement, at a quicker stage than may otherwise be the case. The latter issue is predicated on the view that expediting settlement is the desired aim and that process elements, such as party empowerment, venting and expression of feelings are of less import.

Given judges' predilections for referring to the legal norms relative to the disputes they are mediating, some commentators also perceive judicial mediators (in the same way as lawyer-mediators generally) as an antidote to 'justice' concerns over mediation[171]; particularly in respect of those sessions involving in-court, *pro-se* parties or those for whom mediation was *de facto* the only option.[172] Judicial mediation may also provide disputants with a 'day in court' of sorts at least, which may be beyond the gift of private mediators.[173] Equally, however, judicial mediation may be seen as incompatible with the traditional function of judges within courts, causing a dilution of the court's (and hence judges') public duty to mete out justice in society. The reality of a judge's public office may also dictate that some common mediation traits should remain out of bounds. For example, caucusing and other meetings with private parties may be problematic for the judicial mediator because given the covert nature of discussions therein, in the words of Hon Marilyn Warren AC, Chief Justice of Victoria they may "jeopardise the independence and dignity of the judicial office."[174]

4.4.2 Empirical Evidence

What then do we know about judicial mediation schemes? Is there evidence that the theoretical concerns of Roberts and his ilk have 'contaminated' the process? While it is at times difficult to distinguish clearly between judicial mediation and other, more traditional judicial settlement measures (not least because the nomenclature used is often loose), lawyers generally appear to hold favourable views on such activities. As Judge Cratsley has noted in respect of various US studies from 1984 to 2005, "[w]hile the views of the bar about judicial settlement activity are not

[170] Cranston (2007), p. 204 reflecting on the views of the Vice-Chancellor of the Delaware Court of Chancery set out in Strine (2003), p. 591.

[171] Discussed in Chap. 5 at Sects. 5.2.5.1 and 5.3.3.

[172] See for example, Brady (2007).

[173] See Polster (2007).

[174] Warren (2009), p. 5.

uniform or consistent from state to state, they are far more positive than negative".[175] Similarly, Nadia Alexander has recently pointed to significant research across the common law world revealing that lawyers usually favour judicial mediation.[176] Some evidence also exists suggesting that clients prefer judicial mediators, to their non-judicial counterparts.[177] Nonetheless, in other contexts, judicial mediation, when it has been a voluntary process at least, has failed to attract the attention of potential users.[178]

Research into the views of US attorneys on mediators with judicial experiences and those with no such experience suggests that judicial and non-judicial mediators are recruited for the particular, respective skills or qualities each bring to the table. The study revealed that judicial mediators[179] are seen to be effective primarily because of their abilities to provide case evaluations, whereas non-judicial mediators were generally seen to be effective in view of their process skills.[180] The results suggest then that parties and their lawyers may select mediators (where they have the choice) in line with their own normative preferences for mediator behaviour. In this sense, one is not necessarily superior to the other but each offers something distinct to the market.

Evidence exists suggesting that judge-mediators do in practice tend to cut to the quick in mediation compared to other mediators. One US study compared the practices of sitting judges who mediate with retired judge–mediators, finding that sitting judges devoted generally less time to mediation than their retired counterparts. Moreover, they generally focused less on such wider goals of mediation such as reconciling the parties and party empowerment than retired judges with prevalence being placed on expediting settlement.[181] Similar findings have been found in German research.[182] Perceptions of coercion in judicial mediation may be inevitable. They are prevalent in other forms of judicial dispute resolution. In the US context it has been stated that "counsel from several state judicial conduct organizations have reported receiving complaints of judicial coercion and intimidation in settlement conferences."[183] Concerns have also been voiced regarding the lack of established behavioural norms and ethical rules governing judicial settlement practices, particularly to help ward off undue judicial pressure placed upon

[175] Cratsley (2005), fn 11.

[176] Alexander (2009), Chap. 3, fn 15.

[177] Robinson (2006), p. 351.

[178] For example, in the English context, the spectacular failure of the judicial mediation scheme in the Technology and Construction Court—see Goswami (2007); a Judicial mediation pilot in the context of Employment Tribunals in England Wales has also largely been seen as a failure—see Rayner (2010).

[179] It should be noted that these were former judges rather than sitting judges.

[180] Goldberg et al. (2009).

[181] Burns (1998), p. 363, cited in Alexander (2009), p. 11.

[182] Warwel (2007), pp. 124–133, cited in Alexander (2009), p. 11.

[183] Cratsley (2005), p. 13.

parties to settle.[184] Harking back to the notion that some disputing parties seek direction from their mediators, interestingly, there is evidence from some studies that some judges have been all too quick to shed their judicial robes. Research into judicial mediation in the context of Employment Tribunals in England and Wales revealed that some clients viewed judge-mediators as too 'detached' when a more interventionist approach was preferred.[185]

4.5 Conclusion

It is beyond doubt that significant evidence exists in practice that the interaction of lawyers in the mediation process, both acting as mediators and as party representatives, may have diluted the purity of certain fundamental aspects of mediation, namely: parties' active participation in the process and self-determination of settlement options; the development of creative, interest-based options for mutual gain; and expansion of norms upon which settlement is based beyond legal parameters. Nevertheless, the benefits of lawyer-mediators and lawyer representatives are equally apparent. First, lawyers may possess many of the skills and qualities sought of mediators generally in its classic facilitative guise. Training and education, which has expanded and gained sophistication across the globe, will further assist lawyers (and others) to develop their nous in the field. More importantly and controversially perhaps, lawyers may bring to the table skills, abilities and behaviours, which although might appear strikingly at odds with the ethos of the original vision of mediation, may in fact serve to undergird the process in the legal sense and eradicate some of its perceived weaknesses. We should, of course, be wary when it is lawyers who seek out such attributes in mediators or espouse such values in lawyer-representatives. This is so not least because we may suspect that lawyers' agendas in this regard may at times be serve-serving and not commensurate with that of their own clients in the process. Nonetheless, it is indisputable that in practice clients themselves often seek out what lawyers can offer in mediation. Participants within mediation may value legal information and advice from mediators and seek evaluations as to their legal position. They may feel protected and emboldened by the presence of a lawyer. Clients may prefer a 'day in court' with a judge mediating their case.

While some might argue that such desires emanate from a fundamental misunderstanding of the mediation process (which it is true may be perpetrated by lawyers) the matter is more nuanced than this argument suggests. Yes, 'pure' mediation is a hard sell for clients in dispute. Much more needs to be done in terms of education and promotion throughout the legal profession, business

[184] See Cratsley (2011).

[185] Urwin et al. (2010), pp. 44–46.

community and society in general, so that the promise of mediation becomes more compelling. Equally, clients may in fact reap much more than they perceive is possible from participation in a 'pure' mediation process unblemished by the trappings of lawyers. While this may be so, particularly in circumstances in which mediation is linked to formal legal dispute resolution processes, arguments in favour of lawyer presence and an advocating of the 'contamination' they bring become more compelling. It should not surprise us that a clamour for the bleeding of law and lawyers into mediation in this context exists. When mediation enters mainstream legal disputing environments a balance between preserving purity in the process and recognising the environment within which we now find it, has to be struck.

References

Agapiou, Clark (2011) An investigation of Scottish construction industry participants views on, and experiences of mediation (Unpublished, on file with the author)

Alexander N (2006) Introduction. In: Alexander N (ed) Global trends in mediation, 2nd edn. Kluwer International, Alphen aan den Rijn

Alexander N (2009) International and comparative mediation: legal perspectives. Kluwer International, Alphen aan den Rijn

American Bar Association Section of Dispute Resolution (2008) Task force on improving mediation quality. Final report. http://www.abanet.org/dch/committee.cfm?com=DR020600. Accessed 1 Nov 2011

Barry R, Henaghan M (1986) Mediation in the family court. Family Law Bull 1:84

Brady A (2007) Court mediation scheme: a cause for Concern Law Society Gazette 25 October. http://www.rougemontchambers.co.uk/newsletters/article-courtmediationscheme.html. Accessed 1 Nov 2011

Brooker P (2005) Construction lawyers' experience with mediation post-CPR. Construct Law J 21(1):19–46

Brooker P (2008) An investigation into evaluative and facilitative approaches to construction mediation. Struct Surv 25(3/4):220–238

Brown N et al (2005–2006) The purported rigidity of an attorney's personality: can legal ethics be acquired? J Legal Prof 30: 55–78

Brusegard D (2004) The implications of demographic change in the legal profession. Canadian Bar Association. http://cba.org/CBA/futures/pdf/demographics_feb04.pdf. Accessed 1 Nov 2011

Bucklow A (2007) The "everywhen" mediator: the virtues of inconsistency and paradox: the strengths, skills, attributes and behaviours of excellent and effective mediators. Arbitration 73(1):40–48

Burns S (1998) The name of the game is movement: concession seeking in judicial mediation of large money damages cases. Mediation Q 15:359–371

Clark B, Dawson C (2007) Scottish commercial litigators and ADR: a study of attitudes and experience. Civ Justice Q 26:228–249

Coope S, Morris S (2002) Personal *Injury Litigation*. Negotiation and settlement. HMSO, Edinburgh

Cranston R (2007) Complex litigation: the commercial court. Civ Justice Q 26:190–207

Cratsley JC (2005) Judicial ethics and judicial settlement practices: time for two strangers to meet. http://www.americanbar.org/content/dam/aba/migrated/judicialethics/resources/comm_rules_Cratsley_51605_ddt.authcheckdam.pdf. Accessed 1 Nov 2011

Cratsley JC (2011) Judges and settlement: so little regulation and so much at stake. Dispute Resolut Mag 17(3):4–7

Currie C (2000) Should a mediator also be an attorney? http://www.mediate.com/articles/currie.cfm. Accessed 1 Nov 2011

Daicoff S (1997) Lawyer know thyself: a review of empirical research on attorney attributes bearing on professionalism. Am Univ Law Rev 46:1337–1427

Duve H (2008) Verfahrensdesign – Alternativen zum Dispute Board. Baurecht 39(10):1531–40

Eekelaar J et al (2000) Family lawyers: the divorce work of solicitors. Hart Publishing, Oxford

Enterkin J, Sefton M (2006) An evaluation of the exeter small claims mediation scheme. Executive summary. http://www.dca.gov.uk/research/2006/10_2006excsum.pdf. Accessed 1 Nov 2011

Flood J, Caiger A (1993) Lawyers and arbitration: the juridification of construction disputes. Modern Law Rev 56:412–440

Galanter M (1982) The emergence of the judge as a mediator in civil cases. Judicature 69:257–262

Genn H (1987) Hard bargaining: out of court settlements in personal injury actions. Clarendon Press, Oxford

Golan D (2000) Variations in mediation: how-and why-legal mediators change styles in the course of a case. J Dispute Resolut 2000:41–62

Goldberg SB, Shaw M (2007) The secrets of successful (and unsuccessful) mediators continued: studies two and three. Negot J 23(4):393–418

Goldberg SB et al (2009) What difference does a robe make? comparing mediators with and without prior judicial experience. Negot J 25(3):277–305

Goldfien J, Robbennolt J (2007) What if lawyers have their way? an empirical assessment of conflict strategies and attitudes towards mediation styles. Ohio State J Dispute Resolut 22:277–319

Gordon E (2002) What role does gender play in mediation of domestic relations cases? Judicature 86(3):134–143

Goswami N (2007) Judges told to stick to the day job as mediation pilot fails. The Lawyer. http://www.thelawyer.com/judges-told-to-stick-to-the-day-job-as-mediation-pilot-fails/126749.article. Accessed 1 Nov 2011

Greatbatch D, Dingwall R (1990) Selective facilitation: some preliminary observations on a strategy used by divorce mediators. Fam Court Rev 28(1):53–64

Grillo T (1991) The mediation alternative: process dangers for women. Yale Law J 100: 1545–1610

Grima F, Paille P (2011) Mediation in professional relationships in France: tactics and outcomes. Ind Relat J 42(5):428–452

Guthrie C (2001) The lawyer's philosophical map and the disputant's perceptive map: impediments to facilitative mediation and lawyering. Harvard Negot Law Rev 6:145–188

Heumann M, Hyman J (1997) Negotiation methods and litigation settlement methods in New Jersey: 'You Can't Always Get What You Want'. Ohio State J Dispute Resolut 12:253–310

Hillig J, Huhn M (2010) Construction mediation in Germany. In: Brooker P, Wilkinson S (eds) Mediation in the construction industry: an international review. Spon Press, London

Hoffman D (2003) A primer on successful negotiation. http://www.bostonlawcollaborative.com/blc/205BLC/version/default/part/AttachmentData/data/2005-07-negotiation-primer.pdf?branch=main&language=default. Accessed 1 Nov 2011

Howell R (2005) How lawyers negotiate. Unpublished PhD thesis, University of Technology, Sydney (On file with the author)

Howieson J (2002) Perceptions of procedural justice and legitimacy in local court mediation. Murdoch Univ Electron J Law 9(2):13

Kolb DM, Putnam LL (2005) Negotiation through a gender lense. In: Moffitt ML, Bordone RC (eds) The handbook of dispute resolution. Jossey Bass, San Francisco

Kovach K, Love LP (1998) Mapping mediation: the risks of Riskin's grid. Harvard Negot Law Rev 3:71–110

Kressel K (2007) The strategic style in mediation. Conflict Resolut Q 24:251–283

Kuhner TK (2005) Court connected mediation compared: the cases of Argentina and the United States. ILSA J Int Comp Law 11:520–556

Lande J (1998) Lawyers' routine participation directs shape of liti-mediation. Alternative High Cost Litigat 16:53–62

Lande J (2000) Towards more sophisticated mediation theory. J Dispute Resolut 2000:321–334

Lande J (2008) Doing the best mediation you can. Dispute Resolut Mag 14(3). http://www.law.missouri.edu/lande/publications/Lande%20Doing%20Best%20Mediation%20You%20Can.pdf. Accessed 1 Nov 2011

Lingl JP (2011) Relative effectiveness of mediators and lawyer-mediators in a Court Annexed Mediation Programme. http://www.mediate.com/pdf/MediatedCaseDataStudy.pdf. Accessed 1 Nov 2011

Love L (1997) The top ten reasons why mediators should not evaluate. Florida State Rev 24:937–948

Macfarlane J (2001) Culture change? Commercial litigators and the Ontario Mandatory Mediation Programme. http://dsp-psd.pwgsc.gc.ca/collection_2008/lcc-cdc/JL2-70-2001E.pdf. Accessed 1 Nov 2011

Macfarlane J (2008) The new lawyer: how settlement is transforming the practice of law. UBS Press, Toronto

Maharg P et al (2003) Minority and social diversity in legal education. Scottish Government. http://www.scotland.gov.uk/Publications/2003/03/16713/19583. Accessed 1 Nov 2011

Mantle M (2008) Report on the findings of small claims mediation project in Edinburgh Sheriff Court (Unpublished, on file with the author)

Mays R, Clark B (1996) Alternative dispute resolution in Scotland. Scottish Office Central Research Unit, Edinburgh

McAdoo B (2002) A report to the Minnesota supreme court: the impact of rule 114 on civil litigation practice in Minnesota. Hamline Law Rev 25:401–477

McAdoo B (2004) The judicial perspective on Rule 114 in Minnesota. Report to the ADR Review Board

McAdoo B, Welsh N (1997) Does ADR really have a place on the lawyer's philosophical map? Hamline J Public Law Pol 18:376–391

McDermott P, Obar R (2004) What's going on in mediation: an empirical analysis of the influence of the mediator's style on party satisfaction and monetary benefit. Harvard Negot Law Rev 9:75–114

McEwen C et al (1995) Bring in the lawyers: challenging the dominant approaches to ensuring fairness in divorce mediation. Minnesota Law Rev 79:1307–1411

Melville A, Laing K (2010) Closing the gate: family lawyers as gatekeepers to a holistic service. Int J Law Context 6(2):167–189

Menkel-Meadow C (1985) Portia in a different voice: speculations on a women's lawyering process. Berkeley Women Law J 1:39–63

Menkel-Meadow C (2004) Is the adversary system really dead? dilemmas of legal ethics as legal institutions and roles evolve. Curr Leg Probl 57(1):85–115

Mulcahy L (2001) Can leopards change their spots: the role of lawyers in mediation. International Journal of the Legal Profession 8(3): 203–224

Murayama M (1999) Does a lawyer make a difference? effects of a lawyer on mediation outcome in Japan. Int J Law Pol Family 13:52–77

Myers F, Wasoff F (2000) Meeting in the middle*: a* study of solicitors' and mediators' divorce practice, legal studies research findings No 25. Scottish Executive Central Research Unit, Edinburgh

Nelken L (2005) The myth of the gladiator and law students' negotiation styles. Cardoza J Conflict Resolut 7:1–25

Newman P (1994) The MED-ARB debate: some contributions. Arbitration 60(3):173–183

Ng P (2011) The use of mediation in preventing homelessness in England. Int J Law Built Environ 3(2):146–159

Niemeijer B, Pel M (2005) Court-based mediation in the Netherlands: research, evaluation and future expectations. Penn State Law Rev 110:345–379

Onn, L.S. (2006) Singapore: Non Court Annexed Mediation. International Bar Association Mediation Newsletter 2:1

Peters D (2011) Understanding why lawyers resist mediation. Paper presented at 2nd Asian Mediation Conference, 24–25 February 2011, Kuala Lumpur

Pollack C (2007) The role of the mediation advocate: a user's guide to mediation. Arbitration 73(1):20–23

Polster DA (2007) The trial judge as mediator: a rejoinder to Judge Cratsley. The Mayhew-Hite Report on Dispute Resolution and the Courts. http://www.mediate.com/articles/polsterD1.cfm. Accessed 1 Nov 2011

Rayner J (2010) Judicial mediation in Employment Tribunal cases falls short Law Society Gazette. http://www.lawgazette.co.uk/news/judicial-mediation-employment-tribunal-cases-falls-short. Accessed 1 Nov 2011

Relis T (2009) Perceptions in litigation and mediation: lawyers, defendants, plaintiffs, and gendered parties. Cambridge University Press, New York

Resnick J (1982) Managerial judges. Harv Law Rev 96:374–448

Riskin L (1982) Mediation and lawyers. Ohio State Law J 43:29–60

Riskin L (1996) Understanding mediators' orientations, strategies and techniques: a guide for the perplexed. Harvard Negot Law Rev 1:7–51

Riskin L (2002) The contemplative lawyer: on the potential contributions of mindfulness meditation to law students, lawyers and their clients. Harvard Negot Law Rev 7(2):1–66

Riskin L (2003) Decisionmaking in mediation: the new old grid and the new new grid system. Notre Dame Law Rev 79(1):37–46

Roberts S (1992) Mediation in the lawyer's embrace. Modern Law Rev 55:258–264

Roberts S (1993) Mediation in family disputes. Modern Law Rev 46:537–557

Robinson P (2006) Adding judicial mediation to the debate about judges attempting to settle cases assigned to them for trial. J Dispute Resolut 2:335

Rosen R (2002) We're all consultants now: how changes in client organizational strategies influences change in the organization of corporate legal services. Arizona Law Rev 44:637–683

Rosenberg J (1991) In defense of mediation. Arizona Law Rev 33:467–507

Rueben R (2000) Constitutional gravity: a unitary theory of alternative dispute resolution and public civil justice. UCLA Law Rev 47:949–1104

Rundle O (2008) Barking dogs: lawyer attitudes to direct disputant participation in court-connected mediation of general civil cases. Queensland Univ Technol Law Justice J 8(1):77–92

Sarat A, Felstiner W (1997) Divorce lawyers and their clients: power and meaning in the legal process. Oxford University Press, New York

Saville-Smith K, Fraser R (2004) Alternative dispute resolution: general civil cases. New Zealand Ministry of Justice, Welligton

Schneider AK (2002) Shattering negotiation myths: empirical evidence on the effectiveness of negotiation styles. Harvard Negot Law Rev 7:143–233

Schneider AK, Mills N (2006) What family lawyers are really doing when they negotiate. Family Court Rev 44:612–622

Sela A (2009) Attorneys' perspectives of mediation: an empirical analysis of attorneys' mediation referral practices, barriers and potential agency problems, and their effect on mediation in Israel. Unpublished MSc thesis, Stanford Law School (on file with the author)

Sommerlad H et al (2010) Diversity in the legal profession in England Wales: a qualitative study of barriers and individual choices. Legal Services Board. http://www.legalservicesboard.org.uk/what_we_do/Research/Publications/pdf/lsb_diversity_in_the_legal_profession_final.pdf. Accessed 1 Nov 2011

Stemple JW (2000) Identifying real dichotomies underlying the false dichotomy, twenty-first century mediation in an eclectic regime. J Dispute Resolut 2000:371–394

Stipanowich T (1996) Beyond arbitration: innovation and evolution in the United States construction industry. Wake Forest Law Rev 31(1):65–182

Strine L (2003) 'Mediation only' Filings in the Delaware court of chancery: can new value be added by one of America's business courts? Duke Law J 53:585–596

Urwin et al (2010) Evaluating the use of mediation in Employment Tribunals. Ministry of Justice Research Series 7/10. http://www.justice.gov.uk/publications/docs/evaluating-judicial-mediation-march10.pdf. Accessed 1 Nov 2011

Van Winkle J (2001) Mediation: a path back for the lost lawyer. American Bar Association, Chicago

Vindelov V (2006) Mediation in Danish Law: in retrospect and perspective. In: Alexander N (ed) Global trends in mediation, 2nd edn. Kluwer International, Alphen aan den Rijn

Waldman E (1997) Identifying the role of social norms in mediation: a multiple model approach. Hastings Law J 48:703–769

Warren M (2009) ADR and a different approach to mediation. Law Institute of Victoria Serving up Insights Series Speech. http://www.supremecourt.vic.gov.au/wps/wcm/connect/justlib/Supreme+Court/resources/8/f/8fb3cb004056e0f5a68abee505682c73/ADR+and+a+different+approach+to+litigation_CJ.pdf. Accessed 1 Nov 2011

Waters AE et al (1998) Gender and negotiator competitiveness: a meta-analysis. Organ Behav Hum Decis 76:1–29

Warwel D (2007) Gerichtsnahe Mediation: Empirische Untersuchung der Verhaltens- und Vorgehensweisen von Richtermediatoren in Gerichtsnahen Mediationsverfahren. Lit Verlag, Berlin

Welsh N (2001) The thinning vision of self-determination: the inevitable price of institutionalization? Harvard Negot Law Rev 6:1–96

Wilder GZ (2003) The road to law school and beyond: examining challenges to racial and ethnic diversity in the legal profession. American Bar Association. http://www.lsac.org/LsacResources/Research/RR/RR-02-01.pdf. Accessed 1 Nov 2011

Williams G (1983) Legal negotiation and settlement. West Publishing, Minnesota

Wissler RL (2001) Evaluate or facilitate? A.B.A Dispute Resolut Mag 35

Wissler RL (2002) Court-connected mediation in general civil cases: what we know from empirical research. Ohio State J Dispute Resolut 17:641–703

Chapter 5
The Fusing of Mediation, Lawyers and Legal Systems

5.1 Introduction

Drawing on some key themes developed in preceding parts of this book, this chapter explores a number of complex and contested issues arising from the yoking of mediation to the legal system and the injection of lawyers into the process. With a focus on court-connected mediation, I examine the impact that mediation's repositioning from the outside to the centre of traditional, legal disputing practices has had on the process itself as well as the consequences the same may hold for formal, legal civil justice. To what extent lawyers and the law do and should play a role within mediation in the institutionalised context is also explored.

5.2 Mediation and Civil Justice Concerns

There has been much consternation and gnashing of teeth over the issue of mediation's place within the civil court context. As noted in Chap. 2,[1] fundamental critiques of mediation which emanate from the fusing of mediation with traditional civil justice systems include 'justice' concerns emanating from the replacement of court adjudication with informal processes and the inadequacy of such forums to protect the weak and disempowered. Waves of criticism have also battered the shores of mediation in respect of the suppression of public norms and eradication of judicial precedents and hence legal development caused by an increasing usurping of formal adjudication by private settlement mechanisms. Prior to exploring these issues and to provide a little context to the ensuing analysis, I will first set out an examination of the how and why of mediation's embedding within formal civil justice regimes.

[1] At Sect. 2.1.

B. Clark, *Lawyers and Mediation*, DOI 10.1007/978-3-642-23474-3_5,

5.2.1 *The Shifting of Mediation into the Mainstream*

5.2.1.1 The 'How' of Institutionalisation

In Chap. 1 I mapped out some of the ways that mediation has moved from the fringes into the mainstream of the civil disputing arenas across jurisdictions globally. Mediation may become linked to the litigation process by a number of means. First, mediation may be compulsory—either as a matter of course in certain types of action, for example, as found in Argentina[2] and provided for in recent reforms to the Italian civil court system[3] or at the behest of judges who may retain the right to mandate that disputing parties mediate in particular cases they consider amenable to the process. Mandatory mediation in its different guises is commonplace across the world, found for example, in many US states, in Australia and New Zealand and in parts of South America, and sanctioned (although not mandated) by the recent EU Directive on Mediation.[4] Shy of mandating mediation attendance itself, in other circumstances, parties may be compelled to at least attend compulsory mediation information or 'intake' sessions.[5] A further common way in which mediation may be promoted by courts in jurisdictions in which fee shifting regimes operate (i.e. 'loser pays' systems[6]), which may amount to compulsion 'by the back door', is that an 'unreasonable refusal' to mediate may result in cost penalties awarded against the party concerned.[7] Other financial imperatives, such as rendering an attempt at mediating a prerequisite for eligibility of legal aid or providing tax breaks[8] for mediated settlements may also be used to encourage use. Court fees may also be waived for mediating parties.[9]

In other instances judges may be empowered by specific court rules to refer parties to mediation (i.e. suggest but not mandate that they mediate).[10] Judges may

---

[2] Law nr 24.573 of April 24, 1996 in which mediation became a mandatory first step in cases heard before the Civil and Commercial Courts.

[3] Legislative Decree n. 28/2010.

[4] See Chap. 1 at Sect. 1.2.

[5] From April 2011 divorcing spouses in England and Wales have been compelled to attend an information session on mediation prior to proceeding with their case through the court. See Practice Direction 3a- Pre-action Protocol for Mediation Information and Assessment—http://webarchive.nationalarchives.gov.uk/+/http://www.justice.gov.uk/news/announcement230211a.htm Accessed 1 November 2011. At the time of writing it is proposed to expand this provision to general, non-family civil cases as well as compulsory mediation in small claims—Ministry of Justice 2011, para 25.

[6] Also known as the "English Rule". With the notable exception of the USA, this approach is generally the norm.

[7] Such as has developed in England and Wales under the Civil Procedural Rules 1998—for a review of the case law see generally Shipman (2006).

[8] Found, for example in Italy under Article 20 of Decree 28.

[9] As in Romania—See Romanian Civil Procedure Code 271, Law 192/2006, Articles 62, 63.

[10] In my own jurisdiction such rules have existed for some time empowering judges to suggest mediation in matrimonial actions.

also be equipped to delay cases pending mediation to comply with limitation of claims rules. In some jurisdictions, lawyers may be placed under obligations by professional or court rules to point up the possibility, and discuss the use of mediation with their clients and/or opposing counsel.[11] Additionally, statutory dispute resolution processes in, for example, areas such as planning, employment and education may either provide for, or mandate use of mediation as a step in the prescribed procedure. Statutory consumer dispute schemes also commonly mandate or provide for the use of mediation.[12]

5.2.1.2 The 'Why' of Institutionalisation

In terms of why mediation has gained such prominence within formal justice systems, it is worth recalling the discussion in Chap. 1 setting out the American efficiency proponents' agenda for mediation in the Pound conference era.[13] In short, there was a stark realisation that American civil courts had become blighted by crippling delays and costs to the point that the system was in crisis. A perception arose that this malaise had at least in part been caused by an upsurge in litigious behaviour fuelled by aggressive, adversarial lawyering, and that other, more harmonious ways of resolving disputes should be promoted.[14] Such promotion, not least, would 'save' the civil justice system from itself.[15]

Most other court-based developments in mediation across the globe have in fact emanated largely from such an 'efficiency' priority rather than any particular deep-seated appreciation of mediation *per se*. For example, civil justice reviews across the common law world in countries such as England and Wales, and Hong Kong have promoted the use of mediation at least in part as to alleviate significant costs and delays inherent in their civil court systems.[16] Civil law countries have also looked to mediation as a remedy for struggling court systems: witness, for example, the recent reforms to Italian civil justice with mediation held up as an antidote to the exorbitant delays of the system.[17] Similarly in the Netherlands the final report of

[11] Such as Rule 17 in Missouri—see McAdoo and Hinshaw (2002).

[12] Such schemes are common in the EU—Alleweldt et al. (2009).

[13] See Chap. 1 at Sect. 1.1.

[14] To what extent the 'litigation explosion' in the USA was a myth has been hotly contested –see Galanter (1985).

[15] Although as noted in Chap. 1, many Pound Conference participants were keen to stress the importance of retaining access to justice for all parties, including those diverted into new, alternative programmes, Welsh and McAdoo (2005), pp. 401–405.

[16] Woolf (1996), para 9 (England and Wales); Chief Justice's Working Party on Civil Justice Reform 2004, section 29 (Hong Kong).

[17] Under legislative decree n. 28/2010: D.Lgs. 4-3-2010 n. 28, "Attuazione dell'articolo 60 della legge 18 giugno 2009, n. 69, in materia di mediazione finalizzata alla conciliazione delle controversie civili e commerciali", Italian Official Journal, March 5, 2010, n. 53.

the Platform ADR project of the Ministry of Justice promoted mediation as way to curb overly litigious behaviour on the part of the citizens and help alleviate court loads.[18] In a like fashion, mediation was rendered mandatory for most litigants in Buenos Aires[19] not least to eradicate crippling case loads. Court-connected developments hence often have aims which are tied closely to the economic wellbeing of the formal justice system.[20] Evaluations of in-court projects may thus focus on establishing whether mediation wipes in feet in monetary terms and/or whether it saves judicial and administrative time rather than whether, in qualitative terms, mediation benefits participants or produces better outcomes.[21] In-court mediators may work under pressure to meet settlement targets. By virtue of such goals, settlement and economic efficiency may become overarching aims, with the quality dimensions to such schemes receiving less attention. This is an important issue not least because many of the key benefits which participants may derive from mediation may be lost in an efficiency-driven species of the process—a point developed below.

5.2.2 The Backdrop to Justice Concerns

Most concerns pertaining to the lack of 'justice' found within mediation arise in the context of mandatory referral to the process, or where funding imperatives or a lack of viable alternatives renders mediation *de facto* mandatory for participants. It should be noted that anti-justice assaults have particularly been levied against mediation because, as described above, the process has at times been held out by judges and policy-makers as an antidote for the ills of civil justice systems, crippled by access problems, exorbitant party and state costs, and lengthy delays. Mediation has become a target not least then because a perception has arisen that it is some sort of sticking plaster for the deep wounds that successive lack of public investment has been inflicted upon civil justice systems. In turn this has fuelled a trenchant defence of traditional, adjudicative civil justice systems and the rule of law generally, with mediation cast as the villain of the piece.

While my own view (which I shall elaborate below) is that much of the above criticism is in fact misguided, mediation aficionados are themselves at least partially to blame for the skewering that their beloved process has received from

[18] See the final report: Platform ADR (1998).

[19] By virtue of the Mediation and Conciliation Law—Ley de Mediación y Conciliación [Mediation and Conciliation Law], Law No. 24.573, Oct. 25, 1995, [28258] Boletín Oficial [B.O.] 1 (Arg.). See also Kuhner (2005), p. 29.

[20] Boulle (2000), p. 5; Alexander (2004), p. 17. A separate but related issue is the fact that in-court mediation may have to reflect the aims of formal civil justice systems, discussed below at Sect. 5.3.

[21] Although the evidence is mixed—see Chap. 2 at Sect. 2.6 for a discussion of parties' costs in mediation.

critics. History tells us that faced with a lack of demand for services, grass roots mediation enthusiasts in the USA were quick to abandon their 'alternative', background locale in the arena of dispute resolution and accept the shot in the arm that courts could give their programmes.[22] Allied to this is the notion that mediation as a process may inherently look weak because it often seems that in its voluntary, extra-judicial form, it is generally an unwanted commodity. While this cannot really be disputed—when purely voluntary, the take up of mediation across different jurisdictions and dispute contexts is very often modest—there is certainly a case to be made for mediation promotion nonetheless. This is so because mediation is a rare beast in which the reality may be better than the fantasy. By this I mean that what the process seems to offer to those in the midst of a dispute may pale into insignificance to what is actually experienced (or at least may be potentially experienced) within mediation.[23] Evidence suggests that given the potentially profound impact of the mediation experience, even the most recalcitrant and cynical participants—both lawyers and clients—often walk away from the process satisfied. Nonetheless, there may be an irresistible attraction to the argument that if participants are not queuing up to sample mediation's wares then *ipso facto* there must be deficiencies in the process itself.

Mediation has often been painted as providing second class justice for the disenfranchised in society. In the USA, for example, such views were buoyed by the historical social context against which mediation took root in the civil justice system. Very often it seemed to be cases of a perceived lesser import, in legal or financial terms, mostly involving the poor and disenfranchised that were diverted into newly developed court-connected mediation or other ADR schemes. So, in the aftermath of Pound, "[a]lternative processes suddenly became a panacea for the resolution of consumer disputes, prisoners' grievances, problems of juveniles and the elderly, and the claims of Indians and Eskimos".[24] In the eyes of some, courts were using mediation and other informal dispute resolution mechanisms to 'bin their garbage'. The political context against which such developments were taking place should not be forgotten. In particular, post-Pound developments in court-connected mediation and diversion from the civil courts often took place against a backdrop of recently won legal rights for minorities, the vulnerable and less powerful in society. These hard fought legal gains now appeared to be placed into abeyance as those seeking reliance on the same were corralled into alternatives such as mediation within which rights assertion was not paramount. One of the most articulate critics, Laura Nader noted that within mediation, claims were reframed through a 'harmony'[25] lens into non-legal disputes to be resolved through discus-

[22] See Chap. 1 at Sect. 1.1.2.

[23] See the evidence discussed in Chap. 2 in Sects. 2.6 and 2.7.

[24] Auerbach (1983), p. 124.

[25] Nader (1993), p. 3.

sion and compromise to the detriment of parties seeking rights enforcement.[26] Some suspected profound, cynical forces at play. Auerbach, for example, wryly observed that "[n]othing, it seemed, propelled enthusiasm for alternative dispute settlement like a few legal victories that unsettled an equilibrium of privilege".[27] In this context then, it may have been inevitable that mediation became infected by a rights-suppression discourse. Far from empowering individuals and freeing them from the shackles of political power exercised through law, mediation can in this light rather be seen as a vehicle of state social control to ensure that the disempowered in society remain in their place firmly beneath the privileged.

Against this backdrop of mediation being used to prop up ailing civil court systems and arguments around its 'second-class justice' nature, the next section shall explore in more depth some arising matters including the issue of the justice to be found in court-connected mediation; mediation and power imbalances; and mediation's role in the 'loss of law'. Prior to undertaking this analysis, it is worth briefly reviewing some of the legal controversies that have dogged the process of mandatory mediation. This is especially important as mandatory mediation represents the most obvious affront to parties' pursuance of justice through the civil courts in the sense that they may be precluded from seeking to assert their legal rights at least until they have attempted to mediate the dispute.

5.2.3 The Debate Over Mandatory Mediation

Although given mediation's poor voluntary take up, mandatory mediation has a certain attraction, the practice seems intuitively wrong—a world away from mediation's voluntary, participative roots. On a personal note, compelling parties to mediate is something that I have always viewed with a combination of discomfort and allure. It is fair to say, however, that my own view has shifted more in favour of the practice in recent times than was hitherto been the case. I say this with important qualifications as articulated below in this chapter. It is also important to be clear about what mandatory mediation means. As noted above, the term may be used to denote a number of distinct mechanisms, including blanket rules mandating that all cases of a particular nature are mediated prior to adjudication by the court; discretionary rules bestowed upon judges to refer individual cases to mediation on a compulsory basis; and mandatory recourse in both such senses to preliminary mediation information or 'intake' sessions. Whatever the policy debate regarding the merits or otherwise of mandatory mediation, one of the most fundamental objections to the concept is that it may simply be unlawful and contrary to fundamental constitutional legal rights and protections afforded to citizens.

---

[26] See for example, the discussion in Genn (2010), pp. 114–121; Brunsdon-Tulley (2009).

[27] Auerbach, p. 128.

5.2.3.1 Mandatory Mediation and Fundamental Constitutional Rights

Across Europe there has been significant debate as to whether or not mandatory mediation violates fundamental legal rights of would-be litigants. In particular, arguments have centred on whether mandatory mediation circumvents the right to a fair trial enshrined in Article 6 of the European Convention on Human Rights (ECHR). English jurisprudence on court ordered mediation has especially grappled with this issue. In the aftermath of the Civil Procedure Rules reforms of 1998, and ensuing robust judicial promotion of the process,[28] some initial English judicial flirtation with mandatory mediation occurred.[29] The affair was short lived, however. In a seminal case on the issue, *Halsey v Milton Keynes General Trust NHS*[30] Dyson, LJ in the Court of Appeal opined that compulsory referral by the court to mediation would amount to an infringement of Article 6 of the ECHR. The view in *Halsley* was based on an interpretation of the decision in *Deweer v Belgium*[31] in which the European Court of Human Rights held that where a shopkeeper alleged to have contravened a pricing law was offered the chance to make a payment in 'friendly settlement' which would preclude the case going to trial, this amounted to a infringement of Art 6(1). The *Halsey* ruling was subsequently attacked by a spate of commentators.[32] It was argued in particular that the court in *Halsey* misinterpreted the law in this respect and that an obligation to attempt mediation but with no compunction to settle as a step within litigation procedure would not *per se* infringe Article 6.[33] More recent European Court of Justice (ECJ) jurisprudence on the matter concurs with this viewpoint. In the preliminary ruling in *Alassini*[34] the ECJ held that neither general principles of European Union law nor the specific provisions of the Universal Service Directive (USD) of the EU telecoms

[28] Including the imposition of cost penalties for 'unreasonable' refusals to mediate—see *Hickman v Blake Lapthorn* (2006) EWHC 12. The rules set out in *Hickman* include that: the burden will fall on the unsuccessful party to show that the other party was unreasonable in not mediating; where a party holds a reasonable belief that he has a strong case, then this will be relevant as to reasonableness, albeit that in evenly balanced cases, little weight will be attributed to such a belief; concerns about the cost of mediation may be a relevant factor; a party's view as to whether there is a reasonable prospect of success at mediation is a relevant but not determinable issue regarding reasonableness; the unsuccessful party at trial must to show that there was a reasonable opportunity of success at the mediation; where a party has refused to mediate despite encouragement from the court then that may be taken into account.

[29] In *Shokusan v Danovo* [2004] All ER (D) 61 (Aug) it was held by Blackbourne J. that a court had the power to order mediation even if one party was unwilling to take part.

[30] [2004] EWCA (Civ) 576.

[31] (A/35) [1980] E.C.C 169 (ECHR).

[32] See, for example, Lightman (2007); Clark (2008).

[33] For a discussion of *Halsey* and *Deweer* see Tronson (2006).

[34] Joined Cases C-317/08, C-318/08, C-319/08 and C-320/0, cases made against the introduction of mandatory mediation in Italy.

liberalisation programme[35] prevented member states from providing for mandatory mediation in so far as that any such scheme does not result in decisions binding against the parties, or is subject to substantial costs or delays. This case can be seen to chime with the terms of the recent EU directive on mediation which expressly affirms the legitimacy of the practice of mandatory mediation.[36] Even Lord Dyson, architect of the article 6 based ruling in *Halsey*, has since retreated from his initial position, and has accepted that mandatory mediation will not generally circumvent Article 6 of the ECHR. As Lord Dyson acknowledges though, and echoing the ruling in *Alassini*, a mandatory scheme of mediation may be anathema to Article 6 is it operates in an illegitimate way, in terms, for example, of placing significant costs and delays in the way of parties subjected to it.[37]

Other countries have also grappled with whether, and in what circumstances, mandatory mediation may be anathema to constitutional rights of participants. The United States Constitution, for example, guarantees citizens the right to a trial and in many cases trial by jury.[38] Important other provisions include the right to 'due process' in terms of legal proceedings.[39] It seems clear, however, that such fundamental rights do not, *per se*, prohibit the compelling of would-be litigants to mediate their dispute as a preliminary step in court proceedings. Again, mediation and other pre-trial settlement processes may violate provisions of the Constitution in so far, however, that they represent a substantive hurdle to pursuance of justice through for example, excessive costs or delays. Modern practice, generally recognises, however, the balance to be struck between providing reasonable and viable civil justice systems in the modern world and affording citizens the mechanisms by which to enforce their legal rights. This need to weigh rights of due process for citizens in the pursuance of legal justice against requirements to ration state resources is an issue I shall return to below.[40]

[35] Providing for Directive 2002/22 on universal service and users' rights relating to electronic communications networks and services (Universal Service Directive) [2002] OJ L108/51 of April 24, 2002.

[36] *Mediation Directive (2008/52/EC), Article 5 states that:*"This directive is without prejudice to national legislation making the use of mediation compulsory or subject to incentives or sanctions, whether before or after judicial proceedings have started, provided that such legislation does not prevent the parties from exercising their right of access to the judicial system."

[37] Dyson (2010). It has been argued however, that compulsory references to mediation, on pain of striking out the case or imprisonment for contempt of court, even if there is no compunction to settle therein may be contrary to Article 6 given that good faith requirements to mediate and likely settlements reached in the process may render justice through the courts, *de facto* unattainable—see Shipman (2011).

[38] U.S. CONST. amend. VII ("In suits at common law, where the value in controversy shall exceed twenty dollars, the right of trial by jury shall be preserved, and no fact tried by a jury, shall be otherwise re-examined in any Court of the United States, than according to the rules of the common law.").

[39] By virtue of the Fifth and Fourteenth amendments to the Constitution.

[40] At Sect. 5.2.7.

5.2.3.2 Practical Issues

Leaving aside legal and principled reasons for avoiding mandatory mediation, other more prosaic objections exist. Recognising the worth of mediation in its voluntary form, some commentators have averred that mandatory mediation should be avoided not least on the premise that it simply does not work. In this regard we may, for example, point to evidence gleaned from research into the London County Court scheme into a compulsory court-annexed mediation[41] which suffered a high 'opt-out' rate and very modest levels of settlement. Many parties seemingly resented being corralled into mediation and participated accordingly.[42] Across the globe, mandatory mediation schemes do at times suffer from poor settlement rates when compared to their voluntary counterparts, presumably on the basis that parties, piqued at being denied the right to pursue legal justice, merely go through the motions.[43]

Nonetheless, that is not always the case. In Australia, for example, there is significant research that even mandatory mediation may have a transformative impact on the parties and settlement rates are generally high.[44] Similarly, research in German mandatory court-annexed mediation schemes has also found that parties were generally appreciative of the process and that in many dispute areas, settlement rates were high.[45] Trevor Buck's research into ADR in Australian administrative justice processes detected high rates of user satisfaction, "which [varied] little according to whether the mediation [was] voluntary or compulsory".[46] A study into the mandatory mediation projects in Baden-Wurttemberg, Bayern and Nordrhein-Westfalen found that "[t]he mandatory nature of the conciliations does not appear to have negatively affected this [generally positive] perception" of mediation. Tamara Relis's research into medical negligence, court-connected mediation in Canada also revealed very little differentiation between parties' perceptions and experiences of mandatory and voluntary mediation.[47] Clearly a wide range of factors will affect the success (in settlement and other terms) of mandatory mediation programmes, including such issues as pre-mediation information and guidance for

[41] It was not truly compulsory in that parties channelled into the scheme could opt out.

[42] Often by opting out: Genn et al. (2007), pp. 33–46. Settlement rates were also generally poor, see Fig. 2.15.

[43] Genn et al. (2007); Blomgren Bingham et al. (2008–2009), pp. 253–254 (in a study of civil cases handled by Assistant United States Attorneys, when voluntary mediation was used settlement rates were 71%; when the process was mandatory the rate dropped to 50%). Evidence from a labour mediation scheme in Turin City Council found that settlement rates dropped when participation in the programme shifted from a voluntary to compulsory basis—Chiarloni (2000) cited in De Palo et al. (2003), p. 3.

[44] Hamilton (2005).

[45] Alexander et al. (2006), pp. 246–247.

[46] Buck (2005), pp. v–vi.

[47] Relis (2009), p. 20.

participants, the attitude of lawyers toward the programme and their aptitude for participation, the skill of the mediators,[48] screening to ensure appropriate cases are selected and parties' overall perceptions of the legitimacy of the process itself.[49]

Beyond the impact on individual cases, mandating mediation may also help embed the process generally and lead to its increased acceptance and use. Research into a mandatory court-annexed mediation scheme in Ontario, for example, found that despite initial resistance to the programme by lawyers, judicial compulsion of mediation led to a shift in disputing culture in which some lawyers and their clients began to accept and embrace the process as it became normalised.[50] According to Julie Macfarlane, "[a]lthough mandatory mediation may secure lawyers' obedient conduct without necessarily changing their minds and hearts, the changed conduct may, with further practice and exposure, affect a lawyer's normative values and attitudes towards mediation".[51] Equally there is significant evidence from the USA to suggest that exposure to mandatory mediation increases general deployment of the process, enhances the flow of information from lawyers to disputants about alternative dispute resolution processes and may also over time lead to dilution of some of the less desirable adversarial practices of lawyers.[52] The same phenomenon was reported in England in the context of perceived *de facto* court compulsion to attend mediation.[53] Against a backdrop of low voluntary up take of mediation but potentially high *post-hoc* success and the scope for efficiency contributions to civil court systems, mandatory mediation may represent an alluring prospect for policy makers.

5.2.4 Mediation and 'Justice'

One of the most trenchant critics of an untrammelled roll out of mediation within civil court environments is Professor Dame Hazel Genn.[54] Though her writings have arisen principally in the context of English civil justice, many of the lines of

[48] Including their proclivity for cajoling or pressuring parties into settlement, which clearly may be a hidden danger behind high settlement rates.

[49] In an answer to a question at a 2010 speech on mediation in Scotland and the USA, regarding whether mandatory mediation ought to be supported, Professor John Lande responded that the more important question was one of overall, effective dispute programme design—Lande (2010).

[50] Macfarlane (2001), Chap. III. See Chap. 2 at Sect. 2.5 for a discussion of lawyers' disputing cultures.

[51] Macfarlane (2008), p. 92.

[52] See the discussion by Carrie Menkel-Meadow in Menkel-Meadow (2001), p. xxviii. Nonetheless, coercion into mediation may lead to an increased tactical use of mediation—see Chap. 2 at Sect. 2.6.2.

[53] Brooker and Lavers (2002).

[54] In particular her high-profile Hamlyn Lectures, see Genn (2010).

attack she lays out are applicable to mediation's progress from the margins to the centre of civil justice in all jurisdictions. While Genn's comments have been made with some hyperbole and rhetorical flourish and arguably generated more heat than light, there is a serious core to them. Echoing the views of critical American socio-legal scholars in the post-Pound era, the main plank of her criticism is the notion that diverting litigants into mediation, a process which is not fundamentally concerned with the assertion of vested legal rights, is anathema to the civil courts' role in society to mete out justice. Her now infamous utterance on the topic—"[t]he outcome of mediation is not about *just* settlement, it is *just about settlement*"[55]—has emboldened the anti-mediation brigade and thrown down the gauntlet to the mediation movement. Amplifying this natty little phrase, more explicitly she asks, "[a]re mediators concerned about substantive justice? Absolutely not... Mediation is about searching for a solution to a problem. There is no reference to the hypothesised outcome at trial. The mediator does not make a judgement about the quality of the settlement."[56]

Although the picture of mediation Genn paints may be true in respect of a truly facilitative, 'norm-generating'[57] species of mediation, her assault is somewhat off the mark with regard to many forms of mediation today, particularly those most commonly connected to the court process, which are the primary target of her arrows. As I have discussed in this book, practice norms in mediation may often be more evaluative, with a greater role therein of the law and legal justice than Genn, or much official mediation discourse acknowledges. As Macfarlane has noted recently in the Canadian court-connected environment, the law does and should play a significant role within the mediation process as one of a matrix of factors relevant to settlement.[58] Carrie Menkel-Meadow has noted that "[mediation's] practice often turns to [a] kind of case evaluation... especially in complex legal disputes where the parties seek a third-party neutral 'advisory opinion' in the context of their dyadic negotiations. Parties... often seek guidance from a 'neutral' who combines the mediator's process skills with some knowledge or wisdom, *either about case law and precedents* (my emphasis) or about custom, trade practices and industry insider knowledge"[59] As I elaborated in Chap. 4, the prominent role of legal norms in mediated settlement may be even more acute in lawyer-dominated, court-connected mediation which, experience suggests, tends to be more evaluative in nature and solutions crafted therein more reflective of adjudicative norms than mediation in other contexts. This may especially be the case with judicial mediation but equally has become commonplace in court-connected mediation generally. Moreover, in some contexts, indicative settlements reached must be

[55] Genn (2010), p. 117.

[56] Genn (2010), pp. 116–117.

[57] Waldman (1997), p. 745, in which the parties themselves are responsible for generating the norms upon which the settlement is based.

[58] Macfarlane (2008), Chap. 6.

[59] Menkel-Meadow (2001), p. xxvi. See also Subrin (2002/2003), pp. 218–219.

approved of by the parties' own lawyers or affirmed by the court after agreement to ensure that they are legally acceptable—lending a further, formal justice flavour to the process.

As a caveat to the above, two points must be made here. First, the influence of legal norms by various means within the process does not mean that mediated settlements in the court-connected context can be viewed as 'equal' in formal justice terms with an adjudicated decision taken by a judge. Second, many of the attributes described above which may bring the mediation more in line with formal justice are often decried by purists as damaging and contrary to the ethos of the process. Thus, mediation proponents can hardly make use of such arguments in defence of anti-justice salvos. Nonetheless, there are other ripostes that can be proffered to combat the anti-justice criticism of mediation sceptics.

5.2.4.1 Mediation: an Alternative to What?

In many contexts in which court-connected mediation takes place, a mediated settlement (if the case does resolve) takes place instead of a non-mediated settlement, rather than a judicial decision. This is so because in the general civil court context, absent mediation, cases often settle extra-judicially in any case. If, as has been claimed, there is no formal justice to be found in mediated settlements, it is a pertinent question to ask whether 'justice' is to be found in that which it most often replaces—negotiation in the shadow of on-going litigation, what Marc Galanter termed "litigotiation".[60] Although, given the privacy of such outcomes, there is only limited empirical evidence available on the subject, research has suggested that negotiated settlements through lawyers often do not track the applicable law, but rather are often bare, unprincipled compromises or far more reflective of other applicable norms and considerations such as economic and reputational factors.[61] Against this backdrop then, mediated settlement, which as we have discussed, may often be influenced at least by relevant legal norms, can be seen as arguably superior in formal justice terms to that which will likely take place otherwise. It is also likely that mediation will be perceived by parties as superior in procedural justice terms over lawyer-led negotiated settlements.[62]

While the above analysis may be true in respect of general commercial litigation, involving sophisticated repeat players well versed in the tactical use of litigation to elicit a favourable negotiated settlement, the same arguments may not hold water in

---

[60] Galanter (1984).

[61] Some of the evidence is summarised by Menkel-Meadow (1995), p. 2675, including: a study where it was observed that negotiations carried out by law students rarely made reference to the applicable law (Condlin 1985); a study of offers made by lawyers in the context of civil litigation which commonly made little reference to legal arguments (Kritzer 1991); and a study of securities litigation disputes, in which settlements often did not reflect law but rather other economic or strategic factors (Cooper-Alexander 1991).

[62] See discussion of procedural justice at Sect. 5.2.4.4 below.

other dispute contexts. This is so because civil cases involving individuals such as those in the consumer, housing and family contexts, may more commonly involve parties genuinely seeking a day in court rather than using the litigation process tactically to expedite a favourable settlement.[63] Out of court settlement rates in such actions filed are generally lower than in the general civil/commercial dispute context.[64] Absent schemes to divert such cases from the courts, a significant proportion would otherwise carry forward to judicial determination. So if mediation may truly represent an alternative to adjudicated settlement in such contexts, how does the process square in justice terms with judicial decisions?

5.2.4.2 Justice in Mediation

The latter question leads on to a more fundamental riposte of pro-mediation commentators that focuses on the superiority of the 'justice' that parties might find in mediation as opposed to the formal equivalent delivered by courts. Such positions represent a shot across the bows of lawyers because they attack the notion that the law should be the only barometer of justice. A pluralistic notion of justice recognises that justice is not the monopoly of the law and legal remedies but rather may be found in a whole range of social norms and considerations. In fact, courts, rooted as they are in the application of legal norms to relevant facts, may often fail singularly to deliver justice in the parties' terms. For example, adjudication through the courts may fall down in the eyes of litigants by the way the discourse of the dispute is shaped and compromised by the law,[65] by the fact that parties' participation in the process may be limited[66] and that the legal remedies available may not in fact meet either party's underlying interests. Although as I noted above at least one party in a civil case may be seeking justice in the legal sense, there is in fact significant evidence that individuals who come before the civil courts are not always aware of, and do not seek, the limited remedies that a court can deliver, but rather have significant extra-legal desires which may remain unsatisfied post-adjudication.[67]

---

[63] Although nonetheless, litigants in these settings may in fact harbour significant extra-legal agendas—see Relis (2009), pp. 9–10; Ross and Bain (2010), paras 5.12 and 5.13.

[64] See for example, Hadfield (2005), part 5.

[65] Menkel-Meadow (1995), p. 2674.

[66] Thus contrary to notions of procedural justice—see generally, Lind and Tyler (1998).

[67] Ross and Bain (2010), paras 5.12 and 5.13. Plaintiffs may sue for a whole range of extra-legal factors. Relis's work is important in that it found that parties' extra legal needs are not extinguished by the legal reframing of the dispute which occurs in lawyer-led dispute settlement—Relis (2009), pp. 9–10, 15. Research in Scotland has revealed that while around half of individual disputants surveyed wanted financial compensation, a similar number sought to ensure that the conduct complained of would not happen to others, 43% wanted an apology and 41% wanted an explanation—Scottish Consumer Council (1997), p. 23.

If this is so, then diversion to a mediation session may not represent such an alienation of litigating parties' stated preferences for legal justice as may otherwise be the case.

Following on from the above, it is argued by proponents that mediation may then deliver an outcome which comports better with participants' own sense of justice than a litigated decision. Certainly surveys of those who have participated in mediation often find them satisfied with the process and the outcomes that they have crafted therein. High settlement rates and user satisfaction levels abound across a range of jurisdictions and different dispute contexts.[68] Many users, including those recalcitrant at the outset, report that they would mediate again. Richard Abel has made the point that this kind of evidence is of little relevance on the basis that by the time parties mediate their expectations have been battered down to such a low level by the civil justice system that satisfaction with mediation becomes largely meaningless.[69] The basis for this perhaps mean spirited proposition is questionable, however. Moreover, surveys often reveal that parties are more satisfied with mediated outcomes than those procured in adjudication.[70]

5.2.4.3 Justice and the Durability of Mediated Settlements

Another important justice-based concern in the context of mediation is its perceived lack of coercive power. In short, it may be argued that mediated outcomes lack the legal enforceability of decisions rendered in litigation. The formal enforceability of mediated agreements varies significantly in practice. In some contexts, mediation results in non-legal, principled agreements which are unenforceable at law. In other cases, agreements may be captured in detailed legally binding contracts. Even in the latter case, however, enforcement may require to be sought in subsequent legal proceedings in the same way as would be required in respect of any other contract. Such enforcement may of course be costly, time-consuming and problematic. Remedying such purported defects, in many contexts, mediated agreements reached may be rendered formally binding in the same way as a court judgement. For instance, a variety of such ways of legally legitimising mediated agreements

---

[68] For a thorough review of the US field see Jones (2004), a special double journal issue collection which has chapters on court connected, community, employment, victim-offender and environmental mediation. For UK court-annexed schemes see Prince (2007); Doyle (2006); Ross and Bain (2010); For Dutch evidence see de Roo and Jagtenberg (2006), p. 287; Neimeijer and Pel (2005). Even in the mandatory context mediation is often highly regarded by participants see the discussion in Sect. 5.2.3.2.

[69] Abel (1982).

[70] For Germany see for example, Proksch (1998). Research in court-connected mediation in the Netherlands found that parties were more likely to be satisfied with their mediation processes if they had previously litigated Welsh (2007), p. 21. Similar findings are cited in Neimeijer and Pel (2005), p. 364 and have also been uncovered in Scotland—Ross and Bain (2010), para 5.25.

can be found across Europe, especially in the court-connected context.[71] Of course, judicial pronouncements may not always be adhered to either. Enforcement endeavours through 'diligence' procedures are commonplace, often time consuming and difficult to execute.

Against this backdrop, it can be said that mediated agreements in fact often fare well as compared to judicial decisions in terms of their durability. In the context of Dutch court-connected mediation, for example, Machteld Pel found that mediated settlements were enforced in their entirety in 66% of cases, with a further 22% complied with at least partially. Such rates were high when compared to the enforcement of court judgements in comparable cases.[72] Recorded enforcement rates across a number of UK small claims mediation programmes are also high compared to those cases in which judgement was tendered.[73] The voluntary and participative nature of mediation may lead to an increased acceptance of, and compliance with agreements rendered therein. In McEwen and Maiman's research into court annexed mediation in Maine, they viewed that the high rate of compliance (double that reported in adjudicated cases) was primarily due to the voluntary nature of the programme and active participation of disputing parties.[74] In this sense, there is some evidence that as mediation takes on more of a mandatory hue, compliance rates fall and agreements are more routinely challenged.[75] In the court-connected context in particular, satellite litigation challenging the enforceability of mediated settlements has become commonplace, threatening to undermine the process.[76]

[71] A summary of different approaches across the EU is set out in European Parliament: Non-legislative Resolution of 25 October 2011 on alternative dispute resolution in civil, commercial and family matters. http://www.europarl.europa.eu/sides/getDoc.do?pubRef=-//EP//TEXT+TA+P7-TA-2011-0449+0+DOC+XML+V0//EN&language=EN Accessed 1 November 2011.

[72] Niemeijer and Pel (2005), pp. 363–364.

[73] Ross and Bain (2010), para 5.17 (mediated outcomes enforced in 90% of cases at Aberdeen and Glasgow Sheriff Courts as against 67% through traditional court procedures); ADR Now 2007 (reporting that in research into small claims mediation at Manchester County Court, **all** agreements reached in mediation were complied with); Prince and Belcher (2006) (in an evaluation of the Exeter County Court mediation scheme, only 4% of mediated outcomes required enforcement actions as against 19% in a control group where an adjudicated decision was delivered).

[74] McEwen and Maiman (1984), pp. 40–45. See also Wissler (2004), pp. 65–68. My own work in respect of Scottish commercial lawyers, found few stating that mediation's lack of coercive power is a weakness of the process—see Clark and Dawson (2007), p. 244, fn 75.

[75] See Coben and Thompson (2006), part III (a study of US Federal and State litigation between 1999 and 2003 over mediated cases).

[76] Coben and Thompson (2006); Sussman (2009) pp. 5–9 for a review of US satellite litigation.

5.2.4.4 Procedural Justice in Mediation

Aside from the matter of substantive justice (to be found in settlements reached), mediation also has the potential to score highly in terms of procedural justice. Procedural justice refers to the process by which outcomes are produced. A significant body of literature exists focusing on participants' perceptions of the fairness of decision-making procedures.[77] Parties' perceptions of procedural fairness have consistently been found to impact upon their overall assessment of encounters with decision making bodies, independent of outcomes. Indeed, parties are more likely to view outcomes as fair if they judge that the process by which those outcomes have been arrived at was in itself procedurally fair.[78] While most initial research in the area has focused on criminal justice,[79] procedural justice has more recently become influential in the study of civil disputing.[80] Three primary factors contribute to assessments of procedural fairness: (1) voice: the opportunity to present views, concerns and evidence to a third party, 2) being heard: the perception that the "third party considered their views, concerns and evidence"[81] and 3) treatment: being treated in "a dignified, respectful manner".[82]

Procedural justice norms have been brought to bear in the scrutiny of mediation.[83] In this sense it has been argued that mediation's key promise of party empowerment and self-determination may in fact be its Achilles' heel. In short, it has argued that in procedural justice terms, parties often prefer a decision to be taken by an authoritative third party.[84] There is some evidence from particular research studies that people perceive greater procedural fairness when decisions are made on their behalf by an authoritative third party than in processes in which parties retain decision control.[85] However, the evidence is equivocal and on a nuanced reading of the literature, Nancy Welsh has revealed the importance of embedding procedural justice norms in all types of dispute resolution.[86] By this she means that there seems to be no discernible link between perceptions of procedural justice and decision control *per se*, but that both types of process (i.e. those in which decisions rest with the parties and those where decisions are imposed by third parties) will only be deemed procedurally fair, when the core elements of voice,

[77] "three decades of socio-legal research have demonstrated that citizens also care deeply about the process by which conflicts are resolved and decisions are made, even when outcomes are unfavourable or the process they desire is slow or costly" MacCoun (2005), p. 172.

[78] Lind and Tyler (1988), pp. 66–70.

[79] Tyler and Huo (2002); Tyler (2006).

[80] Adler (2009); Halliday and Scott (2009).

[81] Welsh (2001), p. 820.

[82] Welsh (2001), p. 820.

[83] See, for example, Welsh (2001); Welsh (2002); Howieson (2002).

[84] See Hensler (2002), pt III for a discussion of evidence in this regard.

[85] MacCoun (2005), p. 175.

[86] Welsh (2002), pt II.

dignity and being heard described above are present. There is a danger in the court-connected context in particular, that procedural justice norms may falter in the mediation models that have become prevalent in this setting.

In terms of the impact that lawyers may hold in procedural justice terms, in the setting of court-connected mediation arguably lawyers may both be an aid to ensuring procedural justice norms are adhered to and a barrier to such endeavours. On one level, the participation of lawyers may lead to a usurping of the client's role within mediation (e.g. *in extremis* by replacing clients at mediation or more subtly and commonly by domination of clients within the process[87]). Clients may thus experience a poor perception of their own ability to participate within the process. The issue here, however, is not simply that participants' opportunities for voice will be diminished in such environments but rather that lawyer involvement (either as representative or mediator) may change the rules of the game and lead to an emphasis placed upon settlement and focus upon monetary issues at the expense of acknowledging and meeting clients' own, perhaps multifarious interests and needs.[88] If lawyers behave in an overly adversarial fashion, they may also damage their client's perceptions of dignity within mediation to the determent of parties' perceptions of procedural justice.[89]

By contrast, it is also true that lawyers may enhance procedural justice. First, their presence either as mediators or party representative may lend an air of dignity and respect to proceedings in the eyes of participants. The authority which is part and parcel of the judicial mediator's office may in particular imbue proceedings with dignity and gravitas.[90] Additionally, clients may believe that having a lawyer in tow will ensure that they are being heard by mediators. As articulated in Chap. 4, the assistance of lawyers in mediation may also help clients to find their own 'voice'.[91] While this may be achieved by lawyer encouragement and coaching of clients to assist them to articulate their position well, it is also true that some clients may be happy to sit back and allow their lawyers to do the talking. This feature, in itself, may not (by some parties at least) be seen as limiting client voice. Far from stifling client participation in the process, a party's active participation within mediation may thus be appropriately and perhaps only achieved by some clients through the mouthpiece of their lawyers. Lawyers' presence (on both sides at least) may also increase client's perceptions that the mediation process is fair and even handed—for example, one in which they may make rational decisions in view of the legal parameters of their cases.[92]

---

[87] See Chap. 4 at Sect. 4.2.3.1.

[88] See for example, Relis (2009), p. 14.

[89] There is some evidence that parties are more likely to perceive mediation as procedurally fair when lawyers engage in cooperative rather than adversarial approaches, Wissler (2002), p. 686.

[90] See Chap. 4 at Sect. 4.4.1.

[91] Section 4.2.3.2.

[92] Howieson (2002).

5.2.5 Power Imbalances in Mediation

The argument that mediation is unable to handle and in fact may exacerbate power imbalances between participants has dogged development of the process in recent decades.[93] Power imbalances may take a number of forms, both tangible and intangible, including in terms of parties' confidence, intelligence, eloquence, access to legal resources and financial wealth. On this view, high settlement rates and even party satisfaction may not be enough of a justification for mediation, particularly when it becomes entwined with the values of justice and fairness inherent in the formal civil justice system. A somewhat paternalistic point of view perhaps, but one that holds significant resonance within the court-connected context, is the notion that although parties may be satisfied with an outcome crafted within mediation, nonetheless, it may objectively be seen as unfair and perhaps not commensurate with the legal dimension to their dispute.[94] Although perhaps blissfully unaware of this fact and even basking in a post-settlement glow, a party may be short-changed in mediation. This scenario may arise particularly with *pro se* litigants without access to legal representation or advice (and may be especially pressing where one party is legally represented and the other is not). Equally, however, parties may feel brow-beaten in mediation and fold like a pack of cards to the demands of their opponent, given, for example, their lack of financial clout to walk away from the only settlement in town and take further legal action.

If the mediator does not take steps to alleviate any power imbalances that do subsist between the participants by, for example, aiding the weaker party to articulate their position, providing legal advice, or counselling the more powerful parties to take up more reasonable positions relative to their opponents, then arguably any resolution crafted may not be fair from an objective perspective. Mediators may find it difficult, however, to bridge any perceived power imbalances within mediation given the impartial nature of their role and their inability to take sides. Particularly in classic, facilitative, norm-generating mediation, where parties are the masters of their own solutions unfettered by the imposition of norms reflecting some form of objective fairness, mediators may be left powerless to alleviate power imbalances played out in any settlements crafted by the parties. Seemingly 'unfair' settlements reached for example, under one party's cloak of ignorance as to the legal dimensions of their case or in circumstances in which a party has no real option but to acquiesce to the demands of the other, may thus leave a bad taste in the mouth. Given gaps in access to formal justice and attendant recourse to legal remedies, with mediation used to bridge the divide, a lack of alternative options for recourse may in fact reflect reality for disempowered individuals. With reference to the huge power gulfs that subsist in society, Auerbach noted, "without legal

[93] Rueben (2000); Grillo (1991); Auerbach (1983).

[94] An issue arguably of importance in the court-connected context, see Sect. 5.3 below.

power, the imbalance between aggrieved individuals and corporations and government agencies cannot be redressed.[95]"

The issue of power imbalances has perhaps reared its head most frequently in the setting of family mediation. In particular, it has been argued that women often experience mediation from a position of disempowerment relative to males. Feminist critiques of mediation in this regard were spearheaded by the influential work of Tina Grillo[96] and have remained an enduring concern since, especially in the court-connected context. In particular, it has been argued that power imbalances between the sexes in mediation may arise from such matters as differences in financial standing and hence access to legal advice impacting upon knowledge levels within mediation as well as available options in the event of not settling. It has also been suggested that the general negotiation styles of men may favour them over women in the facilitative, norm-generating, mediation environment.

In line with the above views, some empirical evidence suggests that women are disadvantaged within mediation.[97] Nonetheless, contrary evidence also exists suggesting that Grillo's arguments regarding the impact of mediation upon women have been overstated. Joan Kelly's review of research in the field found little empirical evidence that women were biased against within mediation.[98] Mediation research into family mediation in Germany revealed a 75% settlement rate with some 80% of participants reportedly "very satisfied" with the process. In terms of satisfaction no significant difference was gleaned between the views of men and women.[99] Research by Tilley similarly found no evidence to support the claim that women are disadvantaged by mediation. Indeed the author suggested that the opposite may in fact be true given the opportunity for women within mediation to express their voice and participate equally in discussions. Tilley's study did reveal, however, that some women may be disadvantaged in terms of settlement but only because they do not consider their own interests to the full. Rather they often sacrificed such interests to those of the family as a whole to a greater extent than males.[100] Relis's work suggests that although in general women do not believe that they are disadvantaged within mediation, there is evidence that women are in fact potentially adversely affected by their participation in the process. For example, within mediation it was reported that women were less willing to discuss the compensation aspects of their claims, less prone to meet their adversary face to face within mediation, more likely to suffer emotional distress, less actively participative and more accepting and less critical of mediator behaviour.[101] It was

---

[95] Auerbach (1983), p. 145.

[96] Grillo (1991).

[97] LaFree and Rack (1996); Bryan (1999); Bohmer and Ray (1994), p. 232.

[98] Kelly (2004).

[99] Proksch (1998).

[100] Tilley (2007).

[101] Relis (2009), at p. 25.

recognised in this study that the impact of such matters could be reduced by lawyer representation. In a like fashion, while research in the context of family mediation in the US State of Georgia found scant differences between the ways than men and women experienced mediation, it was noted, however, that the lack of disparity may to some extent be explained by the presence of attorneys as party representatives within mediation.[102]

5.2.5.1 The Power of Lawyers

The findings of the last two studies described above lead to consideration of the general proposition that lawyers represent some sort of remedy to power imbalances in mediation. As discussed in Chap. 4, the presence of lawyers, either as party representatives or as mediators, may go some way to assisting parties to achieve an equal footing relative to their opponent within mediation. So, for example, lawyer representatives within mediation may aid parties' causes by the tendering of legal advice and information to ensure parity of legal knowledge and by acting as a mouthpiece to enhance their client's ability to negotiate effectively. Equally, lawyer mediators may be able to bridge power gulfs between parties by similar means as lawyer representatives. Of course such behaviour on the part of the mediator may place her impartiality in question and lead the mediation along more evaluative, quasi-adjudicative lines, arguably minimising the prospect of wider benefits of the process including creativity and party empowerment.[103] As noted already in this book, in a similar vein, overly robust lawyer advocacy may be to the detriment of the process as it may become too imbued with adversarial, positional tactics.

5.2.5.2 The Power of Mediation

If the view is taken that adding lawyers to the mix is an inappropriate way of resolving power imbalances, what then can classic, facilitative mediation offer in this regard? It has been argued that key traits of standard, facilitative mediation augur well for ensuring a parity of power between participants. It is contended that standard mediation may alleviate power imbalances by the impact of mediators treating both parties with respect and dignity, drawing out ground rules for conduct, allowing both sides 'space' within which to express their positions, listening with care, and such matters as controlling how both parties are greeted, seated and addressed.[104] It is also suggested that mediators within their facilitative guise can

[102] Gordon (2002), Table 1.

[103] See Chap. 4 at Sect. 4.3.6.

[104] Davis and Salem (1984), pp. 18–19.

more actively seek to remedy power imbalances for, example, by such tactics as asking reality testing questions, prompting parties to seek external legal advice where deemed appropriate and supporting a party's negotiating efforts, including assisting in the development of settlement options in caucus.[105] It may of course take a very skilful mediator to tread the fine line between such activities and encroaching over onto the ground of partiality. Such activities may also easily cross over into the realm of evaluative or directive techniques, which may be precluded by standard codes of practice.[106]

It is worth mentioning that one other potential remedy to such concerns about power imbalances is the adoption of a "transformative" approach to mediation.[107] Proponents in the "transformative" school may posit that power imbalances can be more readily alleviated within this model. This is so because within this framework, the mediator's role is primarily to 'support' party interaction, restoring to those in conflict a degree of competence or 'empowerment', which in turn leads to a greater capacity to recognise the perspective of the other. Under this model, settlement is not an aim in itself but rather may be a natural consequence of the focus on improving party interaction. It should be noted though that from a practical perspective, the scope for such a holistic approach in the settlement-focused, time-limited environment of court-connected mediation may be limited, however.[108]

5.2.6 *Mediation and the 'Loss of Law'*

The argument that an overly robust encouragement of mediation is anathema to the public role of the court to promulgate and develop the law through precedent was most famously made in the classic polemic *Against Settlement* published by Owen Fiss in 1984, swimming against the tide of promotion of settlement-based alternatives to the court very much to the fore at that time in the USA.[109] His argument suggests that diversion from traditional dispute resolution processes to mediation will entail a reduction in trials and resultant judicial precedent, leading to a law devoid of necessary judicial development and clarification. Hailing from Scotland, I am very familiar with such concerns. Judges in my own country have, on

---

[105] Davis and Salem (1984), p. 20. See also Chornenki (2004), pp. 164–166 who articulates the notion of "power-with" (the power of the collective) which can be created by the parties and mediator in mediation to help expedite "elegant, economical and efficient solutions".

[106] See Chap. 4 at Sect. 4.3.6.

[107] Bush and Folger (2005).

[108] For one notable exception see Blomgren Bingham et al. (2009) (review of the use of transformative mediation within the context of US Postal Service employment disputes).

[109] Fiss (1984).

such a basis, spoken out in voluble terms against the linking of mediation with court procedures. For example, speaking in the context of proposed reforms to the Scottish legal system,[110] which may herald an increased role for mediation within the civil courts, Lord Rodger[111] recently remarked that "society actually needs litigation... Only a line of authoritative decisions... is ever going to put flesh on the very abstract statutory bones and show how the system is actually meant to work in practice....it would in my view be bad public policy positively to discourage resort to the very courts whose decisions could provide the necessary guidance on the interpretation and application of... Scottish statutes."[112] Other prominent Scottish judges have since echoed such views.[113]

The 'loss of law' issue is of more immediate relevance in common law countries[114] in which strict systems of judicial precedent exist and higher court decisions are recognised as formal sources of law, than in the civil law world. It is interesting that scholars have pointed to evidence of the superiority of common law systems over their civil law cousins that emanates from the application of judicial development and in this light cautioned against the loss of such an advantage which might result from the promotion of private settlement and suppression of developmental court judgements.[115] While identifying any phenomena as portraying a system's superiority may be problematic, such benefits of common law systems linked to judicial advancement of the law are cited as better shareholder and creditor rights; more active enforcement of the law; values of stock-markets as a higher percentage of overall GDP; and stronger protection for intellectual property rights. Promoting private settlement (including through mediation) as a legitimate aim of civil justice systems is, thus against this backdrop, seen as a "misguided policy".[116]

[110] Which, although technically a 'mixed' system, follows a system of judicial precedent in the common law tradition.

[111] A former UK Supreme Court judge. Lord Rodger sadly died as this book was bring written.

[112] Rodger (2008).

[113] Including Lord Reed (Reed 2007) and Lord Hope, currently Chancellor of my (Strathclyde) university (Hope 2011). Other players in the Scottish legal system generally do not it seems share the belief that developments in mediation will impact negatively upon the development of the law through judicial precedent. At a conference debating the potential utility of mediation in the Scottish civil justice system (Civil Justice Conference: Modernising the System, 26th November, 2007, Edinburgh) 75% of conference delegates surveyed disagreed that mediation developments would limit development of the law through judicial precedent; see also Clark and Dawson (2007), in which 69% of Scottish commercial litigators shared this view.

[114] Or in mixed systems that follow judicial precedent.

[115] See for example, Carr and Jencks (1999–2000), pp. 185–188 citing La Porte et al. (1997); Keller (1998).

[116] Carr and Jencks (1999–2000).

Beyond a reduction of judicial precedent, there are arguably other negative fallouts resulting from diminishing trials beyond the disappearance of judgements themselves. In this sense civil courts do not simply provide private dispute resolution but also carry out important public functions. Such other important aspects of litigated trials which may transcend civil and common law nations include: benefits stemming from the public function of jurors[117]; the public promulgation of acceptable norms in society and validation of the rule of law[118]; and the public demonstration of democratic practice in which individuals' power is equalised.[119] On a more practical matter, scholars have also lamented the fact the reduction in civil trials may lead to the loss of key judicial and lawyering skills in disposing with civil cases, as the well of experience in such matters dries up.[120]

5.2.6.1 Mediation and the Vanishing Trial

In many jurisdictions in which mediation has increased in prominence, there has been much consternation over recent trends in 'vanishing trials' and debates as to the extent that diversion to mediation is a contributory factor. To what extent promoting mediation *leads* to a reduction in trials is moot, however. Herbert Kritzer's comparative analysis of the phenomenon of vanishing trials in England and Wales, Canada and the USA found that civil trials have decreased of late in all those jurisdictions.[121] While it has been noted that in some cases, increasing recourse to mediation may be a contributory factor,[122] equally the process can also be seen rather as a beneficiary of a climate in which trials have become rarer and settlement generally has become the norm.[123] In England and Wales, it is

[117] Again rare in the civil law world.

[118] Luban (1994–1995). Disseminating through society in different forms outside of formal precedent itself.

[119] Resnik (2008), p. 806.

[120] See Yeazell (1994); McMunigal (1990); Glasser (1993). These issues lead to the issue of ownership of the dispute at hand. We might pose the question, "whose dispute is it anyway?" If parties seek or might benefit from private resolution to their dispute despite the loss of public benefits which might otherwise be gleaned from a judgement, should the public attributes of the dispute trump private concerns? A full examination of these issues is outside the scope of this book but for a spirited discussion see Luban (1994–1995) and compare with Menkel-Meadow (1995).

[121] Kritzer (2004).

[122] Although as Kritzer notes it is difficult to attribute trial attrition rates to any particular contributory factor—Kritzer (2004), p. 752.

[123] See Galanter (2004), pp. 483–484, 545 and table A.10 who notes that while fewer than five percent of filed cases get to trial, mediation is only fifth on the list of reasons for the "vanishing trial." Most cases get disposed of by or settled after summary judgment.

notable that significant drops in the rates of civil trials took place before the Civil Procedure Rules that sought to expedite settlement practices within the justice system in 1998, prior then to any significant development in the use of mediation, thus signalling that other factors were the primary cause.[124] For the USA, it has been suggested that a key driver in the reduction in civil trials is the fact that would-be litigants, who have become wary of the costs, time and risks attendant to formal civil justice procedures, have increasingly contracted out of the public system.[125]

It is also worth noting that classic American studies of judicial settlement conferences found that their use did not generally lead to a reduction in trial rates.[126] Similarly, pre-trial, mandatory arbitration schemes in the USA, did not generally reduce trial rates. As Deborah Hensler has noted, "most cases that participated in court arbitration would have settled before trial".[127] A general point can hence be made that at least in respect of disputes at the higher end of civil justice spectrum,[128] mediation will often take in place in respect of cases, which absent mediation, would have settled extra-judicially in any instance. [129] The few cases that proceed to trial may continue (in the absence of blanket compulsory rules) to do so, whether mediation has gained in popularity or not. Against this backdrop, the argument that increasing attempts to mediate and the diversion of appropriate cases may in fact lead to an *increase* in trials rather than a reduction is compelling. Promoting mediation (if it is scheduled at an early enough in the life-cycle of a litigated case[130]) may lead to earlier settlements than those in litigated cases which are settled by general (non-mediated) means. Hence a culling of cases from the court's docket at an earlier stage and thus a freeing up of the system to handle those cases in which an adjudicated decision is genuinely sought, may occur.

[124] Kritzer (2004). For trials in the Queens Bench Division of the High Court there is a precipitous drop from the 1988 peak of 3,189 to a mere 600 in 1998. In my own jurisdiction, cases initiated and heard in the Scottish Court of Session and Sheriff Courts have also taken a significant dip in recent times, despite the fact that concurrent civil mediation activity has been steady rather than prolific—for statistics, see http://www.scotland.gov.uk/Topics/Statistics/Browse/Crime-Justice/TrendCivil Accessed 1 November 2011. For more recent English statistics of diminishing civil case loads see Genn (2010), pp. 33–36.

[125] See generally, Smalkin and Smalkin (2005).

[126] Rosenberg (1964); Church et al. (1978) cited in Hensler (2003), p. 176.

[127] Hensler, p. 178.

[128] Where binding precedents may in fact be produced.

[129] As I have previously noted, in most jurisdictions globally at least outside of minor civil cases involving individuals, out of court settlement is the norm. In this sense research into mediation in English construction cases found parties involved in mediation viewing that if they had not mediated they would have settled anyway in 78% of cases. It was suggested that 19% of cases would otherwise have proceeded to trial—Gould et al. (2010), p. 52.

[130] This may not always be the case. Lawyers in particular may prefer mediation post-discovery, which may actually have the effect to elongate cases which would have settled earlier.

The resultant increased speed and economy of the civil justice system may lead to more—not fewer—trials taking place as litigants are drawn back into the system.[131]

5.2.7 *Mediation's Relationship with Formal Civil Justice*

In attempting to discern the appropriate place of mediation within the justice system, it must be recognised that in practice the availability of formal justice is often rationed in any case. To the extent that it should be is clearly a matter of some debate. For decades, however, States have slimmed down formal justice provision in certain contexts. Core due process values may be retained but practical rules putting the flesh on the bones of such overarching norms are often compromised so that any semblance of 'purity' in terms of application of relevant law to facts proven becomes a theoretical notion only. In the reality of scarce state resources, full blown civil trials emblazoned with strict evidential rules and procedures to afford litigants the ability to pursue legal rights become reserved for cases of a higher import. The reality is that a diluted, truncated facsimile of formal justice is served up by the civil courts in many instances. Formal justice will always fall short of its ideals but does so most starkly perhaps in disputes of a lesser value and importance. More generally the prospects of equalisation before the law of parties to formal judicial processes may be slim much of the time. Power imbalances are just as alive and well in formal legal processes as they are in informal ones.[132]

In this light, court-connected mediation may represent an acceptable alternative. As I have noted above, mediation may be pillared because it is often seen as a way in which the state is abrogating its responsibility to fund formal civil justice mechanisms adequately. Nonetheless, while such a roll out of mediation may be seen as a cost cutting measure for States, such monetary savings may be achieved hand and hand with qualitative benefits for participants. Mediation in the court-connected setting may be able to deliver superior process and outcomes for participants than that which can be realistically achieved in the judicial alternatives. Honest debates must be had over the aims and component parts of in-court mediation schemes, however. I will now proceed to discuss the impact that such

---

[131] In certain instances, it can be argued that too much precedent can be counterproductive in that it can create further uncertainty in the law, thus increasing the risks inherent in litigation and dissuading would-be litigants from engaging with the process—Menkel-Meadow (2005), p. 2668; Smalkin and Smalkin (2005), para 42.

[132] For the classic treatment see Galanter (1974). Repeat players and the more affluent may be able to milk the system to the detriment of their less knowledgeable or powerful opponents, for example by using the system to expedite favourable settlement, continually appealing decisions to drain their counterparts' resources, or resisting enforcement. It is also worth noting that power imbalances may be more prone to control in civil law jurisdictions given the generally, more interventionist role of the judge and the more limited freedom of parties to control the litigation process than in common law counterparts.

implantation within the formal dispute resolution context has had and should hold for mediation itself as well as the place of lawyers within the process.

5.3 Mediation Practice in the Institutionalised Context

5.3.1 Problems with Current Court-Connected Mediation

As I have noted throughout this book, models of mediation in its institutionalised setting have developed in ways that diverge significantly from the grassroots origins of the process. Evidence suggests that court-connected mediation in particular has become infiltrated to a significant extent by the dominant culture of litigation, leading to a settlement focus and narrow, lawyerly approach to dispute resolution. It will be recalled that many aspects of typical mediation models in the court connected setting have been caused by the increasing role of judges and lawyers in the process, and more specifically, by such rules as mandating that mediators be lawyers, lawyer preferences for evaluative mediators, lawyer 'shopping' for lawyer-mediators, lawyer attendance as party representatives in mediation with at times clients excluded from participation, and systems requiring the *ex post* approval by the courts of any mediated settlements reached.

I have already explored the fact that the prominence of the law and lawyers in commonly found mediation models may eradicate some of the formal justice concerns relative to its court-connected species, but in the process limit the wider restorative and psychological benefits to be gleaned from the process and diminish party satisfaction, particularly in the realm of procedural justice.[133] Lawyer domination, allied to an overtly settlement focus—which is almost inevitable in the efficiency-driven context of the court, and may harbour time-limited mediation sessions and case disposal targets—may in particular lead to an unsatisfactory party experience in mediation. Given drives for economic efficiency and the quick turnaround of large volumes of cases, mediation in the shadows of the court house, may fail to engage sufficiently with procedural justice norms.[134] Settlement driven processes and lawyer domination therein may lead to more limited client participation within mediation, for example, by affording scant time for parties to express their own 'voice' with even their presence excluded or discouraged. Perceptions of dignity and fairness may also falter within mediation in this context, particularly if parties feel pressurised into settlement in a short time frame are unwillingly sidelined by lawyers and the narrow legal compass of issues deemed relevant to resolution.

[133] Golann (2002), p. 336 suggesting that repairing relationships within court-connected mediation is rare.

[134] Welsh (2002).

While it is clear that much modern mediation practice, especially in the court connected context may thus be unsatisfactory from a number of perspectives, it would be misleading to suggest that the imposition of lawyers and legal norms into the process is always detrimental. Context is everything. What is an appropriate mediation model in one setting may be inappropriate in another. We must also be more nuanced in our discussion of the infusing of mediation with lawyers and the law. How and to what extent this is achieved is fundamental.

5.3.2 Accepting Change in Court-Connected Mediation

At the outset it should be accepted that when mediation is implanted within the civil court system in some form, then it is right that its merits and normative character are reappraised in light of the new context in which it is located. So when mediation takes place within the corridors of the court, for example, the need for the process to be reflective, to some measure at least, of the goals of the court system to mete out and be seen to mete out 'justice' is compelling.[135] The mediation process in this setting can thus no longer be seen as an 'alternative', voluntary extra-legal forum of dispute resolution where the law and lawyers are of little relevance. A classic, facilitative model may in particular not be appropriate when in-court mediation is tightly time-limited; involves *pro-se*, 'one-shotter' parties; those attending under compulsion or with little alternative means of resolving the dispute or seeking redress; and/or where significant power-imbalances exist between the participants. Leaving unrepresented, disempowered litigants, with scant knowledge of mediation or the legal character of their cases, cast adrift in a sea of client self-determination and settlement norm-generation, may simply be unsustainable within the context of court-connected mediation.

The much vaunted principle of confidentiality[136] may also require modification within the court-connected context to ensure that parties are not pressured into settlement or dealt with unfairly within the process. This may be especially so in the context of mandatory or *de facto* compulsory referral where tactical abuse of the process by recalcitrant parties may be expected to rise.[137] Questions over the

---

[135] See for example, McAdoo and Welsh (2005), p. 404, suggesting that for "court-connected mediation to be considered successful, it must help courts deliver... [s]ubstantive justice, including: [o]utcomes that are consistent with the rule of law".

[136] And the related issue of evidential privilege for the mediator.

[137] The linked issue of 'good faith' participation in mediation is also important here. If an obligation to attempt mediation in good faith is seen as important within the court-connected context, for the provision to operate effectively, it may be necessary to depart from normal rules on confidentiality and privilege within mediation. This brings with it inherent dangers, however, in that it may blight mediators' impartiality and damage parties' faith in the process. For a good discussion see Zimmerman (2009).

immunity of mediators[138] also require clarification to ensure that accessible redress is available to disaffected parties.

An appropriate fusing of law within mediation in the court-connected context should not be manifest by creating models of mediation which, as may often currently be the norm, represent some sort of distorted and diminished mirror image of formal adjudication.[139] Such models often serve the interests of lawyers and other repeat players in the process rather than the participants.[140] Much of the current composition of court-connected mediation programmes have developed not by careful design but rather by tactical, professional manoeuvring and the natural, but not necessarily conscious or desirable absorbing of the dominant legal culture within mediation. A more conscious attempt at appropriate programme design in mediation needs to be attempted in the realm of court-connected mediation. The input of lawyers and legal norms into mediation should be done in such a way as to ensure that the process captures the qualitative promise of mediation, captures mediating parties' desires and needs in the process, as well as ensuring an appropriate reflection of the institutional missions of the courts in which mediation is located. So for example, this could mean that the mediation process should encompass mechanisms to ensure, in so far as possible, a level playing field between the parties, and access in some way to legal advice as part of the process either from the mediator or lawyer representatives, especially where this is sought by the parties involved.[141]

Ensuring the informed consent of participants both in terms of entering mediation (where the process is not mandatory) and in agreeing to settlements reached in mediation is also paramount.[142] Parties should also expressly consent to the model of mediation which is to be provided. There should also subsist checks and balances to ensure that certain kinds of parties are not routinely prejudiced within mediation. Efficiency and pursuing settlement at all costs should not be overarching aims, but emphasis also placed upon the qualitative benefits to be gleaned from the process. Norm education and advocating models of mediation[143] may require

---

[138] This may be particularly pertinent for judicial mediators who may, in line with their judicial office, generally hold immunity from law suit in respect of their activities. Claims are more arguably more likely to arise against inappropriate or negligent conduct on the part of mediators in the court-connected context, given the inevitable, settlement-heavy atmosphere of such programmes, evaluative, directive styles of mediation practiced therein and the fact that many parties will have no access to independent legal advice throughout the process.

[139] Although formal adjudicative models in cases of lesser import often provide this.

[140] Such as mediators, court administrators and insurance companies.

[141] As discussed in Chap. 4 at Sect. 4.3.7 there is significant evidence in the court connected context that clients seek out legal evaluation from mediators and are more likely to perceive mediated outcomes as fair when the mediator evaluates the legal strength of parties' cases.

[142] While evidence suggests that courts are none too keen to disregard mediated settlements and typically rely on contract law to determine issues regarding enforceability of settlements reached (see Sussand 2009; Coben and Thompson 2006, pt. III).

[143] Waldman (1997).

implementation in some contexts to ensure that key, underpinning legal norms are captured within mediation agreements.[144] Procedural justice norms should be heeded within mediation imbuing the process with dignity and respect; allowing effective party participation; and ensuring that parties are heard and seen to be heard by mediators.[145] Screening[146] is a necessary element to ensure that inappropriate cases are not routinely diverted to mediation in a blanket fashion.[147] Rigorous research projects should accompany the development of new programmes to ensure that such aims are being met.

What of lawyers then in this brave new world where mediation meets formal civil justice? Lawyers, in various ways, may thus be important components of such court-connected mediation programmes. An unfettered and misdirected involvement may lead to many of the problems which currently blight court-connected mediation in which their domination and narrowly viewed settlement focus can lead to party dissatisfaction, reflecting badly on both mediation and the civil court itself. As noted, however, the absence of legal input into mediation may lead to perceived unfairness, lack of protection of the poor and disenfranchised and thus a process which is an uneasy bedfellow with the role of the court in society. Research tells us that lawyers may sometimes aid party perceptions of procedural and substantive justice. Their presence may also help eradicate power imbalances. The key issue, however, is not whether lawyers are present or not, but rather how they are utilised. Research by Roselle Wissler has revealed that lawyer involvement, *per se*, is not generally a determinative factor in respect of a number of key benefits within mediation such as client control in decision making, voice, settlement rates and party satisfaction but varies significantly depending on the *nature* of lawyer involvement.[148] Determining what such involvement entails is a key task in the design of appropriate court-connected mediation programmes. It strikes me, however, that acting as a lawyer mediator or party representative in private, out of court, commercial mediation, for example, may require a quite different approach from undertaking the same roles within the context of in-court mediation. Training and educational endeavours for lawyers (and others) should countenance this fact to a greater degree than is generally prevalent at present.

As a final point on the issue of requisite training and background for mediators in the court-connected context, I should make it clear that I am not advocating that all mediators be lawyers. Nonetheless, when mediation taken place in the shadow of

[144] Such as in the family context, provisions relative to the rights of children or permissible rules on financial settlements arising on separation or divorce.

[145] Not least because perceptions of procedural justice within mediation will impact upon notions of the legitimacy of the decision making body concerned—the court—Lind and Tyler (1988), pp. 66–70.

[146] And hence adequate education of those carrying out such screening activities.

[147] Even if the programme affords judges or other 'screeners' the right to compel parties to mediate or attend mediation intake sessions in particular instances.

[148] Wissler (2010).

the court, I would contend that mediators should in this context be well versed in appropriate knowledge regarding the legal backdrop to disputes that come before them. In this sense, an understanding of such matters as: the civil court system, remedies available and rules relating to costs in such regimes; rules relating to important process elements of mediation such as financial imperatives to mediate, confidentiality, evidence and enforceability of agreements; an understanding of lawyer-client relationships; and a general understanding of basic underpinning law relative to the legal nature of disputes that they commonly handle, such as contract and tort. While many standard mediation programmes, include minor coverage in respect of these elements, more requires to be done. In many jurisdictions, such programmes focusing on the legal dimension of disputes exist as voluntary, bolt-on training,[149] but perhaps there is a need to render such content a core element of requisite training for court-connected mediators at least. Just as mediators, lawyers included, require to be aware of, and understand, a whole range of other potential factors which influence settlement, such as power, reputation, saving face, participants' needs to vent, be heard and understood by the other party, so too do mediators require an understanding of the importance of the legal dimension to disputes they handle. So where legislation or approved rosters sanction those entitled or given a badge of approval to mediate in court-connected contexts, such rosters should not limit membership to, or favour lawyers. Appropriate legal skills and knowledge should be one box to be ticked in a similar vein to other skills, experience and characteristics that those seeking inclusion must meet.

5.4 Conclusion

There is little doubt that mediation's journey into the centre of formal disputing practices is likely to continue unabated in the near future in many jurisdictions globally. The debate over the impact that the relocation of mediation heralds for civil court systems requires a nuanced, balanced approach. On the one hand we must pay due regard to the practical limits of court systems in achieving the aims of formal justice. In a like fashion we must recognise the deficiencies of formal justice itself and the mismatch between what it can deliver and the needs and aspirations of parties who find themselves before the courts. Equally mediation should not be used as some sort of sticking plaster to cover up the need to provide access to justice to

[149] For England and Wales, see the course provided by CEDR at http://www.cedr.com/skills/flyer/?id=284 (Accessed 1 November 2011) and Chartered Inst of Arbiters at http://www.ciarb.org/education-and-training/course-finder/2010/03/commercial-mediation-module-3—law-for-mediators-128.php (Accessed 1 November 2011). Various programmes are available in the USA, for example at: http://www.mediationincnc.com/; http://www.icmadr.com/conflict-resolution-training/other-training-programs/legal-process/ (Accessed 1 November 2011) and in Canada http://adrresources.com/adr-events/2514/basic-civil-procedure-for-non-lawyer-mediators-adr-ontario (Accessed 1 November 2011).

the disempowered in society. Mediation may rightly be criticised if it fails to deliver either by lawyer domination transforming the process into 'litigation-lite' or by its reluctance to appropriately engage legal norms to protect the vulnerable who find themselves stumbling into the process. Mediation processes in the court setting need to stand on their own feet and be capable of exhibiting the wider, qualitative benefits of the process, while being reflective of the context within which they are now placed. Lawyers, who fully understand the merits and limitations of mediation, may have a key role to play in ensuring that such a balanced approach to its practice is taken. The need for appropriate education, training and mentoring in the lawyer's role in mediation as well as regulation of their involvement (in addition to that of others) in the process is thus a crucial element. In addition, to a range of other relevant issues pertaining to the lawyer's future interaction with mediation, this is a matter that I will explore in the concluding chapter.

References

Abel R (1982) The Politics of Informal Justice. Academic Press, New York.

Adler M (ed) (2009) Administrative justice in context. Hart Publishing, Oxford

Alexander N (2004) Mediation on trial: ten verdicts on court-related ADR. Law Context 22(1):8

Alexander N et al (2006) Mediation in Germany: the long and winding road. In: Alexander N (ed) Global trends in mediation, 2nd edn. Kluwer International, Alphen aan den Rijn

Alleweldt F et al (2009) Study on the use of alternative dispute resolution in the European Union. Final Report. Civic Consulting of the Consumer Policy Evaluation Consortium (CPEC), Berlin 16 October 2009. http://ec.europa.eu/consumers/redress_cons/adr_study.pdf. Accessed 1 Nov 2011

Auerbach J (1983) Justice without law, resolving disputes without lawyers. OUP, New York

Blomgren Bingham L et al (2008–2009) Dispute resolution and the vanishing trial: comparing federal government litigation and ADR outcomes. Ohio State J Dispute Resolut 24: 225–262

Blomgren Bingham L et al (2009) Dispute system design and justice in employment dispute resolution: mediation in the workplace. Harvard Negot Law Rev 14:1–50

Bohmer C, Ray ML (1994) Effects of different dispute resolution methods on women and children after divorce. Family Law Q 28:223–245

Boulle L (2000) Minding the gaps: reflecting on the story of Australian mediation. ADR Bulletin 3(1):3

Brooker P, Lavers A (2002) Commercial lawyers' attitudes and experience with mediation. Web J Curr Legal Issues 4:1

Brunsdon-Tulley M (2009) There is an 'A' in 'ADR' but does anybody know what it means anymore? Civil Justice Q 28(2):218–236

Bryan P (1999) Killing us softly: divorce mediation and the politics of power. Buffalo Law Rev 40:441–523

Buck T (2005) Administrative justice and alternative dispute resolution: the Australian Experience DCA Research Series 8/05

Bush RAB, Folger JP (2005) The promise of mediation: responding to conflict through empowerment and recognition, 2nd edn. Jossey-Bass, San Francisco

Carr C, Jencks M (1999–2000) The privatization of business and commercial dispute resolution: a misguided policy decision. Kentucky Law J 88(2):183–244

Chiarloni S (2000) Stato attuale e prospettive della conciliazione stragiudiziale. Rivista trimstrale di diritto e procedura civile 2:462

Chornenki G (2004) Mediating commercial disputes: exchanging "power over" for "power with". In: Macfarlane J (ed) Rethinking disputes: the mediation alternative. Cavendish, London
Church T et al (1978) Justice delayed: the pace of litigation in urban trial courts. The National Center for State Courts, Williamsburgh
Chief Justice's Working Party on Civil Justice Reform (2004) Final Report. http://www.civiljustice.gov.hk/fr/paperhtml/toc_fr.html. Accessed I Nov 2011
Clark A (Master of the Rolls) (2008) Speech given to 2nd conference of the Civil Mediation Council. http://blog.amandabucklow.co.uk/wp-content/uploads/2008/05/mr_mediation_conference_may08.pdf. Accessed 1 Nov 2011
Clark B, Dawson C (2007) Scottish commercial litigators and ADR: a study of attitudes and experience. Civil Justice Q 26:228–249
Coben JR, Thompson PN (2006) Disputing irony: a systematic look at litigation about mediation. Harvard Negot Law Rev 11:43–146
Condlin RJ (1985) Cases on both sides: patterns of argument in legal dispute-resolution. Maryland Law Rev 44:65–136
Cooper-Alexander J (1991) Do the merits matter? a study of settlements in securities class actions. Stanford Law Rev 43:497–598
Davis A, Salem R (1984) Dealing with power imbalances in mediation of interpersonal disputes. In: Lemmon J (ed) Procedures for guiding the divorce mediation process. Jossey-Bass, San Francisco
De Palo G et al (2003) Mediation in Italy: the legislative debate and the future. ADR Bull 6(3): Article 5, 1–3
De Roo A, Jagtenberg R (2006) The Dutch landscape of court-encouraged mediaiton. In: Alexander N (ed) Global trends in mediation, 2nd edn. Kluwer International, Alphen aan den Rijn
Doyle M (2006) Evaluation of the small claims mediation service at Manchester County Court. Dept of Constitutional Affairs, London. http://www.dca.gov.uk/civil/adr/small-claims-manchester.pdf. Accessed 1 Nov 2011
Dyson L (2010) Speech to the 3rd annual symposium on mediation. Chartered Institute of Arbitrators, London
Fiss O (1984) Against settlement. Yale Law J 93:1073–1091
Galanter M (1974) Why the 'haves' come Out ahead: speculations on the limits of legal change. Law Soc Rev 9:95–160
Galanter M (1984) Worlds of deals: using negotiation to teach about legal process. J Legal Educ 34:268–276
Galanter M (1985) The legal malaise; or, justice observed. Law Soc Rev 19(4):537–556
Galanter M (2004) The vanishing trial: an examination of trials and related matters in federal and state courts. J Empirical Legal Stud 1:459–570
Genn H (2010) Judging civil justice: the 2008 Hamlyn lectures. Cambridge University Press, Cambridge
Genn H et al (2007) Twisting arms: court referred and court linked mediation under judicial pressure. Ministry Justice Res Ser 1/07. Ministry of Justice, London
Glasser C (1993) Civil procedure and the lawyers—the adversary system and the decline of the orality principle. Modern Law Rev 56:307–324
Golann D (2002) Is legal mediation a process of repair or separation? An empirical study and its implications. Harvard Negot Law Rev 7:301–336
Gould N et al (2010) Mediating construction disputes: an evaluation of existing practice. Centre for Construction Law, Kings College, London
Grillo T (1991) The mediation alternative: process dangers for women. Yale Law J 100:1545–1610
Hadfield GK (2005) Exploring economic and democratic theories of civil litigation: differences between individual and organizational litigants in the disposition of federal cases. Stanford Law Rev 57:1275–1328

Halliday S, Scott C (2009) A cultural analysis of administrative justice. In: Adler M (ed) Administrative justice in context. Hart Publishing, Oxford

Hamilton J (2005) Thirty years of civil procedural reform in Australia: a personal reminiscence. Australian Bar Rev 26(3):258

Hensler DR (2002) Suppose it's Not true: challenging mediation ideology. J Dispute Resolut 1:81–100

Hensler DR (2003) Our courts, ourselves: how the alternative dispute resolution movement is reshaping our legal system. Penn State Law Rev 108:165–197

Hope L (2011) Speech of the formal opening of the offices of Digby Brown, Glasgow. http://www.digbybrown.co.uk/digbybrown/opencms/db/news/LordHopeSpeech.html. Accessed 1 Nov 2011

Howieson J (2002) Perceptions of procedural justice and legitimacy in local court mediation. Murdoch Univ Electron J Law 13

Jones TS (2004) Conflict resolution in the field: assessing the past, charting the future. Conflict Resolut Q 22(1&2)

Keller BP (1998) Condemned to repeat the past: the reemergence of misappropriation and other common law theories of protection for intellectual property rights. Harvard J Law Technol 11:401–428

Kelly J (2004) Family mediation research: is there empirical support for the field? Conflict Resolut Q 22(1–2):3–35

Kritzer H (1991) Let's Make a deal: understanding the negotiation process in ordinary litigation. University of Wisconsin Press, Madison

Kritzer H (2004) Disappearing trials? A comparative perspective. J Empirical Legal Stud 1:735–754

Kuhner T (2005) Court connected mediation compared: the cases of Argentina and the United States. ILSA J Int Comp Law 11:520–555

La Porte R et al (1997) The law of the market. Economist, April 19

LaFree G, Rack C (1996) The effect of participants' ethnicity and gender on monetary outcomes in mediated and adjudicated civil cases. Law Soc Rev 30:767–797

Lande J (2010) Lawyering mediation: what can we learn from the USA? 2010 Annual Burgess Lecture, University of Strathclyde. http://video.strath.ac.uk/10/231-10-01.wvx. Accessed 1 Nov 2011

Lightman G (2007) Mediation: an approximation to justice. S.J. Berwin Speech http://www.cedr.com/index.php?location=/library/articles/20070706_208.htm. Accessed I Nov 2011

Lind AE, Tyler T (1988) The social psychology of procedural justice. Plenum Press, New York

Luban D (1994–1995) Settlements and the erosion of the public realm. Georgetown Law J 89: 2619–2662

MacCoun R (2005) Voice, control, and belonging: the double-edged sword of procedural fairness. Annu Rev Law Soc Sci 1:171–201

Macfarlane J (2001) Culture change? Commercial Litigators and the Ontario Mandatory Mediation Programme. http://dsp-psd.pwgsc.gc.ca/collection_2008/lcc-cdc/JL2-70-2001E.pdf. Accessed 1 Nov 2011

Macfarlane J (2008) The new lawyer: How settlement is transforming the practice of law. UBS Press, Toronto

McAdoo B, Hinshaw A (2002) The challenge of institutionalizing alternative dispute resolution: attorney perspectives on the effect of rule 17 on civil litigation in Missouri. Missouri Law Rev 67:473

McEwen C, Maiman RK (1984) Mediation in small claims court: achieving compliance through consent. Law Soc Rev 18:11–49

McMunigal K (1990) The costs of settlement: the impact of scarcity of adjudicating on litigating lawyers. UCLA Law Rev 833

Menkel-Meadow C (1995) Whose dispute is it anyway? A philosophical and democratic defense of settlement (in some cases). Georgetown Law J 83:2663–2696

Menkel-Meadow C (2001) Introduction. In: Menkel-Meadow C (ed) Mediation: theory, policy and practice. Ashgate/Dartmouth, Aldershot

Ministry of Justice (2011) Solving disputes in the county courts: creating a simpler, quicker and more proportionate system. A consultation on reforming civil justice in England and Wales. CP6/2011

Nader L (1993) Controlling processes in the practices of Law: hierarchy and pacification in the movement to re-form dispute ideology. Ohio State J Dispute Resolut 9:1–26

Niemeijer B, Pel M (2005) Court-based mediation in the Netherlands: research, evaluation and future expectations. Penn State Law Rev 110:345–379

ADR Now (2007). 2006 small claims mediation. http://www.adrnow.org.uk/go/SubPage_132.html. Accessed 1 Nov 2011

Platform ADR (1998) Conflictbemiddeling; eindrapport Platform ADR. Ministerie van Justitie, Den Haag

Prince S (2007) Institutionalising mediation? An evaluation of the Exeter small claims mediation pilot. Web J Curr Legal Issues 5

Prince S, Belcher S (2006) An evaluation of the effectiveness of court-based mediation processes in non-family civil proceedings at Exeter and Guilford county courts. Department of Constitutional Affairs, London

Proksch P (1998) Kooperative Vermittlung in streitigen Familiensachen. Kohlhammer, Stuttgart

Reed L (2007) The civil court and the future of dispute resolution. Paper presented to the Scottish Institute of Arbitrators. http://www.scottish-arbitrators.org/z_pdf/articles/the_civil_court.pdf. Accessed 1 Nov 2011

Relis T (2009) Perceptions in Litigation and Mediation: Lawyers, Defendants, Plaintiffs, and Gendered Parties. Cambridge University Press, New York

Resnik J (2008) Courts: in and out of sight, site and cite. Villanova Law Rev 53:771–810

Rodger L (2008) Paper presented to Conference on Delivering Excellence in Scotland's Civil Justice System, the Macdonald Holyrood Hotel, Edinburgh, Friday 20 June 2008 (On file with the author)

Rosenberg M (1964) The pretrial conference and effective justice. Columbia University Press, New York

Ross M, Bain D (2010) In court mediation pilots: report on evaluation of in court mediation schemes in Glasgow and Aberdeen Sheriff Courts. Scottish Government, Courts and Constitution Analytical Team. http://www.scotland.gov.uk/Resource/Doc/310104/0097858.pdf

Rueben R (2000) Constitutional gravity: a unitary theory of alternative dispute resolution and public civil justice. UCLA Law Rev 47:949–1104

Scottish Consumer Council (1997) Civil Disputes in Scotland: A report of consumers' experiences. http://webarchive.nationalarchives.gov.uk/20090724135150/http://scotcons.demonweb.co.uk/publications/reports/documents/CivilDisputesInScotland.SummaryofareportfromtheSCC.September1997.pdf. Accessed 1 Nov 2011

Shipman S (2006) Court approaches to ADR in the civil justice system. Civil Justice Q 25:181–218

Shipman S (2011) Compulsory mediation: the elephant in the room. Civil Justice Q 30:163–191

Smalkin FN, Smalkin FNC (2005) The market for justice, the litigation explosion and the 'Verdict Bubble: A Closer Look at Vanishing Trials. University of Maryland School of Law, Legal Research Paper No. 2005–60. http://papers.ssrn.com/sol3/papers.cfm?abstract_id=827145&. Accessed 1 Nov 2011

Subrin S (2002/2003) A traditionalist looks at mediation: it's here to stay and much better than I thought. Nevada Law J 3: 196–227

Sussman, E (2009) User Preferences and Mediator Practices: Can They Be Reconciled Within the Parameters Set by Ethical Considerations. http://sussmanadr.com/docs/Mediation_preferences_112208.pdf. Accessed 1 Nov 2011

Tilley S (2007) ADR professional: recognising gender differences in all issues mediation. Family Law 37:353–356

Tronson B (2006) Mediation orders: do the arguments against them make sense? Civil Justice Q 25:412–418

Tyler T (2006) Why people obey the law. Princeton University Press, Princeton

Tyler T, Huo Y (2002) Trust in the law: encouraging public cooperation with the police and courts. Russell Sage Foundation, New York

Waldman E (1997) Identifying the role of social norms in mediation: a multiple model approach. Hastings Law J 48(4):703–770

Welsh N (2001) Making deals in court connected mediation: what's justice got to do with it? Washington Univ Law Q 79:788–858

Welsh N (2002) Disputants' Decision control in court-connected mediation: a hollow promise without procedural justice. J Dispute Resolut 1:179–192

Welsh N (2007) The future of mediation: court-connected mediation in the US and the Netherlands compared. Forum Voor Conflictmanagement 01:19

Welsh N, McAdoo B (2005) Look before You leap and keep on looking: lessons from the institutionalization of court-connected mediation. Nevada Law Rev 5:347–432

Wissler R (2002) Court-connected mediation in general civil cases. Ohio State J Dispute Resolut 17:641–703

Wissler R (2004) The effectiveness of court-connected dispute resolution in civil cases. Conflict Resolut Q 22:55–88

Wissler R (2010) Representation in mediation: what we know from empirical research. Fordham Law Rev 37:419

Woolf L (1996) Access to justice. Final Report to the Lord Chancellor on the civil justice system in England and Wales. http://webarchive.nationalarchives.gov.uk/+/http://www.dca.gov.uk/civil/final/overview.htm

Yeazell S (1994) Misunderstood consequences of modern civil processes. Wisconsin Law Rev 631–678

Zimmerman S (2009) Judges gone wild: why breaking the mediation confidentiality privilege for acting in "bad faith" should be reevaluated in court-ordered mandatory mediation. Cardozo J Conflict Resolut 11:353–384

Chapter 6
Conclusion: The Future of Lawyers and Mediation

6.1 Introduction

This book has sought to analyse the interaction of lawyers with modern mediation in the wide panoply of civil disputing. I hope to have captured some of the key issues pertaining to lawyers' engagement with mediation as well as placed a spotlight on current trends, controversies and contradictions in the field. In this sense, as charted in this book, the relationship between lawyers and mediation is a complicated, fluid business. Despite its extra-law origins, in the modern sense mediation can to some extent be seen as the birth child of lawyers, brought into this world at the time of the Pound Conference in the 1970s USA. Lawyers' engagement with mediation and their attitudes, experiences and responses relative to the process, have since followed generally similar patterns in most jurisdictions across the common law and civil law divide. In a global sense many lawyers have moved from ignorance, suspicion and resistance to acceptance and embracement of mediation. Lawyer infiltration, domination and outright 'capture' of mediation markets have taken place in certain settings. Equally, it is true that many lawyers remain unconvinced of the merits of mediation either on principled or practical grounds. Both altruistic and selfish motives doubtless lie behind the lawyer intransigence that continues to exist towards mediation in all corners of the globe. Some of those cynical lawyers have nonetheless taken steps to accommodate mediation (or had little choice but to do so) but in so doing have failed to cast aside their negative attitudes towards the process and remained wedded to traditional adversarial practice norms in their mediation activity. While, sadly most nations share a common trait of limited embedding of mediation within traditional legal education, current professional training for lawyers in mediation varies dramatically in different jurisdictions. Specialised, professional mediation educational and training programmes range from short, practical courses, to sophisticated, rigorous programmes that blend theory and practice. The notion of mediation practice as a 'bolt-on' for lawyers remains strong, particularly in the common law world. This is reflected in the nature of much current training. Despite in the main being rather less well developed in terms of

B. Clark, *Lawyers and Mediation*, DOI 10.1007/978-3-642-23474-3_6,

adoption of mediation, the civil law world can generally be considered ahead of its common law counterparts in the depth of educational requirements set out for mediation practice.

6.2 Treading Carefully: Lawyers' Future Steps on the Mediation Field

As discussed in this book, to some extent the upsurge in interest from lawyers in mediation has been caused by its encroachment upon their traditional turf. Although in its classic form mediation represents an eschewing of the law and lawyers, it has across many contexts become clothed in law, populated by lawyers and relocated within traditional legal dispute resolution sites. Although policy makers, courts and lawyers themselves have been instrumental in bringing about this transformation of mediation, such developments have an air of inevitability about them. The bare fact is that modern mediation in its voluntary, grass roots personae has simply not been especially attractive to those in dispute, despite its proven merits and the *post hoc* satisfaction that those who do attempt it often bask in. Mediation, in its classic form, promises the affirmation of shared values and community norms, which as has been noted by anthropologists, may be sorely lacking in modern day environments.[1] Mediation may appeal for harmony and rationality in terms of resolving a dispute at a time when harmony is not desired and all such rationality on the part of the warring parties has been lost. Mediation promises participant empowerment and self-determination at times when disputing parties may feel more comfortable lining up behind their lawyers and letting others take decisions on their behalf. Against this backdrop of limited appeal and prospects for the process, it was inevitable that mediation proponents would support relocating from outside to inside the arena of legal disputing to gain access to the clients that might use mediation services. It may be hoped that clients (and their lawyers) would be educated in the ways of mediation, experience its joys and even become devotees of, and repeat players within the process. As this book has already noted, that this can be and is in practice achieved is unquestionable. So although mediation may be a medicine[2] that disputants are often reluctant to swallow, many may well benefit from their dose if they can be persuaded to try it.

While mediation use has certainly swelled dramatically as a result, the embedding of mediation within traditional legal dispute resolution mechanisms has very often had the effect to radically alter its normative character. It is mediation's tragedy if its promise remains largely unrealised because lawyer manipulation and the infusing of the dominant legal culture within the process renders it a pale

[1] See generally, Auerbach (1983).

[2] Some may perceive it to be quackery.

shadow of its potential optimum. In this regard, clearly bad practice does exist and often lawyers are to blame. We should not rush to the conclusion, however, that lawyers should have no place in mediation. As I have articulated in this book, lawyers can and do at times add value to the mediation process. Indeed their contribution may go some way to remedying certain defects of mediation that come to light when the process is played out in particular contexts. So, as I have suggested, where mediation takes place in the shadow of the court, explicit recognition of the law and legal norms may be imperative within the process. In all contexts though we need to engage in nuanced, sophisticated debates about harnessing in an appropriate way the qualities that lawyers can bring to mediation without undermining its core principles and values—achieving the best of both worlds as it were.

Lawyers thus need to approach their engagement with this nuanced message in mind. They have not always done so. In chap. 3 I laid out some of the strategic steps that legal professional bodies had taken in respect of appropriating the mediation process through such factors as asserting ownership and entitlement to practice mediation, lawyer 'shopping' for lawyer-mediators, controlling and colonising approved rosters, lobbying governments for exclusive rights to mediate, and pursuing non-lawyer mediators for the unauthorized practice of law as well as the impact that such strategic moves have had on others seeking to gain a foothold in the field. These aggressive steps coupled with the fact that lawyer populated mediation practice models have become infused and twisted by legal norms, speak volumes for the thesis of lawyers' co-option of mediation for selfish, professional aims. They may also have the effect of heightening the anti-lawyer rhetoric in lay communities and ramping up efforts from non-lawyers to guard their mediation turfs vigorously from suspected lawyer attacks. Such developments may in turn fuel the general belief that lawyers are conservative, cynical professionals only concerned with feathering their own nests and protecting their traditional working practices. None of this is likely improve the perceived public perception of lawyers.[3]

By contrast, lawyers need to take (and be seen to take) measured steps in terms of their forays into mediation practice. In this there is a role for individual lawyers, the legal profession, judges and legal academics to set an appropriate tone. Lawyers should rightly value the role that they can play in mediation's many forms and the benefits to the process that their skills and experience can bring. Equally, with humility they must recognise the limits that their traditional legal education and practice norms hold for mediation practice. Lawyers must also acknowledge the

[3] In Chap. 3 I noted some of the evidence that particular lawyers had sought engagement with mediation in a quest for a more palatable professional experience and equally that legal professional bodies had taken up the mantle for the process, to present a more acceptable face to society. With the status and professional status of lawyers at a low ebb in many jurisdictions, mediation activity may represent one small salutary step in aiding lawyers to recover from their current "crisis in professionalism", but only I would suggest if they are seen to enter into the field with an open, conciliatory stance relative to others professional participants in mediation.

cultural and informational prejudices towards the core values of mediation that continue to inhabit legal professions and the resultant need for training and education in the key attributes of, and potential benefits accruing from mediation, which go far beyond the traditional legal disputing paradigm. Lawyers must also face up to and take concerted steps to remedy their conscious or unconscious proclivity for steering mediation practice towards more comfortable lawyerly shores. Similarly, lawyers should recognise the value brought to the process by non-lawyers and the fact that core mediation skills and traits, which lawyers need to acquire, can be found in professionals of all hues (and those from non-professional backgrounds for that matter). It would be misleading to suggest that this is not already happening to some degree. This book has already charted the proliferation of multi-disciplinary mediation bodies and the common practice in some jurisdictions of partnering and co-mediation between lawyers and non-lawyers. Moreover, many lawyers are doubtless able to deftly practice mediation and are cognisant of the full range of qualitative benefits that the process may produce. More needs to be done, however. I will conclude with a few suggestions in this regard.

6.2.1 Reforming Legal Education

Previous chapters of this book have already lamented the lack of underpinning of mediation in standard legal education across the world and I will not repeat that here. Suffice to say that the limited attention paid to mediation, and wider, non-legal and consensual forms of dispute resolution do not bode well for lawyers' aptitude for, and attraction to mediation practice. Although there are signs of change, the traditional psychological composition of law students, competitive experience of law school and absence of the client and her extra-legal needs from mainstream legal education also militate against lawyer propensity towards mediation.

It is clear that mediation classes should become core rather than discretionary, add-on classes within standard law student curriculums. Beyond specific instruction in mediation, the consensual, interests-based ethos of mediation along with the prominent role of clients therein should be systematically embedded within core law school programmes. This would not only aid mediation development itself, but as has been noted by a number of scholars, would comport better with new, more sophisticated models of lawyering, which value collaborative law, preventative law, multi-disciplinary practice, client-centred practice norms and mirror the reality that negotiation and court-sponsored settlement activities have replaced trials as the main staple of litigated outcomes.[4] There is key role to be played here by legal professional bodies and legal academics in helping to shape appropriate content. Law schools should not display a silo mentality to education in this

[4] Menkel-Meadow (1997); Kovach (2003); Macfarlane (2008), pp. 224–232.

regard, however. Greater interdisciplinarity within prescribed education for fledgling lawyers with input from disciples such as business, psychology, economics and sociology to augment core legal learning would better serve to ensure the establishment of lawyers with a more sophisticated appreciation of modern legal practice.

6.2.2 *Regulating Mediation Practice*

Lawyers should desist from promulgating or lobbying for rules that dictate that only lawyers should mediate or provisions that manifestly favour legal professionals by, for example, placing greater hurdles in the place of potential mediators from other professional backgrounds. This is not to say that legal knowledge and experience may not be important for those seeking to practice mediation in certain contexts. I have already argued in Chap. 5 that non-lawyers can acquire such skills where they are seen as necessary to a sufficient level so as to render them fit to practice mediation (such as in court-annexed mediation programmes involving *pro se* litigants). In this sense, the various, optional bolt-on courses in law and legal systems for non-lawyer mediators that currently subsist could be mandated by regulatory provisions for non-lawyers seeking to practice in some settings. Lawyers clearly have a role to play in the design and delivery of such courses, just as they themselves need to learn from non-legal professionals in respect of many aspects of mediation practice.

Linked to the above point is the idea that while ethical codes and practice rules should rightly dictate the conduct of lawyers acting as party representatives in mediation,[5] when acting as mediators, lawyers should not be regulated by their legal, professional bodies (except perhaps to the extent that legal practice rules may place obligations on lawyers to differentiate their legal practice from mediation activity and to avoid conflicts of interest arising in mediation from their standard lawyer activity). Recognising the fundamentally different role of mediation from traditional lawyering activities and emphasising the fact that the mediatory function is one that can be undertaken by suitably trained and regulated personnel drawn from a variety of backgrounds, prescribed training, regulation and oversight, whether established on a self-regulatory footing or by virtue of bodies empowered on a statutory basis, should be undertaken by organisations independent of the legal establishment or for that matter, professional bodies in other disciplines. Codes of practice for lawyers who also happen to practice as mediators should not be promulgated by legal professional bodies. Special features of a lawyer's conduct not common to other professionals such as evidential privilege and immunity from suits should not be applied in this context. Such characteristics, if they are deemed

[5] See discussion below at Sect. 6.2.3.

desirable in the circumstances, should be available to all mediators practising in any particular setting rather than those with a legal background.[6]

Again this is often already the case, with codes of conduct governing mediator conduct for those accredited or approved to practice in certain areas promulgated by bodies which govern mediators drawn from a number of professional backgrounds including lawyers.[7] Nonetheless, numerous codes of practice for lawyers acting in the mediation seat have also been promulgated by legal professional bodies[8] which I would argue conflates mediation practice with the practice of law, and is generally unhelpful in the quest for establishing mediation as a separate profession. It can also be seen as lawyers laying claim to mediation practice. I am not denigrating codes for mediation practice which have been established by lawyers. Legal professional bodies have a wealth of experience in setting forth ethical rules and practice standards for their members. Clearly legal professional bodies and those representing other disciplines can feed into the process of establishing appropriate regulatory frameworks, but any such frameworks should sit outside of any one professional discipline.

As a caveat to the above, I should note that the situation with sitting judges may be different, however. When mediating cases as an adjunct to their traditional function, judges will require to be regulated under the general professional rules which should govern their behaviour. I would argue that judicial mediation will always be sufficiently distinct in normative character—even where those providing the service espouse a purely facilitative model—in view of the fact that is conducted by a judicial officer of the state in a court setting—to render this kind of activity an exception to general regulation of mediation conduct.

6.2.3 Ethical Codes and Rules of Professional Practice for Lawyers Representing Clients in Mediation

While the professional rules applying to lawyers[9] in many jurisdictions now expressly call upon lawyers to discuss mediation with their clients and/or opposing counsel, distinct lawyers' professional rules about conduct within mediation are rare. Lawyers acting as party advocates within mediation often remain subject to

---

[6] In Germany for example, where professional rules of lawyers expressly apply to their mediation conduct (s 18 of the Rules of Professional Conduct for Lawyers), lawyer-mediators can found upon their evidential privilege in seeking to avoid giving evidence in subsequent litigation. Whether such a privilege extends to non-lawyers is questionable (Hillig and Huhn 2010, p.53).

[7] The American Bar Association on Dispute Resolution (ABA) has published model standards of conduct for mediators in combination with the American Arbitration Association (AAA) and the Association for Conflict Resolution (ACR)–AAA, ABA and ACR (2005).

[8] Including the New South Wales Law Society (2008).

[9] Or rules of court.

their general ethical codes or practice rules which govern and set down minimum standards of behaviour in negotiations carried out on behalf of their clients and resulting interactions with their fellow lawyers in this regard. Carrie Menkel-Meadow was one of the first to point to the inapplicability of traditional codes of practice and ethical rules framed in an adversary lense, towards lawyer engagement in mediation and other consensual, dispute resolution processes.[10] In previous chapters of this book I have charted some of the evidence of lawyers' cultural norms that infect their negotiation styles and the practical evidence that exists in this regard. Equally I have recounted some of the adversarial behaviours of lawyers within mediation that may be limiting the utility of the process and the full range of benefits that might accrue from it. General ethical codes and practice rules for lawyers are often based on the premise of the lawyer as 'zealous advocate' for their client.[11] Moreover within negotiation, although lawyers may owe other parties duties of candour, such honesty is often heavily qualified to allow 'puffing' about values of property and/or the intention of the parties they represent. Duties of candour also do not usually extend to disclosure of material facts to the other side.[12] While such codes may be appropriate for standard lawyering practices,[13] provisions governing lawyers' representing clients in mediation may require obligations which better reflect the more collaborative, principled, option-generating, client-centred nature of the process. Some jurisdictions make such express provisions already. The Law Society of New South Wales, for example, has published rules stipulating that within mediation, lawyers should shed their traditional role as party advocate, not act in an adversarial fashion but rather cooperate with the mediator and behave in a courteous manner throughout.[14] Promulgating such codes throughout legal professions may support better practice in lawyer advocacy in mediation. This may particularly be so when such codes are informed by and in turn inform the increased training and educational provision now available for lawyers in representing clients in mediation across the globe.

---

[10] See her classic treatment in Menkel-Meadow (1997); See also Kovach (2003).

[11] Acting within the boundaries of the law. Menkel Meadow pointed out that current professional codes of practice for lawyers are built upon the adversarial model of practice with a prominence given to such notions as "zeal, client loyalty, partisanship and non-accountability"—Menkel-Meadow (1997), p. 430.

[12] Such as the American Bar Association, Model Rule 4.1. This is unlike the case for rules that apply to lawyers when appearing before court or other binding adjudicative processes which tend to require absolute honesty and disclosure of all material facts.

[13] Although this is debatable. It may be argued that current approaches to lawyers' standards of conduct are often skewed in favour of zealous advocacy leading too readily to adversarial behaviours and incivility in general lawyer activity.

[14] New South Wales Law Society (2008), pp. 16–18. See the discussion in the National Alternative Dispute Resolution Advisory Council (NADRAC) report into enhancing standards in Australian Mediation (NADRAC 2011, para 2.5.4) regarding the need to extend such regulations across Australia.

6.3 Final Thoughts

With mediation's future across the globe seemingly secured by such developments as the unrelenting roll out of court-sponsored settlement and increasing embedding of the process within civil court systems, it is likely that lawyers will continue to plough a furrow in the field with more and more of those currently looking in from the outside seeking to take up a seat within. New, non-traditional breeds of lawyers and emerging legal practice models may also comport better with mediation activity. Shifts in traditional legal markets coupled with increasing client awareness of, and receptivity to mediation may also stimulate growth. Amidst this burgeoning activity, the motives and actions of lawyers relative to mediation will continue to be subject to hard scrutiny. The storm over the lawyer's interaction with mediation will doubtless continue unabated. It is of some irony that the mediation debate has become infused with such polarity, dogmatism and disagreement. By taking a leaf out of mediation's book, exploring mutual interests, making appropriate concessions, listening and fostering mutual respect,[15] lawyers and others can together chart growth of the process for the benefit of all in society.

References

AAA, ABA and ACR (2005) Model standards of conduct for mediators. http://www.americanbar.org/content/dam/aba/migrated/2011_build/dispute_resolution/model_standards_conduct_april2007.authcheckdam.pdf. Accessed 1 Nov 2011

Auerbach J (1983) Justice without law, resolving disputes without lawyers. OUP, New York

Hillig J, Huhn M (2010) Construction mediation in Germany. In: Brooker P, Wilkinson S (eds) Mediation in the construction industry: an international review. Spon Press, London

Kovach K (2003) Lawyer ethics must keep pace with practice: plurality in lawyering roles demands diverse and innovative ethical standards. Idaho Law Rev 39:399–430

Macfarlane, J (2008) The New Lawyer: How Settlement is Transforming the Practice of Law. UBS Press, Toronto

Menkel-Meadow C (1997) Ethics in alternative dispute resolution: new issues, no answers from the adversary conception of lawyers' responsibility. S Texas Law Rev 38:407

Moffitt M, Bordone R (2005) The next thirty years: directions and challenges in dispute resolution. In: Moffitt M, Bordone R (eds) The handbook of dispute resolution. Jossey-Bass, San Francisco

NADRAC (2011) Maintaining and enhancing integrity in adr processes: from principles to practice through people. http://www.nadrac.gov.au/www/nadrac/rwpattach.nsf/VAP/(FC77CAE5F7A38CF2EBC5832A6FD3AC0C)~1+Maintaining+and+enhancing+the+integrity+of+ADR+processes+−+From+principles+to+practice+through+people+−+pdf.PDF/$file/1+Maintaining+and+enhancing+the+integrity+of+ADR+processes+−+From+principles+to+practice+through+people+−+pdf.PDF. Accessed 1 Nov 2011

New South Wales Law Society (2008) Mediation and evaluation information kit. http://www.lawsociety.com.au/idc/groups/public/documents/internetcontent/026438.pdf. Accessed 1 Nov 2011

[15] "walking the talk"—Moffitt and Bordone 2005, p. 517.

Index

B. Clark, *Lawyers and Mediation*, DOI 10.1007/978-3-642-23474-3,

Printed by Publishers' Graphics LLC